34TH CONGRESS, } SENATE. { Ex. Doc.
3d Session.   No. 27.

REPORT

OF THE

SECRETARY OF THE TREASURY,

ON THE

CONSTRUCTION AND DISTRIBUTION

OF

WEIGHTS AND MEASURES.

WASHINGTON:
A. O. P. NICHOLSON, PRINTER.
1857.

34TH CONGRESS, } SENATE. { Ex. Doc.
3d Session. } { No. 27.

REPORT

OF THE

SECRETARY OF THE TREASURY,

COMMUNICATING,

In compliance with a resolution of the Senate of the 14th of August, 1856, a report of the progress on the construction and distribution of standards of weights and measures, and supply of hydrometers to the custom-houses; the balances made and distributed to States, and the legislation thereof relative to standard weights and measures.

JANUARY 2, 1857.—Read, and ordered to lie on the table.
JANUARY 21, 1857.—Ordered to be printed. Motion to print 2,000 additional copies, 750 of which to be for the use of the Superintendent. Referred to the Committee on Printing.
FEBRUARY 6, 1857.—Report in favor of the motion, and report agreed to.

TREASURY DEPARTMENT,
Washington, D. C., December 31, 1856.

SIR: I have the honor to transmit herewith, in compliance with a resolution of the Senate adopted August 14th of the present year, a report of progress, made under the superintendence of Professor Alexander D. Bache, on the construction and distribution of standards of weights and measures, and supply of hydrometers to custom-houses; also of balances made and distributed to States, and the laws severally enacted therein, relative to standard weights and measures; all of which is respectfully submitted by—

JAMES GUTHRIE,
Secretary of the Treasury.

Hon. JESSE D. BRIGHT,
President pro tem United States Senate.

Report to the Treasury Department, by Professor Alexander D. Bache, on the progress of the work of constructing standards of weights and measures for the custom-houses, and balances for the States, and in supplying standard hydrometers to the custom-houses, from the 1st of January, 1848, to the 31st of December, 1856.

OFFICE OF WEIGHTS AND MEASURES,
Washington, D. C., December 30, 1856.

SIR: I have the honor to present to the department a report on the progress of the work of constructing weights and measures for the custom-houses, and balances for the States, and in supplying standard hydrometers to the custom-houses since the 1st of January, 1848.

The work on the weights and measures and balances has been, as heretofore, under my general superintendence, but in the immediate charge of Joseph Saxton, esq., who has had eight mechanics and six laborers under his direction in the workshops attached to the office of weights and measures. An aggregate of only eleven hands is at this time in employ on the work. The hydrometers were furnished under the immediate direction of Professor R. S. McCulloh, in 1849, and have been supplied to the custom-houses under instructions from the Treasury Department, or, on application therefor by officers of the customs, directly from the office. A list of the various reports made on these subjects, and of the investigations in relation to the manufacture of sugar, under my superintendence, is appended. (Appendix No. 6.)

The delivery of the hydrometers, and manual for their use, to the custom-houses, gave the opportunity to examine, in some instances, the condition of the weights and measures which had been supplied to them, and to ascertain how far the law requiring comparisons with the standards was carried into execution. The hydrometers which came into the possession of the office from the custom-houses have proved to be more discrepant than had even been supposed. The result of these examinations is given in Appendix No. 7.

The report will be divided into the following heads:
1. Weights and measures for the States.
2. Weights and measures for the custom-houses.
3. Weights and measures—miscellaneous.
4. Division and comparison of standard yards.
 Saxton's dividing machine.
 Saxton's reflecting comparator and pyrometer.
5. Comparison of foreign standards with those of the United States.
6. Balances for the States.
7. Weights and measures and balances for foreign governments, &c.
8. Hydrometers for the custom-houses.
9. Gauging.
10. Laws of the States on the subject of weights and measures.

During the course of the delivery of the hydrometers to the custom-houses between Portland, Maine, and Alexandria, Virginia, by Woods Baker, esq., facts, collected in regard to the method of gauging in use, showed such a want of accordance in principle and practice as to induce the Treasury Department to direct me to have a series of investigations made under my direction by him. These were interrupted by his untimely death in the summer of 1852. Some progress was made in putting this matter into shape by Captain J. G. Foster, corps of engineers, but while engaged in that work he was relieved from duty in the Coast Survey, and I have since had no assistant available for its continuation.

1. WEIGHTS AND MEASURES FOR THE STATES.

At the date to which my last report brought the progress of the work, January, 1848, TWENTY-ONE (21) States of the Union had been

WEIGHTS AND MEASURES.

furnished with a full set of standards, and five (5) others had received a portion of them, the remainder being ready at their call. There remained the States of *Florida, Texas, Iowa, Wisconsin,* and *California,* to be furnished with standards, they having applied to the Treasury Department for them.

The full sets for these States have since been delivered, with the exception of the standard weights for Florida, which remain at the Treasury Department subject to the call of the executive of that State.

The other standards which, at the date of the report of 1847, were at the Treasury Department, have since been called for by the executives of the States for which they were designed, with the exception of the weights and liquid and dry measures for Mississippi.

The full sets of weights and measures thus referred to, consist of—

1. A set of standard weights composed of the following pieces:

One 50 pounds avoirdupois. ⎫ Arranged in one box.
     25   "   "   ⎭

     20   "   "
     10   "   "
      5   "   "
      4   "   "
      3   "   "   ⎬ Arranged in one box.
      2   "   "
      1   "   "
      1   "   troy.

One   10 ounces troy.
      6   "
      5   "
      4   "
      3   "
      2   "
      1   "
    0.5   "
    0.4   "
    0.3   "
    0.2   "
    0.1   "
   0.05   "   of silver wire.
   0.04   "   "   ⎬ Arranged in one box.
   0.03   "   "
   0.02   "   "
   0.01   "   "
  0.005   "   "
  0.004   "   "
  0.003   "   "
  0.002   "   "
  0.001   "   "
 0.0005   "   "
 0.0004   "   "
 0.0003   "   "
 0.0002   "   "
 0.0001   "   "

Those States to which the balances have been delivered have also been furnished at the same time with a set of avoirdupois ounce weights, in addition to the above, consisting of the following pieces:

One 8 oz. avoirdupois.
4 "
2 "
1 "
0.5 "
0.4 "
0.3 "
0.2 "
0.1 "
0.05 " of silver wire.
0.04 " "
0.03 " " } Arranged in one box.
0.02 " "
0.01 " "
0.005 " "
0.004 " "
0.003 " "
0.002 " "
0.001 " "
0.0005 " "
0.0004 " "
0.0003 " "
0.0002 " "
0.0001 " "

2. A standard yard measure with matrix.
3. A set of liquid capacity measures, consisting of the following pieces:

One gallon measure, in its case.
One half gallon measure.
quart "
pint " } Arranged in one box.
half pint "

Each with a ground glass cover.

4. A standard half bushel, with a ground glass cover, in its case.

1. The *actual standard of length*, of the United States, is a brass scale of eighty-two inches in length, prepared for the survey of the coast of the United States, by Troughton of London, and deposited in the Office of Weights and Measures. The temperature at which this scale is a standard is 62° Fahrenheit, and the yard measure is between the 27th and 63d inches of the scale.

The copies or standards made for the Treasury Department, the States, the custom-houses, &c., being of brass, the temperature at which the brass scale of Troughton is a standard is not of practical importance as far as making the copies is concerned. In fact, no differences have yet been detected in the various comparisons made between the expansion of the material of the Troughton scale and of our standards. The number used by Mr. Hassler for the expansion of brass was derived from his experiments made at Newark in 1817, recorded in the second volume new series of the American Philosophical Society's Transactions; it was for the proportional expansion, 0.000,010,509,03, or for expansion in one yard 0.000,378,325,08 of an inch for one degree of Fahrenheit's thermometer.

2. The *units of capacity measure* are the gallon for liquid, and the bushel for dry measure. The gallon is a vessel containing 58372.2 grains (8.3389 pounds avoirdupois) of the standard pound of distilled water, at the temperature of maximum density of water, the vessel being weighed in air in which the barometer is 30 inches at 62° Fahrenheit. The bushel is a measure containing 543391.89 standard grains (77.6274 pounds avoirdupois) of distilled water, at the temperature of maximum density of water, and barometer 30 inches at 62° Fahrenheit.

3. The *standard of weight* is the troy pound, copied by Captain Kater, in 1827* from the imperial troy pound, for the United States Mint, and preserved in that establishment. The avoirdupois pound is derived from this; its weight being greater than that of the troy pound, in the proportion of 7,000 to 5,760; that is, the avoirdupois pound is equivalent in weight to 7,000 grains troy. The pound is a standard at 30 inches of the barometer and 62° Fahrenheit's thermometer.

These standards were adopted by the Treasury Department on the recommendation of Mr. Hassler, in 1832. We shall see in a subsequent part of this report, that their distribution has tended to produce practical uniformity in the weights and measures used in the different States, and that thus the end proposed by Congress is fully answered. The early measures taken by the State of California to procure authentic standards, is strong evidence of the value attached to this practical uniformity, which can be secured in no other way than by the general distribution af authentic weights and measures.

The set of standards furnished to the State of Alabama, having been destroyed by the burning of the capitol, in December, 1849, the Treasury Department, upon application of the executive of that State, directed them to be replaced by new ones; which was accordingly done.

Twenty-four (24) States have directed the distribution of standards to their counties, or provided for the supply of copies of those of the United States. The frequent inquiries addressed by the representatives from the different States, in behalf of their constituents, and from others, induce me to suppose that there is much interest on the subject of establishing thorough uniformity in weights and measures. In a subsequent part of this report abstracts will be given of the laws passed in the various States on this subject, since the date of Mr. Adams' report, 1821. A list of the titles of the laws will be found in the Appendix; the laws themselves being too voluminous to be inserted.

The Territories not being by law supplied with these standards, each new State as it is admitted is so furnished from the stock at the office previously prepared for this purpose. Thus far it appears that the force of mechanics now employed, and which has been diminished

---

* See Doc. No. 299, 22d Congress, 1st session.

by deaths and other circumstances from the first periods of the work, is about adequate to prepare the necessary weights, measures and balances.

COUNTY STANDARDS.

The standards to be furnished to the counties by each of the States should consist of a standard of length, standards of liquid and of dry capacity measures, and a set of troy and avoirdupois weights, with suitable scales and beams, or balances, for testing the town standards.

1. *The standard of length* should be the *yard*, carefully copied from the United States standard yard. The bar to be longer than the scale to be placed upon it, so that the ends may project beyond the lines between which the yard is measured.

The scales of feet, inches of the first foot, and tenths of the first inch, and tenths of yard, with the first tenth divided into hundredths should be marked upon the yard with fine strokes, transversely to the length; the principal divisions being marked by longer lines than the others. The bar should be a line measure, not cut to the length of the yard, because of the greater facility which it will afford for transferring the yard to other bars, by means of a small square, similar to the one accompanying the United States standard yards, with which the yards for the counties should likewise be provided; it will also allow of other yard measures being laid upon this, in order to compare their lengths and divisions more readily.

2. *The standards of liquid capacity measures* should be the *gallon*, containing 231 cubic inches, the half gallon, quart, pint, half pint, and gill all to be made of brass. The body of the vessels to be made of sheet brass, one tenth of an inch in thickness, thickened at the top by a band to one fifth of an inch. The bottom to be made of cast brass, turned, since the effects of use, and of the comparisons if made with water, will make this necessary. The interior dimensions should be the same as the United States standards. The standards should be without handles, as they will be equally convenient for the purpose of comparing the town standards, and it will tend to prevent their being used for other purposes.

3. *The standards of dry measures* should consist of the *half bushel*, to contain 1075.21 cubic inches; the peck, the half peck and quarter peck, to be of a cylindrical form, made of stout sheet brass, one tenth of an inch in thickness, and thickened at the top by a band, to one fifth of an inch. The bottom also to be of stout sheet brass, one fifth of an inch thick, and slightly concave, to prevent the spring in the bottom, which might occur if the bottom were a plane. The interior diameter of each measure, should be equal to the height from the centre of the bottom to the plane of the rim. The half bushel should have handles for the convenience of handling, but it will be better for the others not to have them, for the reasons mentioned in reference to the liquid measures. The thickness of the bottom, one fifth of an inch, will be sufficient for these measures, as the comparisons can be made by filling with small seed, rape seed* is preferable, and "strik-

---

* The seed of the garden cockscomb (*Celosia Cristata*) answers the purpose best, but requires to be cultivated in quantity for this particular use.

ing" it. The form proposed, it is believed, will be found to be preferable to that of shallower vessels, or even to any other. It is similar to the French dry measures. It is more convenient for striking and handling than a shallower measure. It is to be hoped that the introduction of this form will be a step towards the final abolition of the practice of heaping measures.

4. The *weights* should be of the same form and denominations as those furnished to the States, viz: 50 pounds weight, 25, 20, 10, 5, 4, 3, 2, 1 pounds avoirdupois, and 1 pound troy, avoirdupois ounce weights from 8 ounces to $\frac{1}{10000}$ of an ounce, and troy ounce weights from 10 ounces to $\frac{1}{10000}$ of an ounce; all to be made of brass, and the outside to be turned. The large weights from 50 pounds to 1 pound, and some of the larger ounce weights may be cast hollow, and filled with lead to the proper weight, having a knob to be screwed in. This is for economy and the convenience of adjustment. The other ounce weights to be solid. The hundredths, thousandths, and ten thousandths of an ounce, may be made of silver or brass wire in the same manner as the United States ounce weights, the number of sides of the figure into which they are formed, denoting the weight, as a pentagon for *five* ten thousandths of an ounce, a quadrangle for *four* ten thousandths, a triangle for *three* ten thousandths, an angle for *two* ten thousandths, and a small bar for *one* ten thousandth of an ounce. For the purpose of comparing the town standards with those of the county, two balances, or scales and beams, will be necessary, one for large weights from one to fifty pounds, the other for small weights less than a pound. A plain beam, with its knife edges resting on the projecting arm of a single cast-iron column, dishes with proper knife edge supports, an index on the base of the column, and a long index arm attached to the beam, will essentially complete the arrangement. The knife edges with their bearing points should be made with extreme care, to insure the requisite sensibility in balances for verifying standards. The other parts may receive more or less finish, according to the proposed expense. Designs for balances of the above description, suitable for counties, can be furnished, if desired, to the executives of States. The cost of a full set of weights and measures of the kinds described, exclusive of the balances, will come within the limits of one hundred and fifty and two hundred dollars.

2. WEIGHTS AND MEASURES FOR THE CUSTOM-HOUSES.

The complete set of weights and measures for the custom-houses, according to the provisions made by Mr. Hassler, consists of—

1. A set of standard weights, consisting of the following pieces:
One 1 pound troy.
One 1 " avoirdupois.
One 2 " "
One 3 " "
One 4 " "   Arranged in one box.
One 5 " "
One 10 " "
One 20 " "

One 25 pounds avoirdupois. } Arranged in one box.
One 50   "   "
2. One standard yard.
3. A set of liquid capacity measures, composed of—
One gallon, with ground glass cover.
One half-gallon, with ground glass cover.
One quart, with ground glass cover.
One pint, with ground glass cover.
One half-pint, with ground glass cover.

The principal custom-houses were furnished with the above full set of liquid measures; to the others only the gallon was furnished.

4. A standard half-bushel, with ground glass cover.

The detailed list of those delivered, with the dates and places of delivery, which is too voluminous to be embraced in the report, is placed for reference in the Appendix, (No. 9.) Of those remaining in the office, twenty-three gallons are duly packed, and ready to be sent to custom-houses. The list shows that there have been delivered to custom-houses one hundred and four (104) sets of weights, ninety-one (91) standard gallons, twenty-four (24) sets of parts of the gallon, consisting of the half-gallon, quart, pint, and half-pint; twenty-two (22) standard yards, and eleven (11) standard half-bushels.

The records of the adjustment of the measures are given in the appendix, that they may be referred to in case of any accidental loss of the label which accompanies them. Each one is marked with a number, and those issued under my superintendence with the letter B.

The form of label (Appendix No. 5) shows the comparison between the measure sent and the office standard. Mr. Saxton is engaged, when time affords from other duties, in dividing and comparing the yard measures.

The divisions on the matrix of the yard measures are made by a machine of Mr. Saxton's invention, and the comparison of the end measures with the standard by his pyrometer. Both of these beautiful instruments will be found described in a subsequent division of this report.

Directions having been received to furnish standards and balances to San Francisco, and standards to three other ports in California, and one in Oregon, as soon as practicable, in order to satisfy the necessity felt in the new State for reliable standards, and to enable the framers of the new constitution to establish them as the standards of the State, a complete set of avoirdupois and troy weights, of liquid and capacity measures, and the standard yard, were shipped in December, 1849, for San Francisco. In the following April, four other sets of standards, for the towns of San Diego, Monterey, and Sonoma, in California, and Astoria, in Oregon; together with a set of balances for the State of California, and one large balance for Oregon, were shipped on board the revenue cutter "Polk;" the standards to be delivered at their destination, with the exception of those for Sonoma, which were deposited with the collector at San Francisco. Subsequently, sets of standards were sent to Olympia, W. T., and Scotsville, Oregon, on application of the collector, and by direction of the Treasury Department.

The list shows that a very large proportion of the custom-houses have been supplied with standards. Those for the others are chiefly made and in the course of delivery. The custom-houses of the States of Indiana, Illinois, Missouri, Arkansas, Texas, Wisconsin, and Iowa remain to be supplied. Arrangements will be made, as speedily as the office force allows, to complete the full sets for these custom-houses.

The standards of weights and measures at Alexandria, Virginia, having become injured and soiled for want of care, were sent to the office to be repaired, and in lieu of them was returned a new set in September, 1853.

The department has also directed that the standards lost by the burning of the custom-house at Georgetown, S. C., should be replaced.

At the time of delivering the hydrometers, Mr. Baker examined the weights and measures at the following named fourteen custom-houses: Portland, Portsmouth, Newburyport, Salem, Boston, New Bedford, Barnstable, Providence, New Haven, New York, Philadelphia, Wilmington, Del., Alexandria, and Norfolk. While on Coast Survey business there, I examined those of Wilmington, N. C., ascertained the loss of those of Georgetown, S. C., by fire, and had those of Jacksonville examined through the courtesy of Dr. Baldwin.

It was gratifying to find that in general these instruments had been cared for. Those injured by improper use, which were few in number, have been or will be replaced. The standards at Providence, Rhode Island, and at Philadelphia, Pennsylvania, were especially spoken of by Mr. Baker as very carefully preserved. The inquiry into the observance of the law (Appendix, No. 2) requiring the surveyor of each port to compare the weights and measures in use with the standards of the Treasury Department also resulted satisfactorily. The observed irregularities, it is believed, can readily be corrected by a circular from the department.

Mr. Baker's detailed report is given in the Appendix, (No. 7.) It contains, besides his remarks on this subject, the circulars to the collectors in relation to the care of the weights and measures, and other information.

3. WEIGHTS AND MEASURES—MISCELLANEOUS.

Various calls have been made upon the office by departments and officers of the government and of the States for authentic standards of weights and measures, which have been answered under the authority of the Treasury Department; this is not one of the least useful purposes subserved by the office.

The Bureau of Ordnance and Hydrography of the Navy Department having applied for a set of standards to be used at the navy yard in this city, and authority being obtained in February, 1848, the following were delivered, as desired by the bureau, viz: A standard half-bushel, gallon, yard measure, a set of avoirdupois weights from 50 pounds to one pound, and one pound troy, and from 8 ounces to $\frac{1}{10000}$ of an ounce.

Two sets of troy grain weights were also furnished, upon application, August, 1852, for the same purpose.

A standard yard was furnished, upon application, to the Engineer Bureau of the War Department.

Standard yards have also been furnished, by authority, to the general land offices in California, Oregon, Washington Territory, New Mexico, Kansas and Nebraska, and Utah Territory, upon each of which were three scales, as follows: one divided to links, tenths and hundredths of a link; another to feet, tenths and hundredths of a foot; and the third to feet, inches, tenths and eighths of an inch. A precisely similar yard was also prepared for the surveyor general of Iowa, Wisconsin, and Minnesota.

A standard yard, prepared in compliance with the application of the joint commission of the army and navy for the western coast, and not being called for by the commission, was delivered, by authority, to Major I. I. Stevens, governor of Washington Territory, in 1853.

A standard yard was furnished to the Bureau of Topographical Engineers, and five others were temporarily placed at the disposal of the chief of that corps for the purpose of constructing a base apparatus for the survey of the northern lakes. Two standards were furnished to the Mexican boundary commission, with two wooden rods, of ten feet each, marked in feet and tenths.

Twenty measuring rods of two feet each were made and graduated, by direction of the Treasury Department, for use in the construction of public works. A rod graduated in a similar way, in inches and parts, was furnished for the work in progress on the Minot's Ledge light-house.

A set of ounce weights was delivered, with the balance authorized to be furnished, to the Naval Academy at Annapolis.

A copy of the standard yard, in wood, was made and furnished to J. A. Lapham, esq., of Milwaukie, Wisconsin; also the foot measure to Norris Brothers, of Philadelphia.

Three sets of ounce and half-ounce weights were delivered to the General Post Office Department, for the purpose of testing the accuracy of balances for ascertaining the weights of letters.

Twelve copies of the "Manual," to accompany hydrometers (used in the custom-houses) for testing the strength of liquors, were delivered, by authority, to the Smithsonian Institution, to be presented to foreign institutions, and one of each for the Institution.

A hydrometer and tables were furnished to J. L. Gillespie, esq., of Honeyville, Virginia, at his expense.

A copy of the "Manual" and a hydrometer were presented to the chief officer of the British excise, in return for his kindness in procuring several gauging instruments, books, &c., for this office.

Two hydrometers and "Manuals" were furnished to Messrs. Huckerath and Van Damme, New York, at their expense.

The supply of hydrometers being nearly exhausted at the opening of the present year by distributions, twenty-five more were purchased, so as to provide for requisitions from the inspector of customs. These have been tested in the office, and proved to equal in point of accuracy the lot first received of Greiner & Son.

4. DIVISION AND COMPARISON OF STANDARD YARDS.

A machine for dividing the yard measure has been constructed under Mr. Saxton's immediate direction. The necessity for something of the kind to replace the old, laborious, and comparatively inexact mode of dividing the yard by hand was much felt, and elaborate experiments were made to determine the best arrangement of machinery for accomplishing this, as well as the best mode of comparing the length measures. The arrangement referred to for dividing the yard is very accurate, and comparatively rapid in use, needing only some slight modifications to render its operations entirely satisfactory.

Both this machine and the comparator were made in the workshop attached to the office.

The following descriptions of the two instruments are illustrated by plates I and II at the end of the Appendix.

1. SAXTON'S DIVIDING ENGINE FOR YARD MEASURES AND SUBDIVISIONS.

The purpose of this dividing machine is to trace the limiting lines, and the lines of subdivision on measures of length, by means of a travelling tracer, which, at prepared points of stoppage, is made to trace, on a matrix, lines perpendicular to its direction of travel. This machine is adapted to ruling the limits of a yard, for subdividing it into tenths, and the first tenth into hundredths. It also rules off three feet, divides the first foot into inches, and the first inch into tenths.

The main support of the machine consists of a cast-iron, horizontal, plane table, (A A, figs. 1 and 2,) to which a long brass plate, (B B, fig. 1,) is attached by screws at one end, leaving free play for expansion in the direction of the other. Stop-studs, (I I I and J J J, figs. 1 and 2,) are screwed to this plate from below, their positions giving approximately the place of the division lines. The stop-studs, (I I I, &c.,) are arranged for the yard, and tenths of the yard, (J J J, &c.,) for feet, and the inches of the first foot. Through each stud runs a horizontal steel screw, with a plane end, which is accurately adjusted so as to stop the tracer at the line to be drawn. Two brass blocks, (E and F, fig. 1,) are so arranged as to bring the matrix parallel to the travelling grooves in the plate, (D D, fig. 1,) one block, (E,) being loose, and the other, (F, fig. 1,) being screwed fast to the bed-plate. The screw, (G,) through this block, (F, fig. 1,) is so adjusted that the tracer, when its carriage is held by the first stop, shall trace the edge line of the matrix shoulder.

A spring, (K,) keeps this shoulder pressed against the zero adjusting screw. A brass carriage, (C C, figs. 1 and 2,) raised so as to clear the stops, by flanges (N N, figs. 2 and 4,) running in the angular grooves (D D, figs. 1 and 3,) of the plate, bears the tracer and all its fixtures. This carriage is made to traverse the grooves by means of a weight and connecting chain, (L L, figs. 1 and 2,) carried over a pulley at the end. Its motion is governed by an axis, (A, fig. 4,) with stop-arms, (B B,) the whole turned by a lever, (C, fig. 1.) By placing this lever vertical, the carriage traverses clear of all the stops;

by turning the lever *toward* the *tracer*, a stop-arm is made to catch on the yard subdividing stops I I I; and turning it *from* the *tracer*, a stop-arm catches on the foot and inch stops J J J. The carriage is first drawn out by hand.

For laying off hundredths of a yard and tenths of an inch, the tracer carriage is suffered to move by running a subdividing screw (P) back a given number of turns, and correcting this by an inclined plane, (M,) adjusted to cause the bearing point (E, fig. 4,) of the carriage to rotate against the screw. The screw passes through two collars, (R and Q, fig. 1,) in one of which (Q) it slides, and in the other (R) it passes through a ratchet-wheel, with a nut centre, which turns on the screw as well as in the bearing. By means of this ratchet-wheel and a ratchet-arm, the screw is arrested when it has been turned through a distance of nearly a hundredth of a yard or a tenth of an inch.

This distance is corrected by moving an inclined plane, (M,) by means of the small button, (O,) so that it will cause the bearing point (E, fig. 4,) of the carriage to rotate around a fixed point (N) in the bed-plate; the amount of correction being fixed by adjusting the inclined plane bar. Two facets give the button, (O,) and of course the inclined bar, (M,) the two positions required. When the button is turned to the left, it gives hundredths of a yard; when turned to the right, tenths of an inch.

The weight for running the tracer carriage is suspended by a flat link steel chain, (F, fig. 3,) one end of which is fixed to the table, from which it runs under a pulley fixed to the weight, up to a drum axle, (K', figs. 1 and 3,) around which it winds. Sliding on the same axle is a drum, (A'', figs. 1 and 3,) moved along the axle by an endless screw (Z, figs. 1 and 3,) working in a fixed rack, so as to keep the carriage chain vertical at the winding point. Connected with this axle by a double gearing at B', (fig. 1,) is a flat plate fly (K'', figs. 1 and 3,) to regulate the velocity of the carriage.

The movements of the tracer are governed by a horizontal crank, (G', figs. 1 and 2,) on a vertical axle, which bears an eccentric (H', figs. 1 and 4,) to push out the tracer, and a circular cam (G, fig. 4,) to bear down the rear end of the lever (C', fig. 4,) and lift the tracer. The tracer has a double joint, for horizontal and vertical motion. The tracer is loaded at will. Above it is a micrometer microscope frame, (L', figs. 1 and 4,) for comparing the stops with the standard.

In using this machine, the tracer carriage is moved to the left and arrested by the last stop. The matrix is carefully placed against the blocks and zero screw. The subdividing screw (P, fig. 1,) is carried out one-tenth of a yard, and fastened in the latch collar. The division of the yard is then traced. The stop-arm (B, fig. 4,) is then disengaged by means of the lever, (C', fig. 1,) and the carriage travels to the next stop, and so on until the yard is divided into tenths. The hundredths are then marked by using the crank and ratchet movement of the subdividing screw. The feet, inches, and tenths are engraved by a second traverse of the carriage. The length of division lines is controlled by a stop-plate, (M, fig. 4,) with notches on the circumference, in which an adjustable stop of the tracer frame enters to trace long lines; while to trace short lines the stop rests against the circumference of the stop-plate. A ratchet-wheel, (J', fig. 1,) moved by a detent on the axle of the tracer crank turns the stop-plate. The temperature is regulated by governing the heat of the room.

FIG. 1.—PLAN OF THE YARD DIVIDING MACHINE.

A A. Cast-iron table.
B B. Brass bed-plate.
C C. Brass carriage bearing tracer, and sliding in the grooves D D.
E F. Brass blocks screwed to bed B, against which the matrix to be divided is placed; F bears the zero screw G.
H H. Matrix to be divided.
I I I. Stops-blocks, with adjusting screws, for yards and tenths.
J J J. Same for feet and inches.
K. Spring to keep the matrix up to the zero screw.
L L. Flat link steel chain leading over the pulley N'' to the weight.
M. Adjusting inclined plane bar.
N. Centre of motion of tracer carriage when guided by the inclined bar.
O. Adjusting button with two facets: when the button is turned against the right facet, the tracer marks tenths of an inch; when turned to the left, it marks hundredths of a yard.
P. Subdividing screw and rod.
Q. Fixed collar.
R. Latch collar for latching screw.
S. Toothed click plate turning on the projecting nut of the ratchet-wheel U.
T. Fixed collar in which the central nut of the ratchet-wheel turns.
U. Ratchet-wheel turning as a nut upon the screw P, and itself turned by the click of the click plate S.
V. Crank of toothed wheel W for subdividing. By turning this a certain number of times to the left, the tracer carriage is moved forward the requisite distance for the subdivision. It is first turned to the right until the crank strikes against the stop Y.
X. Sliding rod with slide supports, and a nut arm (M', fig 3,) resting on the screw axle of the crank V.
Y. Folding stop on the sliding rod X for arresting crank V. When this catch is turned out it gives tenths of an inch; when folded in, hundreds of a yard.
Z. Endless screw, working in fixed rack, and sliding the chain drum on the axle to secure vertical winding as the weight chain runs off at A''.
B'. Gearing to drive fly-wheel.
C'. Small lever turning an axle, on which are two stop arms to catch on the stops and arrest the carriage.
D'. A spring with a roller on its end, which, when the lever C is vertical, catches in a notched cam on the horizontal axis and holds it steady.

E′. Bed-plate of tracer frame.
F′. Tracer.
G′. Crank to turn a horizontal eccentric H′ for pushing out the tracer, and also to turn a circular cam which lifts the tracer by bearing down a lever.
I′. Weight to draw back the tracer.
J′. Ratchet-wheel turned by detent on the vertical axle.
K′. Drum axle, K″ fly, O′ ratchet arm.

Fig 2.—SLIDE ELEVATION OF YARD DIVIDING MACHINE.

A A, &c. Cast-iron bed.
B B, &c. Brass bed-plate.
H H. Matrix to be divided.
I I I & J J J, &c. Stops for subdividing.
N′ N′. Flanges of the tracer carriage.
L L. Chain for drawing carriage by weight.
G G. Wheels for driving fly K″.
P. Subdividing screw.
V. Crank for running screw back through a subdivision.
M. Bar for correcting screw.
G′. Crank for running out and raising the tracer F by an eccentric and circular cam.
P. Subdividing screw.
M′. Crank to ditto.
V. Crank for running the carriage through a subdivision.

Fig. 3—END ELEVATION OF YARD DIVIDING MACHINE.

A A. End support of iron bed.
B B. Brass bed-plates.
D D. Angular grooves.
L. Chain connecting with weight.
Z. Endless screw on sliding chain drum.
F. Weight chain wound on drum K at A′.
K″. Fly.
M′. Crank of subdividing screw.
V. Crank for running the carriage through a subdivision.
O′. Ratchet arm.
U. Ratchet-wheel.
L′. Click.

Fig. 4. PROJECTION OF TRACER CARRIAGE FROM UNDERNEATH.

A′. Axis bearing stop-arms B B.
C. Pin to slide on inclined bar.
D. Centre of motion.
E. Bearing point.
H′. Eccentric for pushing out the tracer.
G. Cam for lifting tracer.
C′. Lever on which the cam acts.

F. Tracer.
L′. Micrometer microscope mounting.
P′. Weight to draw the tracer back.
M. A stop plate, having upon its circumference notches at certain intervals, so that a stop projecting from the tracer frame enters the notches at the proper time, and thus allows the tracer to mark the long lines necessary to indicate the foot, six inches, &c.; the stop rests against the circumference in marking the short lines.

FIG. 5.

U. Ratchet-wheel.
S. Click-plate in contact with ratchet-wheel.
C. Central nut of ratchet-wheel.

II. SAXTON'S REFLECTING COMPARATOR AND PYROMETER.

This very ingenious instrument has been applied to comparing the yard of the kind called end measure, in which the distance between the two ends of the bar is the length of the standard yard. One end of the bar to be compared abuts against a fixed support, the other end is free to move, the whole bar being supported horizontally on rollers. The free end presses against a small horizontal bar or slide connected by a chain with a vertical axis carrying a small mirror. As the free end of the bar moves, the slide moves also and turns the mirror. A scale placed horizontally at any convenient distance from the bar and in the same general direction, is reflected in the mirror, the image being viewed by a telescope placed at the same distance as the scale, and directly over it. The distance of the reflected image of the scale being twice that of the scale from the mirror; the motion of the mirror is shown as on a divided circle of that radius, and the smallest movement of the mirror is measurable.

The same principle is applicable to other forms of length measure, and has been also applied to detect eccentricity of the axis or pivots of instruments, and of motion.

Fig. 1, plate II, shows the general arrangement of this apparatus, and figs. 2, 3, 4, 5, and 6, give the parts more in detail. Fig. 1 shows the arrangement of the bar, its supports, the mirror, and other parts connected with it at A A; the scale at R S; the telescope for observing at T. Fig. 2 gives the details of the telescope and support for it, and for the scale shown by fig. 3. Fig. 4 is the elevation; and fig. 5 the plan of the mirror and connected apparatus, and of their support. Fig. 6 shows the connection of the mirror and of the stem which communicates movement from the standard bar to the mirrors.

The following is a detailed description of the arrangement of the parts: In fig. 1, plate II, A A represents the plan of the stone supports and frame, on which the bar is placed, drawn on a scale of one-sixteenth of the actual size. (A) A, A, are three stone piers which rise two and a half feet above the floor of the comparing room, but not connected with it, and support the instrument. C C is the position of the bar which is placed horizontally on the rollers B, B, B, one end resting against the abutting screw D, and the other acting on the mirror M to turn it. The lower part of the fig. (A) shows the arrangement of the telescope T and attached scale R S.

Fig. 2, plate II, represents the plan of the telescope and part of the attached scale drawn one-fourth of the full size. The telescope rests in Ys (Y Y) attached to a movable bed-plate, and adjusted by the screws S.

Fig. 3, plate II, is the elevation of the scale of its full size, the line above the division indicating the side of the zero, which corresponds to diminishing lengths. Each of the small divisions of the scale, as used in the office comparisons, corresponds to a difference of $\frac{1}{25000}$th of an inch on the bar. The small reflector is represented of full size by figs. 4 and 5—fig. 4 being the elevation, and fig. 5 the plan of the reflecting apparatus. E represents the plan and elevation of the plate, by which the apparatus is fastened to the stone post, on which it rests. G represents a slide in which the abutting screw S is inserted, and against which the end of the bar is placed; this slide moves on two uprights firmly fastened to the plate F. The mirror M, on a vertical axis, turns on hardened steel centres, and is supported above by a bracket fastened to the plate F. A small fusee chain passes once round the axis, and is secured from slipping by an arrangement represented at fig. 6. Both ends of this chain are fastened to the slide—one by a small bracket at H, on the edge of the slide, and the other by the small spring I which keeps it stretched. Thus, when the slide moves, a rotary motion is communicated to the axis of the reflector. The spiral spring I, attached at one end to the slide, and at the other to one of its bearings, serves to draw the slide close against the end of the bar to be measured. The abutting screw S has one hundred threads to the inch, and a micrometer head (N) divided into ten equal parts. One turn of the screw would, therefore, increase or diminish the length by one-hundredth of an inch, ten turns by one-tenth, &c.; while each division on the head would correspond to one-thousandth of an inch. Whole turns of the screw are shown by a small scale on a sliding bar K, which is kept in contact with the side of the slide G by a spring L. The bar carries an arm which, rising to the top of the micrometer head, gives the means of setting.

The manner of comparing a bar with the standard may now be explained. The standard is placed upon the rollers of the frame, one end resting against the fixed abutting screw D; the other adjusted against the abutting screw of the pyrometer in such a manner that when the observer looks through the telescope T, he will see the zero of the scale reflected by the small mirror. The standard being removed, the bar to be compared is inserted in its place, the end resting against the fixed screw D; if its length differs from that of the standard, the mirror is moved, showing no longer the zero, but some other division; and the number of divisions moved over, gives, in twenty-five thousandths of an inch, the difference in length between the bar and standard. The mode of using this instrument as a pyrometer is obvious.

5. COMPARISONS OF FOREIGN STANDARDS WITH THOSE OF THE UNITED STATES.

A. *Comparisons of British Standards.*

Copies of the new British standards of length and weight have been presented to the United States by the British government, through G. B. Airy, esq., Astronomer Royal. They are accompanied by the following statement:

Copies of the British standards of length and weight enclosed in box No. 10, and addressed to the United States of America.

Bronze standard of length No. 11.
Malleable iron standard of length No. 57.

At the bottom of each of the two holes near the extremities of each bar is a gold pin, upon which are drawn three transversal lines and two longitudinal lines. The length one English yard is defined by the distance from the middle transversal line in one hole, to the middle transversal line in the other hole, using the parts of those lines which are central between the longitudinal lines, the temperature of the bronze bar No. 11 being 61°.79 Fahrenheit, and that of the iron bar No. 57 being 62°.58 Fahrenheit. The expansion of the bronze bar is 0.000342 inch, and that of the iron bar is 0.000221 inch, for each degree of Fahrenheit.

Standard weight No. 5.
This weight is heavier than the (commercial) British pound of 7,000 grains by 0.008 grains.

G. B. AIRY.

December 21, 1855.

The bronze standard No. 11 has been compared with the United States standard, viz: the yard from 27 to 63 inches, on the 82-inch Troughton scale. The comparisons were made by Mr. Saxton, in part, by means of the Troughton comparator, and mainly on the dividing machine. The following are the results of the comparisons by the former method:

May 8, British bronze standard shorter 0.00093 inch, temperature 59°.0
    8   "   "   "   "   0.00090 "   "   59°.0
    9   "   "   "   "   0.00090 "   "   63°.0

Mean of three comparisons............0.00091 "   "   60°.3

A considerable number of comparisons were made on the dividing machine described in a former part of this report, the details of which are given in Appendix No. 22, Table I. A microscope-micrometer was mounted on the tracing-frame, and its wires brought into contact with the lines on the standards, while the carriage rested against the stops defining the yard on the machine.

The expansion given for the bronze bar is slightly less than that assumed for the brass of which the dividing machine and the United States standards are made. The comparisons, however, are made at

Ex. Doc. 27——2

temperatures so near that at which the bars have their standard length, that no correction on that account would be sensible.

The following is an abstract of the results :

British bronze standard shorter than the American yard.

Means of comparisons May 1, 1856	0.00065	inch.
May 2	0.00069	"
May 8–9	0.00091	"
Oct. 14	0.00088	"
Oct. 15	0.00088	"
Mean	0.00080 ± 0.00004	inch.

In these comparisons the two standards are virtually at the same temperature, as long as we assume the expansion of the comparator to be the same as that of the bars compared. The British standard, however, is at its true length at a temperature of $61°.79$ Fahrenheit, or $0°.2$ less than the standard temperature of the American yard. The above difference requires, therefore, to be increased by the corresponding expansion of the British standard $= 0.00007$ inch, and we find thus that the British standard is shorter than the American yard by 0.00087 inch—a quantity by no means inappreciable. A difference in this direction, amounting to about one-thousandth of an inch, has long been indicated by indirect comparisons; but a full discussion of the subject must be postponed until after the publication of the report of the committee having charge of the construction of the new British standard.

Comparisons of the British iron standard are still in progress.

The copy of the British standard commercial pound was compared with the American standard commercial pound—the weight used being that made by Mr. Hassler from the troy pound in the United States mint, and marked with a star, (commonly designated as the *star pound*.)

By forty weighings, (see Table II, Appendix 22,) Mr. Saxton found the British weight No. 5 heavier than the American pound by nine one-thousandths of a grain; and since it is stated to be heavier by eight one-thousandths of a grain than the British commercial pound of 7,000 grains, there is but a thousandth of a grain outstanding between the American and British standards of weight—an agreement quite surprising when we consider the process of subdivision and addition by which these pounds of 7,000 grains were, in both instances, derived from the respective troy pounds, which were assumed equal; the United States mint pound being a copy of the imperial troy pound made by Captain Kater in 1824.

B.—Comparison of French standards.

The brass kilogramme, forming part of the set of weights and measures presented to this country by France in return for a set of United States standards, (see a subsequent part of this report,) was compared by Mr. Saxton with the original brass kilogramme bearing the stamp of the French committee on weights and measures, and belonging to the American Philosophical Society, having been originally brought to this country by Mr. Hassler.

The comparisons are given in Table III of Appendix 22. It appears from them that the committee kilogramme is lighter than the new one, by Mr. Silberman, by 0.170 grain, and, consequently, lighter than the French standard is at present by 0.125 grain, or eight milligrammes—an amount by which the several copies made by the committee probably did not differ originally. The weight in question is in excellent preservation, but the casting appears to have some imperfections, and moisture or oil which has since evaporated, may have originally been contained in the small holes.

The same committee kilogramme was compared with the platinum kilogramme, by Fortin, procured by Mr. Gallatin, and certified by M. Arago not to differ by one milligramme from the platinum kilogramme in the archives of France. Table IV, of Appendix 22, gives the comparisons made by Mr. Saxton, from which it appears that the platinum kilogramme is heavier by 1,626 grain. The difference of buoyancy in air is stated by the French committee at 88.4 milligrammes, which is equal to 1.30 grain. The committee kilogramme would thus be 0.326 grain lighter than the platinum kilogramme.

The same weights were compared by Mr. Hassler, (see H. Doc. No. 299, 1832, Schedule M, p. 33.,) and the difference found to be 1.404 grain.

Comparisons of the new French measures and weights with the American standards are in progress.

C.—*Comparison of the Mexican Vara.*

A Mexican vara, the standard of length, brought from Mexico at the close of the war, by Major Turnbull of the Topographical Engineers, was presented to the office by Colonel Abert, chief of the Topographical Engineers; a careful comparison of its length with the standard of this country was made under my direction, which gave its length to be $= 32.9682$ inches at $58°.7$ Fahrenheit. The results of the comparison are appended. (Appendix No. 22.)

This measure was made by soldering sheet brass upon the tinned surface of an iron bar.

The comparison showed a variation from temperature similar and nearly identical with that of an iron bar; and it was this circumstance that first drew attention to the brass covering of the vara, which was intended, no doubt, as a protection against the corrosion of the iron bar. The division lines on the vara were too coarse to admit of a good comparison, and it was necessary to take the edges of the divisions as the true division, as it was impossible to define the centre of the coarse line. It is understood that this vara was one of a number prepared for distribution to the several states of the Mexican republic, and deposited in the archives of the capital at the time it was captured by the American army.

6. BALANCES FOR THE STATES.

These are constructed by direction of Congress, under the joint resolution of 1838, and are intended to furnish to the States the means of adjusting standard weights and smaller capacity measures.

Report has been made from time to time of the progress of the work by the first superintendent, Mr. Hassler, and by myself. The progress up to 1845 was stated in my first report, and that to January, 1848, in my second.* As there stated, the yearly progress on the work is about thirteen per cent. of the whole, when the workmen are employed steadily on the work, and are not drawn off to execute the weights and measures. Since that date, the per centage has been very nearly the same, although the work upon the large balances for the United States mint at New Orleans and Philadelphia, involving, from their size, the necessity for entire new patterns, tended to lower the per centage in the aggregate.

At the date of that report, the whole number completed was eighteen (18) of the first class, nineteen (19) of the second, and thirteen (13) of the third class. At the present time, the whole number completed is thirty-one (31) of the first class, thirty-one (31) of the second class, and thirty-five (35) of the third class.

As soon as there were on hand enough balances to make it safe to do so, I issued the circular marked A, (Appendix No. 4,) to the governors of the different States, informing them that the balances were ready for delivery, and that they would be put up at the State house, recommending, at the same time, that a fire-proof room should be prepared for them, of which a drawing was given, and that they should be placed, with the standards of weights and measures, under the charge of some scientific person who would attend to their use and safe-keeping.

This circular has been re-issued occasionally, and has met with increasing attention, the executives of many of the States having induced the legislatures to make suitable provision for keeping these instruments and the standards.

At the date of my report, in 1848, eight States had been furnished with a set of balances, namely : New York, New Jersey, Delaware, Ohio, Texas, Maryland, Massachusetts, and South Carolina ; since that time, Maine, Pennsylvania, Virginia, Connecticut, Iowa, Kentucky, Tennessee, Wisconsin, and California, have each received a full set, and one first class balance has been sent to Oregon, two large and two of medium size with the Japan expedition ; one large and one small balance to the government of France, and two of the largest size, specially adapted to weighing of coin, have been sent to the mints at Philadelphia and New Orleans.

---

*Letter from the Secretary of the Treasury, communicating the report of Prof. Alexander D. Bache, relative to standard weights, measures, and balances, February 27, 1845. Doc. No. 159, House of Representatives, Treasury Department, 28th Congress, 2d session.

Letter from the Secretary of the Treasury, transmitting a report of the progress made in the construction of standard weights, measures, and balances during the years 1846 and 1847, August 12, 1848, 30th Congress, 1st session. Ex. Doc. No. 84, House of Representatives.

The balances for the State of Pennsylvania were set up in the capitol by Mr. Saxton in August, 1850. Those for Virginia were delivered also by Mr. Saxton, in November, 1850, and placed in the capitol at Richmond. The balances for Maine were sent to the order of the executive, in November, 1850. Those for California were shipped from New York, with the weights and measures, on board the revenue cutter Polk, in 1850, to be delivered at San Francisco.

The set of balances forwarded to the State of Texas, in 1848, under the charge of Mr. Fauntleroy, assistant United States Coast Survey, were delivered by him to the collector at Galveston. They remained there until so much corroded as to render extensive repairs necessary. They were brought back to the office, and now remain subject to the call of the executive of that State, having been put in perfect order again.

The number of balances on hand being greater than the calls for them, I again, in August, 1853, addressed a circular, of the form previously used, to the governors of those States yet to receive balances, (Appendix No. 4,) informing them that they were ready for delivery, and recommending again a suitable form for a fire-proof building that should be provided for them. In answer, applications were received from the executives of Kentucky, Louisiana, Alabama, and Michigan. The balances for Kentucky were accordingly sent by express to the direction indicated by the governor. They were accompanied by a set of avoirdupois ounce weights, from 8 ounces to $\frac{1}{10000}$ of an ounce. The balances for Louisiana and Michigan are ready to be forwarded as soon as I am advised of the mode by which it is desired to have them sent and the persons appointed to receive and take charge of them. Those for Alabama will be sent at an early day, when a person can be spared from the office to put them up in the place designed for their reception. Indiana was not then prepared for their reception. The executive of Rhode Island awaits the action of the legislature in regard to preparing a suitable place of safety for the standards and balances. No answers have been received from the other States to which the circular was sent.

A balance made from the same patterns which were used in those of the mints at Philadelphia and New Orleans, was sent, by direction of the Treasury Department, with copies of the standards of weights and measures, to the World's Fair, London, where a medal was awarded to the articles of the highest class that an instrument not claiming to be an invention could receive. This balance was entirely from original designs by Mr. Saxton.

The first and third class balances sent to the government of France have been placed in the "Conservatoire des Arts et Metiers," of Paris, and are the subject of an elaborate and highly favorable report (Appendix No. 17) by the distinguished curator of that establishment, M. Silberman. The balance designed by Mr. Saxton, and those by Mr. Hassler, modified by Mr. Saxton, and made in the workshops of the office, have thus received the approval of the highest European authorities.*

---

*These balances and weights and measures were, by the kindness of M. Vattemare, placed in the French Exhibition of the Industy of all Nations, and received the award of a complimentary medal.

The city of Washington has applied for balances, the delivery of which has been authorized. They remain subject to the call of the mayor, as I understand no safe place has been provided for their reception.

A small balance, with the necessary weights, was authorized, (Nov. 1851,) upon application, to be loaned to Prof. Henry, of the Smithsonian Institution, for the use of the commission appointed to examine the building stone offered for the extension of the Capitol. It was to be returned at the termination of the investigations.

A medium-sized balance of the kind constructed for the States was authorized to be loaned, (Nov., 1853,) upon application of the Navy Department, to J. H. Alexander, esq., of Baltimore, for the purpose of conducting a scientific investigation upon the character of alimentary substances used as subsistence in the navy. The balance and weights are to be returned when the investigation is completed.

A table is appended (Appendix No. 8) showing the States, foreign governments, &c., to which balances have been delivered under authority, with the dates of their delivery, &c., together with a list of the balances in use in the office of weights and measures. By reference to this table, it will be seen that sixteen States have been furnished with a set of balances, comprising the first, second, and third sizes, exclusive of Texas, from which State the balances were subsequently returned, and the Territory of Oregon, to which a large size balance was furnished. Four foreign governments have each been presented with one or more of the balances included in the set for the States; making, in all thus delivered, four of the large size, two of the medium, and one of the small size.

The total number delivered is twenty of the large size, sixteen of the medium, and the same number of the small size.

Assuming thirty-five as the number of sets to be constructed for the States, there yet remain to be constructed, to complete this number, and supply the place of those presented to foreign governments, four of the large and four of the medium-sized balances.

In the work upon the balances, the castings are made, and the rough filing of the different pieces executed, as far as practicable, by the laborers, after which the pieces for a number of balances (say three at a time, with the present force of five mechanics) are taken up and carried through the different processes of smooth filing, or turning, fitting, grinding, polishing, &c., until they are finished and ready to put together. Several instruments are thus in progress at once; and when the parts are complete, they are assembled, and each instrument is placed in its case and adjusted.

Since the 1st of January, 1848, thirteen of the first class balances, twelve of the second, and twenty-two of the third size, have been made at the office.

Adding to the above the construction of fifty-one sets of small capacity measures, consisting of the half gallon, quart, pint, and half pint; of forty sets of avoirdupois ounce weights, from 8 ounces to $\frac{1}{10000}$ of an ounce; of fifty-four sets of troy ounce weights, from 10 ounces to $\frac{1}{10000}$ of an ounce; and the construction of the yard-dividing machine—the sum presents the production of the establishment, as far as the workshops are concerned, for the past nine years.

7. WEIGHTS, MEASURES, AND BALANCES FOR FOREIGN GOVERNMENTS.

After the burning of the Parliament houses in London, and the destruction at that time of the English standard of measures deposited there, from which our own is derived, Congress ordered, by a resolution of both houses, that a complete set of the standards of the United States be prepared and presented to the British government; which was accordingly done, and the standards, together with one of the largest size balances, were transmitted by our minister in London. (See Mr. Hassler's report, November 12, 1843.) Judging that similar presents to the other governments of Europe would aid in obtaining and diffusing a correct knowledge of the actual standards of different nations and tend towards the attainment of the great object of international uniformity of weights and measures, and France being in importance next to be considered, Congress, by a joint resolution, approved June 30, 1848, "*Resolved,* * * * that the Secretary of State be directed to furnish to Alexander Vattemare one complete series of the standard weights and measures of the United States, now in the Department of State, to be presented to the Department of France." In accordance with which, and with the direction of the Treasury Department, of November, 1848, a complete set of the standards, after a careful re-comparison with the standards in this office, was delivered to M. Vattemare,* in November, 1850, to be presented to his government. Correspondence in relation to this subject will be found in the Appendix, No. 17. The following is a list of the standards thus sent:

List of weights and measures sent to France, November, 1850.

1 large size balance. } The different parts being packed in seven
1 small size balance. } boxes.

Capacity measures.

1 half bushel. } Contained in a mahogany box with velvet fittings, which was placed in an outer packing box.
1 gallon measure. Fitted as above.
1 half gallon.
1 quart.
1 pint.
1 half pint.
} Contained in one box.

NOTE.—Each of the capacity measures was provided with a ground glass cover.

Avoirdupois weights of 50, 25, 20, 10, 5, 4, 3, 2, 1, and 1 pound troy, fitted in two mahogany boxes, and both placed in one packing box.

---

* Agent for international exchanges.

WEIGHTS AND MEASURES.

Set of avoirdupois ounce weights, from eight ounces to $\frac{1}{10000}$ of an ounce, packed in a mahogany box.

Set of troy ounce weights, from ten ounces to $\frac{1}{10000}$, packed in a mahogany box, and placed with the box of avoirdupois ounce weights in one of the boxes containing the parts of the large balance.

Standard yard, with matrix of brass, fitted in a mahogany box, in an outer packing box.

The following tables show the comparisons of the weights and measures sent to France with the standards in this office:

WEIGHTS AND MEASURES. 25

Table of the comparisons of the capacity measures.

Name of standard.	No. of standard.	Date of comparison.	Barometer.	Temperature of water.	Difference of weight from standard.	Corrections for temperature.	RESULT. − Too large; + too small.			Remarks.
							Single.	Mean.	Corrected mean.	
			Inches.	*Fah't.*	*Grains.*	*Grains.*	*Grains.*	*Grains.*	*Grains.*	
Gallon........	140	1844. Feb. 6	29.89	48.4	− 4.80	− 4.928	− 0.13	....	....	The gallon was packed with velvet fittings in a mahogany box, which was enclosed in a packing box.
		7	29.90	47.2	− 5.60	− 5.599	+ 0.00			
		8	29.90	48.5	− 5.00	− 4.867	− 0.13			
		20	30.14	47.2	− 4.25	− 5.599	− 0.45			
		21	29.98	49.0	− 4.25	− 4.526	− 0.28			
		22	30.00	50.6	− 4.05	− 3.019	+ 1.03			* Using glass plate belonging to measure.
		28	30.23	49.2	− 5.02	− 4.345	− 0.67*			
		1849. Jan. 9	30.00	48.7	+ 4.5	+ 4.87	+ 0.37	} − 0.116	....	} Recompared by Prof. Bache.
		Mar. 23	30.30	52.7	+ 0.4	+ 0.11	+ 0.51			
Half bushel...	62	1845. Jan. 25	29.47	52.3	+ 4.1	+ 3.60	+ 0.50	....	....	The half bushel was enclosed in a mahogany box with velvet fittings, and this box placed within a packing box.
		Mar. 7	30.22	53.5	+ 6.5	+ 5.79	+ 0.71			
		1849. Jan. 9	30.00	49.5	− 20.6	− 18.99	+ 1.61	+ 0.10	− 0.38	
		Mar. 23	30.33	52.9	+ 2.0	+ 1.41	+ 0.59			
		24	30.30	53.8	+ 9.5	+ 8.2	+ 1.30			
Half gallon...	58	1851. Mar. 10	30.20	48.2	− 2.6	− 2.534	− 0.076			
		13	30.13	52.6	− 0.25	− 0.1587	− 0.0913			
		15	....	54.4	+ 1.3	− 1.460	− 0.150			
		Nov. 13	30.26	52.5	+ 0.3	− 0.2355	− 0.645	− 0.24	....	
		Mar. 4	30.30	49.8	− 2.05	− 0.954	− 0.096			
		14	30.29	53.6	− 0.22	− 0.348	− 0.128			
Quart........	58	Nov. 13	30.20	52.9	+ 0.12	+ 0.0761	− 0.044	− 0.06	....	
		Nov. 15	29.70	53.8	+ 0.35	+ 0.174	− 0.076			
Pint..........	58	Nov. 13	30.20	53.8	+ 0.38	+ 0.220	+ 0.16	+ 0.083	....	
		17	30.20	52.9	+ 0.05	+ 0.0380	+ 0.012			
Half pint.....	58	Nov. 10	30.15	48.6	+ 0.3	+ 0.30045	+ 0.00045	− 0.077	....	
		18	....	51.1	+ 0.2	+ 0.1491	− 0.0509			
		13	29.55	53.0	+ 0.15	+ 0.031	− 0.181			

WEIGHTS AND MEASURES.

Comparison of the weights with the standards in this office at 62° Fahrenheit.

Denomination.		Difference from standard.	M'n result. —too large, +too sm'll.	Corrected result.	Denomination.		Difference from standard.	M'n result. —too large, +too sm'll.	Corrected result.
No.	Weights.				No.	Weight.			
	Lbs. avoir.	*Grains.*				*Lbs. avoir.*	*Grains.*		
35	50	+ 1.5			35	4	0.00		
35	50	+ 0.45			35	4	+ 0.02	+ 0.013	
35	50	+ 0.85	+ 0.93		35	3	0.00		
35	25	+ 0.15			35	3	— 0.01		
35	25	— 0.43			35	3	0.00	— 0.003	
35	25	— 0.27	— 0.183		35	2	+ 0.05		
35	20	— 0.23			35	2	+ 0.04		
35	20	— 0.17			35	2	+ 0.05	+ 0.046	
35	20	— 0.17	— 0.19		35	1	— 0.01		
35	10	+ 0.18			36	1	— 0.005		
35	10	+ 0.15			35	1	0.00	— 0.005	
35	10	+ 0.17	+ 0.17		35	Troy 1 lb.	— 0.01		
35	5	— 0.01			35	1	— 0.005		
35	5	0.00			35	1	— 0.005	— 0.007	
35	5	+ 0.01	0.00		1	{ 10 oz. / + 2 oz. }	— 0.005		
35	4	+ 0.02			1	...do...	0.000	— 0.002	

Set of avoirdupois ounce weights.—No. 19.

One 8 oz	One 0.1 oz	One 0.003 oz. silver wire
One 4 oz	One 0.05 oz. silver wire	One 0.002 ......do
One 2 oz	One 0.04 ......do	One 0.001 ......do
One 1 oz	One 0.03 ......do	One 0.0005 ......do
One 0.5 oz	One 0.02 ......do	One 0.0004 ......do
One 0.4 oz	One 0.01 ......do	One 0.0003 ......do
One 0.3 oz	One 0.005 ......do	One 0.0002 ......do
One 0.2 oz	One 0.004 ......do	One 0.0001 ......do

Set of troy ounce weights.—No. 44.

One 10 oz	One 0.3 oz	One 0.004 oz. silver wire
One 6 oz	One 0.2 oz	One 0.003 ......do
One 5 oz	One 0.1 oz	One 0.002 ......do
One 4 oz	One 0.05 oz. silver wire	One 0.001 ......do
One 3 oz	One 0.04 ......do	One 0.0005 ......do
One 2 oz	One 0.03 ......do	One 0.0004 ......do
One 1 oz	One 0.02 ......do	One 0.0003 ......do
One 0.5 oz	One 0.01 ......do	One 0.0002 ......do
One 0.4 oz	One 0.005 ......do	One 0.0001 ......do

NOTE.—The above agree with the standard to within an appreciable difference.

Comparison of the standard yard and matrix.—No. 118.

By three comparisons made at this office, the distance between the lines formed by the junction of the yard with matrix is 0.0001 inch less than the standard at 62° Fahrenheit. And by three comparisons of the scale on matrix, the distance between the extreme divisions is 0.0002 of an inch less than the standard at 62° Fahrenheit.

Table showing the probable error of a single weighing, and of the mean of several weighings.

Denomination.	No. of standard.	No. of weighing.	Probable error of single weighing.	Probable error of the mean.	Remarks.
			Grains.	Grains.	
Half bushel	62	5	.779	.349	
Gallon	140	9	.546	.115	
Half gallon	58	4	.031	.015	
Quart	58	3	.059	.033	
Pint	58	3	.05	.028	
Half pint	58	3	.062	.036	

Weights.—(Avoirdupois.)

Denomination.	No. of standard.	No. of weighing.	Probable error of single weighing.	Probable error of the mean.	Remarks.
			Grains.	Grains.	
50 lbs	35	3	.357	.205	
25.do	35	3	.19	.114	
20.do	35	3	.023	.013	
10.do	35	3	.009	.005	
5.do	35	3	.006	.003	The lower denominations were adjusted so as to agree with the standards to within an appreciable quantity.
4.do	35	3	.0077	.004	
3.do	35	3	.0036	.002	
2.do	35	3	.004	.002	
1.do	35	3	.003	.002	
1 lb. troy	35	3	.002	.001	

By direction of the Treasury Department, one of the balances of the largest and one of the smallest class were sent to the government of France with the weights and measures.

The high terms of praise in which M. Silberman, than whom there can be no better judge in Europe, speaks of the weights and measures and balances received from the United States, is a rich reward for the labor bestowed upon them. His appreciation of the balances was shown by the gratifying fact that he used the smaller one, especially adapted to the purpose, to compare the platinum kilogramme which he sent to the London World's Exhibition. He remarks that its sensibility and constancy of results are beyond all reproach, and that his weighings have been made with certainty "to half a milligramme." This praise is the more highly appreciated that it is exceedingly discriminating--the parts selected for special notice, and the qualities attributed to them and to the instruments, being so well chosen. As the praise applies to Mr. Hassler and to Mr. Saxton, I may speak thus unreservedly in regard to it. (Appendix No. 17.)

The government of France, in return for this courtesy on the part of the United States, presented, through M. Alexander Vattemare, a complete sets of weights, measures, and balances, consisting of three different series: the first being composed of a standard metre of steel upon a brass base, and a standard kilogramme of brass gilt; the second, of a brass metre divided, and of a litre, both made by Gambey; and the third of the series of weights and measures which compose the assortment of a bureau of verification of the first order, in which was also included the apparatus for weighing, measuring, and sealing, necessary to these bureaus.

This was accompanied by a valuable article by M. Silberman, the director of the National Conservatory of Arts and Trades, upon the verification of the standards, and also describing his new process for determining the expansion of metal bars. This process was employed for the first time in the comparison of the standard metre for the United States.

The process which had previously been used with satisfaction as regards the accuracy of the results gave the expansion to a sixteenth of a millimetre; but the process of M. Silberman carries the accuracy to the one hundredth of a millimetre. In order to trace the exact length of a metre upon the bar at the temperature of $0°$ and $100°$ centigrade, a new method was designed and used by M. Silberman, and consists, essentially, in using a beam compass with very solid points, (the extreme points of which are of tempered steel, turned and sharpened with extreme care, and are at the distance of a metre apart,) which is placed in a trough filled with melting ice, having holes to allow the points to project. The bar upon which the distance is to be marked is also put in melting ice, and after remaining two hours, is taken out and the points of the beam compass applied. This gives the length upon the bar of a metre at the temperature of melting ice. The bar is then placed in boiling water for two hours, and then the invariable length of the beam compass again applied. The difference gives the expansion for the difference of temperature of melting ice and boiling water. The full description of this method, as well as the apparatus for and process of verification, is given in the translation of M. Silberman's article. (Appendix No. 18.)

The absolute expansion of the metre of annealed steel sent to the United States was found to be 1.0502 millimetres between the temperature of $0°$ and $100°$ centigrade ($32°$ and $212°$ Fahrenheit.) Compared with the standard of plantinum deposited at the Conservatory of Arts and Trades, the annealed steel metre was found to be 0.0226 millimetres too short, while the brass metre (by Gambey) also sent to the United States, is 0.299 millimetres too long at $0°$ centigrade ($32°$ Fahrenheit.)

The comparison by M. Silberman of the gilt kilogramme, No. 6, sent to this country, with the platinum kilogramme deposited in the Conservatory of Arts and Trades, and of the latter with the platinum kilogramme of the archives of State, gave: gilt kilogramme No. 6 $=$ 0.00047 × weight of platinum kilogramme of the conservatory $=$

1,000.00291 grains of the standard kilogramme of the archives. To render the system complete, the relation of the money standard, the *franc* is given by its weight, which is five grammes, and by law consists of an alloy of nine parts of pure silver and one of pure copper.

To the description and results of the several verifications, were added, at the request of M. Vattemare, interesting extracts from a letter from M. Silberman to him, (see Appendix No. 17,) in which the learned director of the conservatory expresses the satisfaction and pleasure which the examination of the United States standards, and especially the balances, gave him; paying a high compliment to the precision and sensitiveness of the latter. A brief history is given of the first idea of the metrical system, springing up amid the errors and discrepancies of the various systems of weights and measures then tolerated in Europe, of the authors of the first movement and the actual steps taken during the revolution, with the final triumph of science, art, and energy, in its adoption by France, and its extension and adoption by several nations of Europe and of America.

The earnest hope is expressed that at no distant day the United States and France, nations so closely united on so many accounts, may also cherish the bond of union of uniform weights and measures, by the adoption of the common unit, the metre. Interest thus expressed, and the generous appreciation of the efforts and progress made in this country towards perfecting a system of weights and measures, coming from a philosopher so worthily at the head of a department embracing that subject in France, cannot but be gratifying to the people of this country. M. Silberman has truly labored to present to us types of the French standards of exceeding exactness, to the verification of which the products of his own invention have lent additional precision.

The value of this beautiful present of the French government is heightened by this circumstance, and by the courtesy shown by M. Vattemare in transmitting the collection to this government, as well as in his unsparing exertions in the matter.

8. HYDROMETERS FOR THE CUSTOM-HOUSES.

The act of Congress of January 12, 1825, authorized the Secretary of the Treasury, under the direction of the President, "to adopt and substitute such hydrometer as he may deem best calculated to promote the public interest in lieu of that now prescribed by law, for the purpose of ascertaining the proof of liquors; and that after such adoption and substitution, the duties imposed by law upon distilled spirits shall be levied, collected and paid, according to the proof ascertained by any hydrometer so substituted and adopted." (See Appendix No. 3.)

An examination of some of the principal custom-houses having shown that there were great irregularities in proving, consequent on the use of hydrometers which did not agree in the indications, either from original defects in construction, or from injury to the instruments, I was requested to direct a series of researches to furnish an instrument which should be unexceptionable in theory and practice, to have a sufficient number of these made to supply the principal custom-houses, and to cause them to be duly distributed. Professor R. S. McCulloh, now of Columbia College, New York, undertook the researches, which he executed with great industry and ability, and reported upon in part in 1845, and in full in 1847.* Tralles' hydrometer, recommended therein, was adopted by the department, and a number of sets of the instrument sufficient for immediate use were obtained from Greiner, of Berlin, and after being carefully compared by Professor McCulloh, were distributed in part to the principal custom-houses. A manual for use with this instrument was prepared by the same scientific gentleman and printed in a very neat and portable form, and with very plain directions for use. In order to facilitate the introduction of this new and perfect instrument, and of the manual, my assistant, Woods Baker, since deceased, delivered them in person to the custom-house officers by whom they were to be employed, and explained and illustrated their use. In a subsequent visit to the same custom-houses, Mr. Baker reported: "I was informed by the surveyors, as well as by the subordinate officers using the instruments, at the Boston, New Haven, New York, and Philadelphia custom-houses, that the new hydrometers are considered greatly superior to the old ones in point of simplicity." The markers at all these places were instructed in their use, and performed the operations properly. Having delivered these instruments personally at Wilmington, North Carolina, Georgetown, South Carolina, and Savannah, and examined that at Charleston, I can unite in bearing testimony additional to that of Mr. Baker in regard to the ease with which the officers of the customs learned the use of the instruments and of the tables.

The hydrometer for testing the strength of liquors imported at the custom-houses is a combination of the alcoholometer of Tralles, with a Fahrenheit's thermometer, made by J. C. Greiner, sr., & Son, of Berlin. It consist of a tube, closed at each end, the part near one end being swelled to contain a Fahrenheit's thermometer, with a carefully graduated scale. The other portion of the tube has within it an accurately graduated hydrometer scale. When placed in the liquid to be tested, it is held vertical by the weight of the large end, and the transparency of the tube allows both the hydrometer and thermometer scales to be easily read.

The directions for the use of the above instrument, together with a "manual of tables," by which the *true per cent.* of alcohol contained in

---

*The titles and dates of these reports are as follows :

1. A report of chemical analysis of sugars, molasses, &c., and of researches on hydrometers, made under the superintendence of Professor A. D. Bache, by Professor R. S. McCulloh, February 17, 1845, Senate Doc. 165, 28th Congress, 2d session.

2. A report of scientific investigations relative to the chemical nature of saccharine substances, and the art of manufacturing sugar, made under the direction of Professor A. D. Bache, by Professor R. S. McCulloh, February 27, 1847, Senate 209, 29th Congress, 2d session.

3. Second report on inquiries and researches, relative to hydrometers, &c , made under the superintendence of Professor A. D. Bache, by Professor R. S. McCulloh, May 29, 1848.

There are two reports from the Treasury Department, dated June 15, 1844, and July 31, 1846, relating to this subject. The first communicating copies of regulations in relation to the importation of foreign sugar and molasses, Senate Doc. 12, 28th Congress, 2d session. The second relative to frauds in recent importations of sugar and molasses from the West India islands, and the measures necessary to prevent their recurrence. Senate No. 467, 29th Congress, 1st session.

any gauged volume of imported liquor could be ascertained for any observed temperature, from 20° to 100°, and for any indication of the hydrometer, were delivered with the instruments.

The "manual" contains three tables, of which the first shows the "true per cent." of alcohol by volume, or the number of gallons of pure alcohol in 100 gallons of spirit, for every indication of the hydrometer from 20° to 100° of Fahrenheit's thermometer, the number of gallons or the volumes being measured at the standard temperature of 60° of Fahrenheit's thermometer.

The second table shows the "volume" which 1,000 gallons of pirit, measured at any temperature from 20° to 100° Fahrenheit, would become if brought to the temperature of 60° Fahrenheit, the true per cent. or strength being known.

The third table is a combination of the first and second; it gives by inspection, for any gauged quantity, particular temperature and corresponding indication of the hydrometer, the proportion, or *per cent.*, of that quantity which is pure alcohol. As the "*commercial values*" of liquors are proportioned to their quantities and strengths, or to the total amount of alcohol they contain, this table is consequently one by which spirits may be bought and sold, and duties justly levied. Table III is therefore the only one that the gauger and prover need use; but in its use it should be particularly observed that both the gauging and proving must be performed at one and the same temperature. If this is impracticable, resort must be had to the other tables to reduce the result of observation to the standard temperature and volume.

The Tralles hydrometer and manual have been delivered at the following named custom-houses:

Portland, Maine,
Portsmouth, New Hampshire,
Newburyport, Massachusetts,
Salem, Massachusetts,
Boston, Massachusetts,
New Bedford, Massachusetts,
Barnstable, Massachusetts,
Providence, Rhode Island,
New Haven, Connecticut,
New York, New York,
Philadelphia, Pennsylvania,
Wilmington, Delaware,
Baltimore, Maryland,
Alexandria, Virginia,
Richmond, Virginia,
Petersburg, Virginia,
Norfolk, Virginia,
Wilmington, North Carolina,
Georgetown, South Carolina,
Charleston, South Carolina,
Savannah, Georgia,
New Orleans Louisiana.

In addition, they have been sent to the following named customhouses on the western coast, by direction of the Treasury Department:

    San Francisco, California,
    Benicia, California,
    Monterey, California,
    San Diego, California,
    Astoria, Oregon,
    Puget's Sound, Washington Territory.

The first set sent to San Francisco was destroyed by fire, and on application from the collector a second set was transmitted. The detailed report on the delivery of these instruments and manuals, by Woods Baker, esq., is given in the Appendix, (No. 7.) It contains valuable matter in reference to the subject, including the circulars of the Treasury Department and of the Office of Weights and Measures to the officers of the customs. Mr. Baker embraces in the same report a statement of the performance of his duty in receiving the old hydrometers and in examining the weights and measures which had been delivered to the same custom-houses. The last named portion of the report I have already referred to. "The old hydrometers" (as reported by Mr. Baker) "collected at the several customhouses visited were of various constructions, though chiefly of Dycas' patent, and with but few exceptions, in a most dilapidated condition."

A detailed statement in reference to all these instruments and to the comparisons of them subsequently made in the office will be found in Mr. Baker's report. The table of comparison "shows conclusively the unreliability of the instruments, and the great necessity of withdrawing them from use, and substituting for them instruments more simple in principle and less liable to become deranged." It is better that an instrument should be broken, than that, being injured, it should be used, while giving false indications. The glass instrument is therefore to be preferred to that of thin metal, and several glass hydrometers can be purchased for the cost of a single metallic one. In a mixture of alcohol and water of 80 per cent. strength, (of alcohol,) different instruments marked from 253 to 234; in a 50 per cent. mixture, from 177 to 112; in a 24 per cent. mixture, from 107 to 49. These results are in accordance with those previously obtained by Professor McCulloh, and which he thus summed up: "From the preceding statements, it will be evident that, with but few exceptions, I found the instruments now in the hands of the officers of the customs wholly unfit for use, by reason of accidental injuries which they have suffered, so that generally it would be impossible to determine with them the true strength of any liquor imported and subjected to their examination."

The remaining hydrometers will be delivered as occasion may serve, or as calls are received for them from other custom-houses, and as the instruments now in use may be broken. The experiment of introducing them has been successful beyond the most sanguine expectation.

9.—GAUGING.

By an act of Congress passed in 1799 it is made the duty of the "surveyor" of each port of entry to "examine and try, from time to time, and, particularly on the first Monday in January and July of each year, the weights and measures and *other instruments* used in ascertaining the duties on imports, with standards to be provided at the public expense," &c. (See Appendix No. 2.)

This law had for its object to carry out the provision of the constitution, by establishing in all the custom-houses a uniform system of weights and measures, and of gauging casks containing imported liquors. It was, however, clearly shown, by the learned report of the Hon. John Quincy Adams upon weights and measures, in 1821, that a great want of uniformity in weights and measures and the methods of gauging existed at that time in the States and custom-houses.

Few of the States had passed laws regulating the gauging of casks, and the implements used were even more various than the diversified sources from which the weights and measures had been derived.

The report of Mr. Hassler, and of the Secretary of the Treasury in 1832, described the same irregularities to exist as were referred to in the report of Mr. Adams.

The direction of the Secretary of the Treasury of June 18, 1831, to Mr. Hassler to make standards for the custom-houses, was the first step towards uniformity in weights and measures; but its effect, in connection with the subject of gauging casks, was merely to fix the uniform value of the *gallon,* without correcting the discrepancies in the methods used. In fact, no act of Congress, or regulation of the Treasury Department, had defined the proper method to be followed.

In the delivery of the new hydrometers and manuals of tables to the custom-houses in 1850, the agent appointed by the Treasury Department for this purpose, Woods Baker, esq., also improved the opportunity to gather the details of the methods of gauging practised at the several ports.

In his report upon this subject, Mr. Baker remarks that "on inquiry into the different modes for estimating the capacity and contents of casks containing imported liquors, oils, molasses, &c., I found a great want of uniformity among them, the same process not being followed by the gaugers at any three custom-houses. *No allowance* is made for differences of temperature, and other irregularities are found," &c.

Upon a report of the result of this examination to the Secretary of the Treasury, authority was obtained to make the necessary investigation with a view to the establishment of a uniform system of gauging throughout the country.

As a first step in the investigation, measures were taken for obtaining all the information necessary concerning the precise methods practised at our principal ports, as well as the system followed by the official gaugers in Europe.

For this purpose, circulars were addressed to the collectors of the ports of Boston, New York, and Philadelphia, desiring them to

Ex. Doc. 27——3

furnish certain detailed information in a tabular form. The returns have been received, and furnish valuable data in the investigation.

Letters were addressed to the United States representatives at London, Paris, Berlin, Brussels, and the Hague, requesting them to procure and forward the official regulations of the respective governments to which they were accredited in relation to the measurement of the capacity of the casks, together with descriptions of the processes now and formerly in use, and the instruments and tools employed by the official gaugers. In reply to this circular, the Hon. Abbott Lawrence forwarded instruments, books and regulations, presented by the chief of the British excise department; the Hon. Geo. Folsom sent instruments, with papers and instructions on gauging; papers were also received from Berlin. The correspondence upon this subject is given in Appendix No. 15.

Subsequently, (October, 1853,) letters were addressed to D. K. McRae, esq., consul at Paris, and W. H. Vesey, esq., consul at Havre, for the purpose of obtaining information of the French method of gauging; prompt and satisfactory replies were received, accompanied by books, papers, and instruments, fully illustrative of the subject of inquiry.

In procuring the requisite information in Paris, Mr. McRae was under many obligations to the Prefect of the Seine and M. Alexandre Vattemare for the facilities which their kindness and assistance afforded him.

The information and data thus collected, affording a concise view of the methods of gauging practised by the principal governments of Europe, will be of much value in arriving at a decision in regard to the most suitable method to be recommended for adoption.

Some experiments have been made to determine the weight, specific gravity, and expansion of various liquid articles of importation, such as molasses and oils, with a view to the ultimate determination of the best practicable method of gauging casks, under all the circumstances of variation of bulk, at different temperatures.

The experiments consisted in weighing the same volume of a substance at different temperatures, ranging from 32° to 76° Fahrenheit, and were made by the late Mr. Woods Baker and Mr. E. Liomin, extending from the summer of 1852 to the following winter, no artificial temperatures being resorted to. A discussion of the results having shown further inquiry to be desirable, additional experiments were made under my direction by Mr. Liomin during the summer of 1854 and the ensuing winter. All these experiments are given in Appendix No. 26, and are graphically represented on plate No. 3. An inspection of the diagrams will show that a very great degree of accuracy is attainable by the method employed, and that practical results of value have been obtained bearing directly upon the subject of gauging by weight.

10.—LAWS OF THE STATES OF THE UNION RELATING TO WEIGHTS AND MEASURES.

The legislation in regard to this subject up to 1819 is given in full and in abstract, in the learned and elaborate report made in 1821 by the Hon. John Quincy Adams, then Secretary of State. It may not however, be out of place here to give briefly a synopsis, derived from that report, of the legal provisions in force at that time in the several States in relation to standards of weights and measures.

In *Massachusetts*, the standard weights and measures were derived from the exchequer of England; the measures were of the *Winchester* standard, and both avoirdupois and troy weights were established. The preparation of county and town standards was provided for.

In *New Hampshire* and *Vermont*, the weights were derived from the exchequer of England, and the measures were of the *Winchester* standard. No troy weights were established by law. In New Hampshire, town standards were to be provided, and in Vermont both county and town standards.

In *Rhode Island*, the weights and measures were required by law to be according to the standards of the exchequer of England, and copies were to be provided by the towns. The practice of "gauging" was established by law.

In *Connecticut*, the standard bushel was to contain 2,198 cubic inches, (copy of an old English bushel, not the *Winchester*, which contains 2150.42 cubic inches,) and the gallon to contain 231 cubic inches. No troy weights were established. All gauging was to be done by "Gunter's" rule.

In *New York*, the weights and measures were to be according to the standards in the office of the Secretary of State, at the time of the Declaration of Independence, (which were themselves derived from the exchequer standards,) until Congress should provide others. Both avoirdupois and troy weights were established, and counties and cities were to provide copies of the standards.

In *New Jersey*, the standards were, by law, to be according to those of the exchequer of England, including avoirdupois and troy weights.

In *Pennsylvania*, also, the weights and measures were to be according to the exchequer standards and kept in each county. Those used, and at that time in the possession of the keeper of the weights and measures, were brought over to this country by William Penn.

In *Delaware*, the standards were to be copies of those in the exchequer of England, and the counties were required to provide copies.

In *Maryland*, the *Winchester* bushel was adopted and used. English standards were required by law to be procured for adoption. Troy weights were recognized. Each county was required to procure copies of the standards. The mayor and council of the city of Baltimore were authorized to fix the standards for that city.

In *Virginia* and *North Carolina*, the standards were to be according to the exchequer standards of England, and copies to be provided by the counties.

In *South Carolina*, the *London* standards were adopted, copies of which were to be provided by the counties.

In *Georgia*, the standards of *Savannah* and *Augusta* were declared to be those of the State. An ordinance of the city councils of Augusta prescribed *avoirdupois* weights, *wine* measure for liquids, and the *Winchester* bushel for dry measure.

In *Kentucky*, the standards of Virginia were adopted as those of the State. The governor was required to procure the standards, and to furnish copies to the counties. The bushel was required by law to contain $2,150\frac{2}{3}$ solid inches, and the wine gallon 231.

No standards had been established in *Tennessee*.

In *Ohio*, the law required a half bushel, to contain $1,075\frac{2}{10}$ solid inches, to be made and kept as a standard, and copies to be procured by each county.

The law of *Lousiana* directed standards to be provided to conform to those in use by the United States revenue officers, and copies to be furnished to each parish. In *Indiana*, copies of the English standards, comprising the half bushel, to contain $1,075\frac{1}{5}$ cubic inches, a gallon to contain 231 cu. in., and avoirdupois weights, were to be procured and distributed to the counties. This law was to remain in force until Congress should otherwise provide.

The standards established by the law of *Mississippi* were defined to be the *English avoirdupois* weights, and standard measures of length, and dry measures of capacity, and *wine* measures for liquids ; copies of which were to be furnished to each county. These were to continue as the standards until Congress should fix a standard for the United States. The standards established in *Illinois* were precisely similar to those of Indiana, with the exception of the pound avoirdupois, which, in Illinois, was to contain 7,020 grains troy.

Alabama adopted the standards of Mississippi, *Missouri* established the same standards as Indiana. In the *District of Columbia*, the standards were required to be conformable to those of the State of Maryland.

It will be seen, from the above, that the weights and measures in use in all the States of the Union at that time were derived from the English. The colonists that came to this country brought with them the weights and measures of their country, but they were rather those of the law, than of any particular section or district.

The standards in the exchequer of England remained the same from the first settlement of Jamestown up to 1826, with the exception of the wine gallon, which was of the time of Queen Anne; and it was from the standards of the exchequer that all the weights and measures of the United States were derived, until Congress fixed the standard. Louisiana at first recognized standards derived from the French, but in 1814 the United States revenue standards were established by law. In Tennessee there does not appear to have been any law at the time fixing the standards, but those in use were derived from Virginia.

The actual standards in use by the several States and in the customhouses, although thus legally derived from the English standards, were, however, ascertained and reported by Mr. Adams to be very defective, and wanting in agreement with the recognized standard, as well as in uniformity. The distribution of carefully constructed standards, made in this office, to the custom-houses, in 1836, furnished the means of uniformity in the collection of the customs ; and the resolution of Congress of 1836, directing the distribution of complete sets of standards to each of the States, fixed the standard for the Union.

The beneficial results and the progress towards greater uniformity, arising from this distribution, will be apparent from a comparison of the legal provisions in the several States at the date of Mr. Adams' report with those in force at the present time, an abstract of which is here given.

Since the distribution of these standards, most of the States have adopted them by new enactments as the standards of the States respectively, and actually distributed, or provided for the distribution of, copies to the counties, and in many instances to towns also.

Such has been the action of the following States, viz:

Maine, New Hampshire, Vermont, Massachusetts, Connecticut, New York, New Jersey, Pennsylvania, Delaware, Maryland, Virginia, North Carolina, South Carolina, Georgia, Alabama, Mississippi, Kentucky, Ohio, Illinois, Iowa, Wisconsin, Texas, California, Tennessee—24; and in the Territories of Washington and New Mexico, (26.)

Louisiana (27) has adopted the standards in use by the United States revenue officers, and provided for the distribution of copies to the parishes, but has not adopted the State standards furnished by the federal government. These are, in fact, derived, however, from the same source. Of the above States, several of them have, by their elaborate and carefully drawn acts, and the actual steps taken to distribute copies to the counties, manifested great interest in the subject. This may particularly be said of New York, Pennsylvania, Massachusetts, and Maryland.

The States of Indiana, Missouri, and Arkansas, still recognize by law the old territorial standards, which were derived from the English exchequer standards. Rhode Island also recognizes the exchequer standards.

Michigan and Minnesota Territory retain the laws adopting the standards in use in New York at the time of their passage, though the State of New York has altered her standards to conform to those of the United States.

To collect the necessary information in order to give a connected history of the legislation upon this subject, from the time at which it was left by the Hon. John Quincy Adams to the present time, it was desirable to obtain more complete copies of the laws enacted by the several States during this period than could be obtained from the libraries of the State Department and of Congress.

To obtain these copies in the reliable and authentic form desirable, circulars of the form appended (No. 11) were addressed to the governors of the several States of the Union.

Answers were received from thirteen States, and upon repeating the circular in July, 1853, replies were elicited from nearly all. In June of the present year the circulars were renewed; and also subsequent to the adoption of the Senate resolution of August 14th, calling for this report. Bound volumes of the Revised Statutes were received from the States of New Hampshire, Georgia, Alabama, Kentucky, Indiana, and Missouri, in 1853, and from Wisconsin, Mississippi, Georgia, Tennessee, and Rhode Island, within the present year. Certified copies of all the laws on weights and measures, from 1819 to 1853, were received from Massachusetts, Rhode Island, New York, Pennsylvania, Maryland, Virginia, Louisiana, Ohio, Texas, and California; and copies of laws on the subject, then *in force*, from the

States of Maine, Vermont, Connecticut, New Jersey, North Carolina, South Carolina, Michigan, Illinois, and Iowa.

The calls made by circular within the present year have been met by all the States of the Union, excepting Louisiana, and Texas; and copies were received of acts passed in Kentucky, Massachusetts, New York, New Jersey, Tennessee, South Carolina, Vermont, Mississippi, Wisconsin, Georgia, North Carolina, Missouri, Indiana, Illinois, Rhode Island, and from Minnesota, New Mexico, and Washington Territories. Official advice was received, also, that no legislation subsequent to 1853 had occurred in Connecticut, Maine, Maryland, Michigan, Ohio, New Hampshire, Virginia, Pennsylvania, Alabama, Iowa, Arkansas, Delaware, and California.

By a letter from the secretary of state of Florida, it appears that no laws on weights and measures have been passed by the legislature of the State. From Delaware, Mississippi, Tennessee, and Arkansas, no laws were received in 1853; and copies of the laws of those States, as well as the acts subsequent to 1819, of those States which only sent copies of the laws then in force, were obtained, as far as possible, from the Congressional and State Department libraries.

The information thus obtained of the legislation of the several States upon the subject of weights, measures, and gauging, during the period from 1819 to the present time, will be seen in the following abstract of laws:

MAINE.

The first law on weights and measures passed by the State of Maine, to be found on her statutes, dates its approval on the 5th of February, 1821, although the phraseology of the first section indicates a previous act.

This law is modelled upon a law of Massachusetts enacted in 1800, and, in fact, is nearly a literal copy of it. A brief account of it may, however, be given here, as it will be referred to in the account of the laws of the States of New Hampshire and Vermont, which were, with the exception of those of a recent date, likewise copied from the laws of Massachusetts.

The first section of this act of 1821, "for the due regulation of weights and measures," declares that "the brass and copper weights and measures heretofore adopted, used, and allowed as standards, be and remain the public allowed standards throughout this State," &c., and that the treasurer, at the expense of the State, provide the standards, as follows: "One bushel, one half bushel, one peck, one half peck, one *ale* quart, one *wine* gallon, one wine half gallon, one wine quart, one wine pint, and one wine gill. Said measures to be made of copper or pewter, conformable, as to contents, to said standard measures, and as to breadth, that is to say, the diameter of the bushel, not less than eighteen inches and a half, containing thirty-two *Winchester quarts*; the half bushel not less than thirteen inches and three quarters, containing sixteen *Winchester* quarts; the admeasurement to be made, in each instance, withinside the measure: also, one *ell* or *yard*; one set of brass weights to four pounds, computed at *sixteen ounces* to the *pound*, with fit scales and steel beams: also, a good beam and scales, and a nest of *troy* weights, from one hundred and twenty-eight pounds* down to the lowest denomination," &c.; each to be stamped with its weight or its measure, and sealed by a seal to be kept by the treasurer : and, in addition, "one fifty-six pound weight, one twenty-eight, one fourteen, and one seven pound weight, made of iron."

It may be well here to remark, that, as this description of the standards is an exact copy from the law of Massachusetts passed in 1800, which also adds that said " brass and copper measures [were] *formerly sent* out of England, with certificate out of the exchequer to be approved *Winchester* measure, according to the standard in the exchequer," &c., there can be no doubt that the standards of Maine were likewise imported from England, or copied from those of Massachusetts which had the seal of the exchequer standard.

The county treasurers were required to procure and keep, for county standards, exact copies of the State standards, (with the exception of the bushel,) to be tried and sealed by the State sealer, and every ten years to be tried and sealed anew. For neglect of this duty, the county sealer to be fined.

The treasurers of towns were likewise required to procure and keep exact copies of the State standards, except the half bushel, and with the liberty to have the half bushel, peck, and half peck of wood, and to be excused from providing a nest of troy weights other than from the lowest denomination to eight ounces. Town sealers, appointed by the selectmen, were to keep the standards, and once in every year try and seal the weights and measures of the inhabitants, after giving public notice of their appointment, and the place where, and time when, they would attend for that purpose. The town standards were to be re-compared, by the State or county standards, once in every ten years. The law also specifies the fines for neglect of duty on the part of sealers, their fees for sealing, and the penalties for any citizen using weights and measures not sealed by the town or county sealers. A particular section prescribes the manner in which the weights used in *banks* should be tested and sealed.

A resolution of the legislature, passed February 6, 1822, authorizes the treasurer to delay or omit the purchase of the State standards until the next meeting of the legislature.

By "An act regulating the weight of hoops, staves, and other articles," approved February 25, 1828, the *hundred weight* of *one hundred pounds* and *ton* of *two thousand pounds* were established.

The State standards enumerated in the law of 1821 were directed to be purchased by the State treasurer, by a resolution of the legislature, approved March 22, 1831, provided that the largest troy weight should be of one hundred and twenty-eight ounces, and the two largest iron (avoirdupois) weights should be, one of fifty pounds and one of twenty-five pounds. Five hundred dollars were appropriated for this purpose.

The United States standards of weights and measures were adopted by the act approved March 2, 1839, and entitled "An act additional

---

* Altered to ounces by resolution approved March 22, 1831.

to an act for the due regulation of weights and measures." This declares that such standards of weights and measures as should be furnished to the State by the United States, in addition to such weights and measures as should be necessary to make complete sets, (which were to be procured by the treasurer, and to be in perfect accordance with the United States standards,) should be the standards of the State.

The State sealer of weights and measures was directed to procure a suitable gold balance, and a balance for avoirdupois weights, to be kept at the State House, for the trial of weights and measures and for no other purposes. The county sealers to procure standards at the expense of the county, and to have them compared every ten years with the State standards. The town sealers were also to procure town standards, and to have them compared with the county standards every ten years.

In July, 1841, the Revised Statutes of the State were adopted. They contained such laws on weights and measures, passed in previous years, as had not been repealed, with the addition of some sections. Chapter 73 declares that "the standard of *weights recently furnished* by the United States, and adopted by this State, shall be continued and used as the standard of weights instead of those formerly used; and the measures adopted by the United States as standard measures, *when furnished* to this State, shall be adopted and used as standard measures of this State."

In the meantime, the State sealer was to procure and preserve the following measures: "One bushel, one half bushel, one peck, one half peck, one *ale* quart, one wine gallon, one wine half gallon, one wine quart, one wine pint, one wine half pint and one wine gill," to be made of copper or pewter, conformable as to measure to the United States standards, and as to diameter, to the dimensions given in the law of 1821.

He was also required to procure the smaller denominations of weights, both avoirdupois and troy, so as to make complete sets as described in the same law. The *yard* and *ell* were preserved as length measures. All the previous laws, as regards the providing of county and town standards, their comparison, and the trying and sealing of the weights and measures of the inhabitants, were re-enacted. The following special acts, passed in previous years, were also re-enacted: Act of March 10, 1821, prescribing the quality and dimensions of casks in which *pearl ashes* were to be packed for exportation; act of same year, March 19, prescribing the form and dimensions of casks, kegs, and firkins, in which *butter* and *lard* were to be exported; act of March 22, same year, regulating the form, quality, and dimensions of casks for containing *fish* of different kinds, and the manner in which they should be salted, or pickled, and packed. For salt fish, the tierce was to contain 300 lbs., the barrel 200 lbs., the half barrel 100 lbs., quarter barrel 50 lbs., and kids (tenths of barrels) 20 lbs. For pickled fish, the tierce was to contain between forty-five and forty-six gallons, the barrel from twenty-nine to thirty gallons, and smaller kegs to be in the same proportion.

Other acts of the same year establish the measurement of coal, wood, and bark, of lime and lime casks, of tobacco and onions, of nails, of hogshead hoops, of shingles, clapboards and staves, of flaxseed, of hair at eleven pounds, and of oats at thirty pounds, to the bushel: act of January 24, 1824, fixing the dimensions and manner in which shingles shall be sawed; of March, 1835, establishing the weight of a bushel of potatoes at sixty pounds; and of March, 1839, establishing the dimensions of boxes to contain herrings for exportation.

The Revised Statutes of 1841, of which a particular description has been given, are now in force in this State. Chapter 73, section 1, provides that the United States standard weights and measures be adopted as the State standards. The weights furnished by the act of Congress had not at that date been received. Since then, the complete set of weights and measures have been furnished to the State, with three balances, which, by the terms of the law, were to be deposited in the State House and used only as standards. The clause in a previous law declaring the *hundred weight* to be 100 lbs., the *ton* to be 2,000, the *quarter* twenty-five pounds, &c., is also re-enacted in the law of 1841.

No laws have been enacted in relation to standard weights, measures of length or capacity, or relative to gauging, in this State, since July 31, 1841.

NEW HAMPSHIRE

The law of 1797, entitled "An act regulating scale-beams, steelyards, weights, and measures," requiring the standards to be in accordance with the approved *Winchester* measures, allowed in England in the exchequer, remained in force, with some alterations, until the year 1848; one of the changes in the law was made by the "act regulating the weighing of merchandise and other commodities," approved July 6, 1827, which enacts that "all commodities which now are and usually have been sold by the one hundred and twelve pounds or one hundred weight avoirdupois shall, when exposed to sale and actually sold, be weighed by the *decimal hundreds* and pounds of avoirdupois," &c., and all weighers are directed to weigh accordingly, under pain of fines.

By an act passed December 29, 1828, in addition to the act of 1797, the contents of the basket for measuring charcoal was fixed at eighteen gallons, level measure, the average diameter not to be less than twenty inches. This law was re-enacted and approved January 1, 1849.

By a resolution of the legislature, approved December 17, 1840, it was resolved "that the set of standard weights now in the capitol, received from the Secretary of State of the United States, be deposited in the office of the treasurer of this State, who is hereby directed to receive and preserve the same."

The act of 1848, entitled "An act in amendment of chapter 110 of the Revised Statutes, relating to weights and measures," requires each county sealer, within three months after the passage of the act, to try and prove the county standards in their possession by the standards furnished to the State by the United States, and now deposited with the treasurer. Such as were not already provided with standards were to procure them and have them tried and proved in the above manner within the three months.

The town sealers were likewise required to procure town standards and have them tried and proved by the county standards within six months, both county and town standards to be re-compared every three years.

Chapter 706 of the Revised Statutes, approved January 1, 1849, re-enacts the preceding, and provides for the appointment by the governor of county sealers; for the election by the towns of town sealers of weight and measures; and for seals to be used by each. It also prescribes the penalty for the selectmen of towns failing to provide town standards, for the neglect of duty on the part of sealers, and the penalty for using weights and measures not tried and sealed by the public sealers. The *hundred* weight was directed to be understood and weighed as *one hundred pounds*, the *ton* two thousand pounds &c., A subsequent chapter (1130) approved in 1851, fixes the weight of a bushel of oats at 30 lbs., a bushel of potatoes at 60 lbs., excepting special contracts, and regulates the weight and marking of loaves of bread.

Since July 2, 1851, no alterations have been made in this State in the laws concerning weights and measures.

VERMONT.

The first law of Vermont in relation to weights and measures was passed March 8, 1779, entitled "An act relating to weights and measures." It declared that the standards of the State should be "according to the *approved Winchester measures*, allowed in England in the exchequer," but omitted to include the denominations of *troy* weight. A copy of this law, which appears to have been modelled upon an old colony law of Massachusetts, passed in the year 1647, was given in the report of the Hon. John Quincy Adams, in 1821.

An amendment to this law passed in November, 1816, entitled "An act regulating and directing the measurement of charcoal, lime, and ashes," specifying that a bushel of these substances should consist of 38 quarts of *ale* or *Winchester* measure, was afterwards repealed in October, 1828.

"An act relating to weights and measures," passed November 18, 1824, prescribes the standard weight of a bushel of Indian corn and rye to be fifty-six pounds, and of oats thirty-two pounds.

In November, 1830, "An act in addition to an act relating to weights," passed March 8, 1797, "required the selectmen of the several towns to procure the additional weights of fourteen and seven pounds." Another amendment to the law of 1797, with the same title as the above, passed November 9, 1831, established *one hundred pounds* as the hundred weight in weighing all gross articles. Thus amended, the old law of 1797 continued in force until 1839, when it was re-enacted, with some changes, the most important of which was in the first section, which declared that "the public standards of weights and measures in this State shall be the *standards adopted by the gov-*

ernment of the United States."* After this section comes the whole law of 1797, with slight modifications.

As it stands, this law presents some singular incongruities. The first section adopts the United States standards, the second enumerates the different denominations which were to be procured by the treasurer of the State and preserved as standards, as follows :

One set of iron weights consisting of one fifty-six pound, one twenty-eight pound, one fourteen, one seven, one two, and one one pound weights, and a suitable scale and beam necessary for the use of the same ; also, one set of brass weights, from one ounce to four pounds, at the rate of sixteen ounces to the pound ; also, one half bushel, one peck, one half peck, one *ale* quart, one *wine* gallon, one two quart wine measure, one quart, one pint, one half pint, one gill, one half gill measure ; *one English ell, one yard ;* which shall be the standard by which all weights and measures shall be tried, proved, and sealed," &c., thus establishing *two* liquid measures, and two measures of length; whereas the United States standards recognize but *one* standard of liquid measure, the wine gallon ; *one* of dry measure, the Winchester bushel ; and *one* of length, the yard.

The law, moreover, does not establish *troy* weights, upon which the troy pound, the United States standard of weights, depend for their unit ; and the denominations that are specified, 56, 28, 14, 7, 4, 2, and 1 pounds, correspond to the "hundred weight," of 112 pounds ; whereas the concluding section declares that "*one* hundred pounds shall constitute the hundred weight," and two thousand pounds the *ton.*

It was made the duty of the treasurer of each county to provide and keep copies of the State standards, with a seal, and to prove and seal the town standards, which were to be provided by the selectmen of the towns.

The State and town standards were also to be stamped in a prescribed manner.

The law also prescribes the fines for neglect of the requirements of the law, fees for sealers of weights and measures, and penalties for using weights and measures not sealed by public sealers.

A subsequent law, in conformity with the standards furnished by the government of the United States, was enacted in 1850, and the above law, with subsequent additions, fixing the weight of a bushel of wheat at sixty pounds, of rye or Indian corn at fifty-six pounds, of barley or buckwheat at forty-six pounds, of oats at thirty-two pounds, of potatoes sixty pounds, is now in force, and the measure of apples the same as lime or ashes, remains as fixed by the law of 1842.

In 1855 it was enacted that "a pile of wood or bark four feet wide, four feet high, and eight feet long, well packed, shall constitute a cord," the length of all cord wood exposed to sale being so estimated as to include only half the kerf.

No law on the subject of weights or measures has been passed in the State since the act last mentioned.

---

* Re-enacted in 1850.

MASSACHUSETTS

The law in force in Massachusetts at the date of Mr. Adams' report on weights and measures was enacted February 26, 1800,* and was a compilation and revision of all the laws enacted previous to the Revolution, reaching back as far as the colonial law of 1647.

It declared, as formerly established by the law of 1692, "that the brass and copper measures *formerly* sent out of England, with certificate out of the exchequer to be approved Winchester measures, according to the standard in the exchequer, and which have been adopted, used, and allowed in this State, shall remain the authorized public standards, by which all weights and measures shall be tried, proved and sealed," &c.

It made it the duty of the treasurer to preserve these standards, which were to be deposited in the treasury of the Commonwealth, being as follows, viz: one bushel, one half bushel, one peck, one half peck, one ale quart, one wine gallon, one wine half gallon, one wine quart, one wine pint, one wine half pint, and one wine gill; also, one ell and one yard; also, one set of brass weights to four pounds, computed at *sixteen* ounces to the pound, with suitable scales and steel beam, and one set of iron weights consisting of one fifty-six pound weight, one twenty-eight, one fourteen, and one seven pound weight; and also a good scale and beam for *troy weights*, and a nest of troy weights from one hundred and twenty-eight ounces down to the last denomination.

It prescribes that all weights and measures which may be procured from time to time to replace the above shall be made and preserved in the same form and of the same dimensions—that is to say:

The diameter of bushel not less than		18½ inches,	to contain	32	Winchester quarts.
Do.	half bushel	"	13¾ "	"	16	" "
Do.	peck	"	10¾ "	"	8	" "
Do.	half peck	"	9 "	"	4	" "

The measurements to be made inside the measures, and the measures to be of copper or pewter. Duplicates were to be provided for a deputy, who was to be appointed by the treasurer. Copies, with the exception of the bushel, were to be provided by the treasurer of each county, with a seal, for testing and sealing the town standards, and the treasurer of each town to provide, at the expense of the town, similar copies, with the exception of the bushel and the troy weights, other than from the lowest denomination to 8 ounces, with liberty to make the dry measures of wood, instead of pewter or copper.

The county standards were to be re-compared with the State standards once in every *ten years;* the town standards with the county every ten years likewise, and the weights and measures of the inhabitants† to be tried and proved by a public sealer of weights and measures once in every year.

In the year 1847, having received the weights and measures and balances from the federal government, the legislature enacted that, "the several avoirdupois and troy weights and balances procured from the government of the United States for this Commonwealth, by the commissioners appointed for that purpose in the year one thousand

---

* Revised Statutes of November, 1835.
† Excepting those used in Boston.

eight hundred and thirty-five, and also all weights, measures and balances that have since been received from the said government for the purpose of being used as standards, shall hereafter be used as the sole authorized public standards of weights and measures of this Commonwealth, and shall be in the care and custody of the treasurer of this Commonwealth." The full set of weights, measures and balances for the State were then enumerated, with a description of the seal to be used by the treasurer in sealing county standards, or by a deputy to be appointed by him, for whose use the treasurer was to procure exact duplicates of the State standards.

The treasurer of each county and of each town was required to keep, at the expense of the county, town or city, a complete set of the aforesaid weights, measures and balances, except the troy weights; the weights of four pounds and under to be made of brass; the others might be made of iron—all to be turned and finished; the liquid measures to be made of brass or iron of durable thickness, to be turned on the inside and on the top edge or rim; the balances to be made of brass, steel or iron, and in all cases the edges and bearings to be made of hardened steel or agate; said weights and measures to be sealed by the State or county sealer; the county standards to be recompared with the State standards at least once in every ten years; the town standards with those of the county once in *every five years*; and both county and town treasurers to keep seals with which to seal the weights and measures of the towns, of public sealers, and of the inhabitants.

The sealers of weights and measures were, every year, after giving public notice of the time and place at which they would attend for the purpose, to try and prove the weights and measures of the inhabitants; the fees for which, as well as the penalties for the use of any weights and measures not thus sealed, are specified.

The hundred weight was declared to be understood to mean the net weight of *one hundred pounds* avoirdupois, and contracts were to be construed accordingly.*

By a resolution of the legislature, approved April 20, 1847, the weights, measures and balances received from the United States were to be removed from Harvard University to the State House in Boston. The treasurer was also authorized to procure two sets of *dry measures* of the following dimensions, being aliquot parts of the half bushel, viz: "two of eight quarts, two of four quarts, two of two quarts, and two of one quart; one set to complete the standard of the Commonwealth, and the other as a duplicate for the use of the deputy State sealer."

An act of 1852 prescribes that the measures of charcoal shall be cylindrical, and of the following dimensions: eighteen inches diameter at bottom, twenty inches at top, and nineteen inches in perpendicular height, which measure shall be of the capacity of two bushels, and shall be filled *level full*.

In 1853, however, this was amended so as to make the dimensions of the charcoal basket nineteen inches in diameter in every part, and eighteen and one-tenth inches in depth.

---

* Chapter 30, sec. 25, Revised Statutes of 1835.

The law of 1847, thus amended, remained in force in 1853.

An act approved April 14, 1855, fixes the weight of a ton of anthracite, bituminous or mineral coal at two thousand pounds avoirdupois, "the seller thereof to cause the same to be weighed by a sworn weigher of the town." A certificate, signed by the weigher, must be given at the time of the delivery.

It was enacted, April 26, in the same year, that the bushel of wheat shall be sixty pounds, of corn or rye fifty-six pounds, of oats thirty-two pounds, of barley or buckwheat forty-eight pounds, and of ground corn or ground rye fifty pounds; that contracts shall be made only for delivery by the bushel, and that a certificate shall be given of the number of bushels, as ascertained by weight, signed by the town measurer of grain.

The last act passed in this State, and approved June 4, 1856, fixes the legal weight of a bushel of onions at fifty-two pounds.

RHODE ISLAND.

In the code of laws of 1647 it was enacted that "the measure shall be one and the weight one throughout the whole colony, and that every town shall have a common balance and weights, and a common measure, that every person may measure and weigh thereat," and that every town shall be careful in the observance of the law in this respect. The penalties for any person whatsoever using false weights and measures that are not according to *the standard* are prescribed. The standards referred to were those established by the statutes of England, or rather the *exchequer standards*.

It does not, however, appear that any standards were actually procured until 1663; for by an act of March 1, of that year, it was enacted that a "general sealer of weights and measures" should be annually chosen, who should procure, at the expense of the colony, a half bushel, a peck, half peck, *ale quart, wine quart*, wine pint, wine half pint, a yard, and weights, which should be "according to the *standard of his Majesty's exchequer* in the kingdom of England."

The towns were also required to procure suitable standards.

By an act passed May, 1698, penalties were prescribed for such towns as failed to procure standards and to have them sealed by the general sealer.

In February, 1728, the act of 1663 was substantially re-enacted.

By an act of June, 1731, the assize of barrels was fixed at thirty-one and a half gallons.

The "digest" of 1767 contains an act fixing the measure of firewood the same as at present.

By act of June, 1751, re-enacted in 1767, the subject of gauging was regulated. It was directed to be done by "Gunter's rule," and the act of 1767 established the rule for finding the mean diameter "by multiplying the difference between the head and bung diameters, by 0.65, and adding the product to the head diameter, or, which is the same, otherwise expressed, by adding six-tenths and a half of the difference between the diameter at bung and head to the diameter at the head."

By act of October, 1784, the weight of Indian meal which should be sold for a bushel, and which had previously been 50 pounds, was fixed at 54 pounds. This was re-enacted in 1798.

The above act regulating gauging was further explained by an act passed January, 1820, which enacts that in measuring the head and bung diameters, the measure shall be taken both in a horizontal and vertical direction, and the mean of the two measures taken as the true diameter of the heads. The act of 1767, as thus amended, was re-enacted in 1822.

The legal dimensions of a cord of wood and of baskets for measuring charcoal were established by an act passed in the same year; and the weight of a bushel of rye meal was established at 50 pounds. In October, 1823, the weight of a bushel of potatoes was fixed at 64 pounds.

By an act passed June, 1825, substituting net for gross weight in sales, and contracts relating to articles of merchandise, an important change was made in this respect, by establishing 100 pounds as the *hundred weight*, and 2,000 pounds as the *ton*. This act was amended by an act in addition to it, passed January, 1830, fixing a penalty of ten dollars for every violation of its provisions.

An act passed October, 1830, fixed a penalty for selling charcoal in any other than the kind of baskets specified by the act of 1822*. By an act passed October, 1836, the weight of a bushel of Indian meal was fixed at 50 pounds ; and by acts of January, 1838, a bushel of potatoes was fixed at 60 pounds, and of onions at 50 pounds.

The "digest" of 1844 contains, in a connected form, such of the above mentioned laws as were still in force.

In June, 1847, a new gauging act was passed, entitled "An act in relation to gauging, and for the appointment of gaugers," which specifies that all casks shall be gauged by "Gunter's rule," computing the *gallon at* 231 *cubic inches;* and that the mean diameter of casks be found according to the principles laid down in "Daniel Anthony's work on gauging, published in Providence, A. D. 1817." The law also specifies the manner of appointing gaugers, their fees, and the penalties for non-compliance with the provisions of the law.

No copy of laws adopting the standard weights and measures of the United States has been sent for the files of this office, although the State, several years since, was furnished with reliable and carefully prepared copies of the government standards. The standards imported from England, after being sealed at the exchequer, have been, and it is presumed now are, the legal standards of the State.

The gauging law of 1847 fixes the *gallon* at 231 *cubic inches*, which in general terms is the standard gallon of the United States, but no definition is made of the unit of length or of weight.

In January, 1852, it was enacted that the city council of Providence should appoint weighers of cotton, and that all cotton sold throughout the State should be first weighed by the agents so appointed. This is the last act of legislation, except the adoption of a resolution providing means for the deposit in a room in Brown University of the standards received from the general government.

---

* Nineteen inches in diameter, and seventeen and a half in depth ; the measure to be well heaped.

CONNECTICUT.

"An act relating to weights and measures," passed in 1827, was modelled upon a former law passed in October, 1800, and contains the following provisions:

"That there shall be kept at the treasurer's office, to be in the custody and under the care of the treasurer for the time being, the following measures and weights—that is to say: a half-bushel brass measure of the capacity of *one thousand and ninety-nine* cubic inches; also a brass peck measure of one-half of the said capacity, and a brass half-peck measure of one-quarter of said capacity, to be called by these names respectively, which shall be the standard of *corn measure;* also a brass vessel of the capacity of 231 cubic inches, which shall be the standard *ale* or *beer measure;* also a brass or iron rod or plate of one yard in length, divided into three parts, one foot in length, and one of these parts subdivided into twelve equal parts for inches, which shall be the standard of those measures respectively; and, also, brass weights of one, two, four, seven, fourteen, twenty-eight, and fifty-six pounds, which shall be the standards of avoirdupois weights."

The bushel thus established as standard would contain 2,198 cubic inches, and was entirely different from the *Winchester* bushel, containing 2,150.42 cubic inches, and, in fact, different from any standard bushel in the English exchequer.

It was, therefore, not derived from the standards of Massachusetts, as her standard bushel was the *Winchester,* which was also the standard of New Hampshire and Vermont.

The *gallon* established as *ale* or *beer* measure is the standard *wine* gallon derived from the exchequer of England.

In the enumeration of the town standards to be provided by the selectmen of the several towns, is given, in addition to the above standards, measures of the following dimensions for corn: "a two-quart measure, the bottom of which, on the inside, is four inches wide on two opposite sides, and four and a half on the two other sides, and its height from thence seven inches and sixty-three hundredths of an inch; a quart measure, which is three inches square from the bottom to the top throughout, and its height seven inches and sixty-three hundredths of an inch; a pint measure, the capacity of which is, from bottom to top, three inches square throughout, and its height three inches and eighty-two hundredths of an inch."

By these dimensions the two quarts would contain 137.34 cubic inches, the quart 68.67 cubic inches, and the pint 34.38 cubic inches, which are aliquot parts of the half bushel of 1,099 cubic inches.

Upon the receipt of the weights and measures from the United States, the legislature passed an act in May, 1850,* adopting them as the standard weights and measures of the State, and directing them to be kept in the treasury, under the care of the treasurer, who was to try the weights and measures of the counties when presented to him for that purpose, and, if found true, to seal them with the letters "S. C.," (State of Connecticut.)†

Every county treasurer was to provide county standards, "corre-

---
* Title LVIII, Revised Statutes. † Act of 1827.

sponding to all the aforesaid standards and of like material," with which he was to try the weights and measures of the towns, and, if true, seal them with a prescribed seal. The selectmen of each town were likewise required to procure and keep, as town standards, weights and measures conformable to the State and county standards, made " of good and sufficient materials," the standards for liquid measures to be of "copper, brass, or pewter;" and to procure, in addition to the half bushel, "a two-quart, quart and pint corn measures," "of the same proportionate dimensions and capacity as those furnished by Congress," meaning the United States half bushel. The town standards to be in the custody of the sealer of weights and measures, who was to be responsible for their safe-keeping, and to try, in the month of April of every year, all weights, measures, or steelyards, used by any person in the town, and if found true to seal them with his official seal, and if faulty to destroy them.

The law prescribes penalties for the failure of the county treasurers and selectmen to comply with its requirements, for neglect on the part of the sealers of weights and measures, and for any citizen using weights, measures, or steelyards, not thus tried and sealed.

It requires the town standards to be compared with the county, and the latter with the State, but does not prescribe the intervals of time at which the comparisons must be made.

The hundred weight was declared to be understood, in the sale of articles by avoirdupois weight, one *hundred pounds*, and the *ton* two thousand pounds.

"In the sale of charcoal, fruits, vegetables, shell-fish, and all other articles sold in heaped measure, 1,282 cubic inches shall constitute a half bushel."

This is the same capacity for the charcoal bushel as that established in Massachusetts by the laws of 1835 and 1853, viz: 2,564 cubic inches.

By "An act in addition to an act concerning weights and measures," approved June 22, 1850, the weight of a bushel of different kinds of grain was established as follows:

Indian corn, rye, and wheat.......... 56 lbs. avoirdupois one bushel.
Buckwheat............................. 45   do.   do.
Oats.................................. 28   do.   do.
Irish potatoes........................ 60   do.   do.

No acts concerning weights and measures have been passed by the legislature of this State since 1850.

NEW YORK.

The act passed by the legislature of this State, March 19, 1813, entitled "An act to regulate weights and measures," remained in force with no considerable modifications until 1851, at which time the standard weights and measures of the United States were adopted as those of the State.

This law of 1813 declares "that there shall be one just beam, one certain weight and measure for distance and capacity—that is to say, avoirdupois and troy weights, bushels, half bushels, pecks, half pecks, and quarts and gallons, half gallons, quarts, pints, and gills, and one certain rod for long measure, according to the standard in use in this State on the day of the Declaration of the Independence thereof; and that the standard of weights and measures now in the office of the secretary of this State, *which is according to the standard of the court of exchequer in that part of Great Britain called England*, shall be, and is hereby, declared to be and remain the standard for ascertaining all beams, weights, and measures throughout this State until the Congress of the United States shall establish the standard of weights and measures for the United States."

"An act authorizing the election of measurers in the counties of Queens, Kings, and Richmond," passed February 9, 1821, is local in its character, as are also the six following, viz:

"An act respecting the sealers and inspectors of weights and measures in the city of New York, March 27, 1821."

"An act for the payment of the officers of government therein mentioned," passed April 3, 1821.

"An act directing certain counties to be supplied with standard brass yard measures," passed March 22, 1822.

"An act respecting measures in the counties of Essex and Clinton," passed April 5, 1822.

"An act to authorize the appointment of a weigher at the quarantine ground on Staten Island," passed March 26, 1826.

"An act to provide for the purchase of standard weights and measures for the assistant State sealer in the city of Albany," passed April 18, 1826.

In the Revised Statutes of the State is "An act concerning the territorial limits and divisions, the civil polity, and the internal administration of this State," passed December 3, 1827, the nineteenth chapter of which is of the computation of time, of weights and measures, and the money of account." The second title of this chapter, viz: "of weights and measures," declares that there shall be but one standard of measure of length and surface, one of weight, and one measure of capacity, throughout the State; and that the standard of length and surface shall be the "yard as used in this State on the *fourth day of July*, 1776."

It defines this yard in order that it may be recovered, in case of loss, to have been formed from experiments made with a pendulum with a brass rod at Columbia College, in the city of New York, in the latitude of forty degrees, forty-two minutes and forty-three seconds, to bear to the pendulum of that place vibrating seconds in a vacuum at the temperature of melting ice, the proportion of one million to one million eighty-six thousand one hundred and forty-one, (1,000,000 to 1,086,141.) "The standard yard thus defined shall be measured in a straight line between two points" engraved upon golden disks inserted into a straight brass rod, &c., enumerating its division into feet and inches.

This standard yard was imported from England, (having been engraved and sealed at the exchequer,) by the corporation of the city of New York, in 1803, and afterwards presented to the State, and deposited with authentic public documents in the office of the secretary of state.

The law directs the subdivisions of the yard into feet and inches and halves and quarters, and establishes its multiples rods, furlongs, miles, and acres.

The *unit* of *weight* was defined to be the pound, of such magnitude that the weight of a cubic foot of distilled water, at its maximum density, weighed in a vacuum, with brass weights, shall be equal to sixty-two and a half such pounds.

It was to be made of brass, its equal subdivisions to be sixteen ounces.

The standard of liquid measures to be the *gallon*, to be made of brass, and to contain at the mean pressure of the atmosphere at the level of the sea *ten pounds* of distilled water at its maximum density, to be subdivided by the number *two* into half gallons, quarts, pints, half pints, and gills, and multiplied by the same number, to form the peck, half bushel, and *bushel;* the latter of which would, as the law declared it should, contain *eighty pounds* of distilled water at its maximum density.

All commodities to be sold by the heaped measure were to be measured by this bushel or its parts. The vessel to be "made round, with a plain and even bottom, and to be of the following diameters: at top, measured from *outside to outside*, the bushel nineteen and a half inches, the half bushel fifteen and a half inches, and the peck twelve and a third inches."

It does not specify the *thickness* of the above measures; therefore the above dimensions, measured from *outside*, to *outside* are indefinite in a legal point of view, although in fact the measures, being derived from the actual standards which had been deposited in the office of the secretary of state, were undoubtedly of uniform size.

This law was derived from the law which went into force in Great Britain in 1825, establishing what are denominated the "imperial standards" of that country.

It contains the same units of measure as established by that law, and in most instances the identical wording, even including the somewhat vague definition of the *bushel*. The "imperial yard," defined as the standard of length, was the same previously established in 1760, in England, and on which the distance was measured between the centres of the two points of the gold studs near each extremity.

The "imperial gallon" contained *ten pounds* of distilled water at its maximum density, and had a capacity of 276.48 cubic inches.

The "imperial bushel" was to contain eight gallons, or eighty pounds of distilled water, and be of the capacity of 2211.84 cubic inches.

That part of this law which specified the one standard for liquid and dry measures was repealed by "An act concerning standard measures of capacity," passed April 29, 1829, which declares that "there shall continue to be *two kinds of gallons*, one for the measure of *all liquids*, and one for the measure of *all other substances* not measured by heap measure," &c.

The gallon for liquids was to contain eight pounds of distilled water at its maximum density at the mean pressure of the atmosphere at the level of the sea.

The gallon for dry measure to contain, under the same circumstances, *ten pounds* of distilled water. Both vessels to be made of brass, and in case of loss to be replaced by the above proportion.

By this law the *liquid gallon* would contain 221.184 cubic inches, or about ten cubic inches less than the wine gallon of 231 cubic inches, made in Queen Anne's reign, in 1705, and at present the standard gallon of the United States.

A list of several local laws passed at different periods by the legislature relating to the regulations of weights and measures in particular towns and counties will be found in the Appendix No. 12. In May, 1836, "An act to regulate the selling of grain" fixed the *weight* of a *bushel* of *wheat* at 60 *pounds*, of *rye* or *Indian corn* at 56 *pounds*, of *barley* at 48 *pounds*, and of *oats at* 32 *pounds*

On the 13th of April, 1843, the building in the city of Albany in which were kept the copies of the State standards issued by the assistant State sealer was burned, and these copies injured or destroyed.

An act of March 25, 1844, directs them to be replaced, provided the cost did not exceed the sum of $150.

On the 11th of April, 1851, an important act was passed adopting the United States standard weights and measures as the standards of the State of New York.

The act is entitled "An act in relation to weight and measures." The first section enacts that " the standard weights and measures now in charge of the secretary of state, being the same that were furnished to this State by the government of the United States, in accordance with a joint resolution of Congress, approved June 14, 1836, and consisting of one standard yard measure, one set of standard weights, comprising one troy pound, and nine avoirdupois weights of one, two, three, four, five, ten, twenty, twenty-five, and fifty pounds, respectively; one set of standard troy ounce weights divided decimally from ten ounces to the one-ten-thousandth of an ounce; one set of standard liquid capacity measures, consisting of one wine gallon of two hundred and thirty-one cubic inches, one half gallon, one quart, one pint, and one half pint measure, and one standard half bushel, containing one thousand and seventy-five cubic inches and twenty-one-hundredths of a cubic inch, according to the inch hereby adopted as standard, shall be the standards of weights and measures throughout this State."

The " standard yard " was directed to be divided into feet and inches, for the measure of cloth, &c., also into halves, quarters, eighths, and sixteenths. The unit or standard of weight was defined to be " the standard *avoirdupois* and troy weights," &c., their proportion to each other of 7,000 to 5,760 being enumerated.

The barrel was to consist of thirty-one and a half gallons, and two barrels to constitute a hogshead. The standard for dry measure, the half bushel, was to be divided by two to form the peck, half peck, quarter peck, quart and pint measures.

The measures to be made cylindrical, with plain and even bottom, and to be of the following diameters: " from outside to *outside* the bushel, nineteen and a half inches, half bushel fifteen and a half inches, and the peck twelve and a third inches." The bushel of wheat was to consist of *sixty pounds*, of *rye* or *Indian corn fifty-six pounds*, of *barley forty-eight*, and of oats thirty-two pounds

The foregoing standards were to be in the custody of a superintendent of weights and measures, to be chosen by the governor, lieutenant governor, and secretary of state. He was to have copies made of the original standards with which to try the county standards, the originals themselves only to be used to try these copies or for scientific purposes, and to be *deposited in a fire-proof building belonging to the State*, from which they were in no case to be removed.

In thus providing for the safety of the elaborate standards furnished by the government, New York, in common with a few of the other States, has shown an appreciation of their value which should recommend a similar action on the part of the remaining States.

The State superintendent was to provide standards, balances, &c., for the cities and counties, and as often as *once in every ten years* compare them with those in his possession.

The county sealers were to provide the towns with standard weights, measures and balances, and compare them with the county standards as often as *once in every five years*.

The duty of the town sealers was to see that the weights and measures used in the towns agreed with the standards in their possession. The law further specifies the duties, fees and penalties for using weights and measures not conforming to the standards.

This is the law now in force in the State of New York, fully adopting the United States standards, providing for furnishing the counties with copies and extending the decimal division of the unit of weight to constitute one hundred pounds as the *hundred weight*, and two thousand pounds as the *ton*.

The most recent act passed by the legislature (April 15, 1854) authorizes the State superintendent of weights and measures to contract for the manufacture of standards for the several counties not yet supplied.

NEW JERSEY.

Up to the date of Mr. Adams' report, as appears from a letter of Governor Williamson, contained in the appendix to that report, no laws had been passed by the legislature of the *State* of New Jersey, regulating weights and measures, although the standards which were tolerated by custom were the same as those in the exchequer of England, as ordained by an old *colony* law of 13th of August, 1725. It appears that no law was enacted by the State up to 1844, as the first act to be found bears date of March 13th of that year. The act is entitled "An act to establish a uniform standard of weights and measures in this State." It enacts "that the standard of weights and measures of the United States, now deposited in the secretary's office, at Trenton, shall be the standard of weights and measures of this State, for the approving and sealing of the same in the several counties thereof; and the said secretary of state is hereby enjoined to preserve and take care of the same," &c. It was made the duty of the secretary to try the county standards, and, when true, to give his certificate to that effect, and seal the standards with the imprinted letters "S. S.," (State standards.) It directed the "chosen freeholders of each and every county" to provide county standards within ten months after the passage of the act, of the following denominations: of weights, from half an ounce to fifty pounds avoirdupois; of measures, from one pint to one gallon, and from one quarter of a peck to half a bushel, and a yard stick; all to be tried and sealed by the secretary of state; also to provide a seal to imprint the letters C. S., (county standards.) The above standards and seal were to be in the custody of the county clerk, who was to be county sealer of weights and measures, and to take an oath or affirmation of a prescribed form for the faithful performance of his duties. He was required, on the first day of the following March, and on the same day every seventh year thereafter, to give public notice in newspapers, &c., at least thirty days previous to the time, when he would attend for the purpose of trying and sealing the weights and measures in use by the inhabitants.

The fees of the sealer are prescribed; also the penalty for any use of weights and measures not thus tried and sealed.

It does not appear that the county standards directed by this law to be prepared for each of the counties were actually provided; for, an act entitled "An act to establish a uniform standard of weights and measures in this State," approved April 17, 1846, which re-enacts the whole of the previous law, with an additional clause, specially directs that the county standards shall be provided by the 20th of March, 1847.

The additional clause defines the denominations of avoirdupois weights, as follows:

"Sixteen drachms,..............one ounce;
"Sixteen ounces................one pound;
"Twenty-five pounds..........one quarter;
"Four quarters.................one hundred;
"Twenty-hundred. ....one ton;

except such as may be used in the weight of *coins* and *apothecaries'* drugs."

The bushel was to contain of wheat, sixty pounds; of rye or Indian corn, fifty-six pounds; of buckwheat, fifty pounds; of barley, forty-eight pounds; of oats, thirty pounds; of flaxseed, fifty-five pounds; and of clover-seed, sixty-four pounds. An act of 1855 (Pamphlet Laws, p. 288) fixes the bushel of potatoes in weight at sixty pounds. No law relative to weights or measures has since been passed by the legislature.

PENNSYLVANIA.

The law in force in this State in 1821, dated as far back as the year 1700, ordained that "brass standards of weights and measures, according to the standards for the exchequer, should be obtained and kept for the county," and "that a brass half bushel, then in Philadelphia, and a bushel and peck proportionable, and all lesser measures and weights coming from England, being duly sealed in London, or other measures agreeable therewith, shall be accounted good till the standard should be obtained."

By "An act establishing a standard weight for grain and foreign salt," passed March 10, 1818, the weight of a bushel of those substances was established as follows:

A bushel of Wheat shall consist of 60 lbs. avoirdupois.
"   Rye or corn   "   58   "
"   Barley   "   47   "
"   Buckwheat   "   48   "
"   Oats   "   32   "
"   Coarse salt   "   80   "
"   Ground salt   "   70   "
"   Fine salt   "   62   "

It was not, however, intended to prevent any one from selling or buying by measure, if they chose.

Such portion of the foregoing as relates to rye and Indian corn was amended by "An act to regulate the standard weight of Indian corn," passed April 16, 1845, which fixed the weight of a bushel at 56 lbs.

By "An act to regulate the standard weight of charcoal," passed January 22, 1847, the standard measure was established at 2,571 cubic inches for each bushel. (The charcoal bushel of Massachusetts and Connecticut is 2,564 cubic inches.)

Several acts of a local nature were passed in the years 1822, 1825, 1827, and 1830.

On April 15, 1834, was passed "An act to fix the standards and denominations of measures and weights in the Commonwealth of Pennsylvania," drawn with much care and attention to details.*

It declares that the standard unit of length "shall be the 'yard,' to conform to that in use in this Commwealth at the date of the Declaration of Independence," and that it shall be the duty of the Governor to procure "a standard yard to constitute the positive standard of length in this Commonwealth, said standard to be equal in length at the temperature of melting ice to the distance between the eleventh and forty-seventh inches on a certain brass scale of eighty-two inches in length, procured for the survey of the coast of the United States."

The standard of liquid measure to be the *gallon*, to contain 231 cubic inches of the aforesaid standard, and no more.

The standard of dry measure to be the *bushel*, to contain 2,150.42 cubic inches; both measures to be made of cast brass.

The standard of weight to be the *pound*, "equal to the troy pound of the mint of the United States;" and the avoirdupois pound of this

---

* It was derived from the report made in 1834, by a committee of the managers of the Franklin Institute on the subject of a law for regulating the weights and measures of the Commonwealth, referred to the managers for the purpose of investigation by a resolution of the House of Representatives, April 5, 1833. The draught of a bill, as reported by the committee, was adopted by the legislature and became a law under the above title.

Commonwealth shall be greater than the troy pound in the proportion of 7,000 to 5,760.

It was made the duty of the governor to procure, within three years from the passage of the act, the above positive standards of length, weight, and capacity, and within ten years, "or when he shall deem it expedient," to have tested the conformity of said positive standards of measure and weight to the foregoing provisions of this act, or *to the natural invariable standards*, and to deposit in the office of the secretary of the Commonwealth the authentic certificates of such reference, with the apparatus by which it was made. The "length of the standard yard was to be compared with that of vibrating seconds, at a certain and defined spot in Independence Square," &c. ; "the standard of weight to be compared with that of 100 cubic inches of water at its maximum density," &c.

The governor was also, within three years after the passage of the act, to provide county standards for each of the counties at their expense, to be made of like material with the State standards, and to be delivered to the county commissioners, who were, at least once in every ten years, to try and prove them by the State standards, and to use them for the adjustment of weights and measures, and for no other purpose.

The denominations of linear, superficial, dry, and liquid measures are enumerated ; those for liquid measures are as follows :

    Four gills make one pint.
    Two pints " quart.
    Four quarts " gallon.
  Thirty-one and a half gallons make one barrel.
    Two barrels   " hogshead.
    Two hogsheads " pipe.
    Two pipes   " tun.

An act "to provide for the ordinary expenses of government, and for other purposes," passed September 29, 1843, authorizes the secretary of the Commonwealth to provide suitable cases for the weights and measures in his office, and to publish the terms upon which standards of approved construction, carefully compared with the State standards, should be furnished to the commissioners of the counties in accordance with the above law of April 15, 1834.

By "An act authorizing the secretary of the Commonwealth to distribute copies of the standard weights and measures, and for the appointment of sealers," passed April 15, 1845, it is directed that the standard weights and measures received from the government of the United States, and those in the office of the secretary of the Commonwealth, should remain in the cases provided for them, which should only be opened for the purpose of comparing the county standards, by the secretary, or by a joint resolution of both houses of the legislature, or on a call of either house, or by the governor, for scientific purposes. Copies of these original standards, to be made of such materials as the governor or secretary should direct, were to be transmitted, upon application therefor, to the commissioners of the several counties, at the expense of the counties, after being stamped with the letters "Pa.," and such additional device as should be suitable for each county. These copies to be re-compared with the State standards every five years or oftener.

The governor was authorized to appoint sealers of weights and measures for such counties as apply for and obtain copies of the standards, whose duty should be to try all weights, measures, scales, beams, &c., used by the inhabitants of such city or county, and, if found true, to seal them. The law prescribes the fees of the sealers, and penalties for using weights, measures, or scales and beams, not sealed by a public sealer, and by a supplementary act of April 21, 1846, the penalty for altering such after they have been sealed; one-moiety of the forfeiture to be for the use of the poor.

By "An act to provide for the establishment of true meridian lines, and of standard measure for surveyors' chains, and to regulate the practice of surveyors in the Commonwealth," passed April 26, 1850, it is provided that in every county there shall be established, upon some inalienable public property, a true meridian line, and a "four pole chain" measure, (22 yards,) by which every surveyor in each county was required, in the month of April in every year, to adjust his compass and surveying chains, so that upon all returns of surveys the true and not the magnetic bearing should be given.

Some subsequent laws of a local character have been enacted, but the above law of April 15, 1845, adopting the United States standards as the standards of the State, remains in force, as supplementary to the act of April 15, 1834, fixing the denominations of the weights and of the measures.

No general laws in reference to the subject of weights and measures have been passed since April 26, 1850.

DELAWARE.

"An act fixing the standard of weights and measures, and regulating the same within this State," passed February 18, 1837, enacts that Samuel M. Harrington and John R. Bostic be appointed commissioners to procure, at the expense of the State, three complete sets of weights and measures, to be in exact conformity with those established by law or regulation of Congress, or to those which might be delivered to the governor of the State, in conformity to the resolution of Congress, of June 14, 1836.

The weights and measures to be made of such metallic or other substances as to them should appear most suitable. These sets, when procured, were to be delivered to, and deposited for safe-keeping in, the offices of the prothonotaries of the three counties of the State—one set to each county—and to constitute the duplicate standards of the State, by which the weights and measures in use by the citizens were to be tried and sealed.

The United States standards, when delivered, were to be deposited in the office of the secretary of state, who was to see that the above county standards corresponded with them. County commissioners for each county were to be appointed by the governor, whose duty it was to go through the county, once in every two years, and examine all the weights and measures in use, and try them according to the county standards; for which purpose, the commissioners were to have free access to the standards deposited in the office of the prothonotary of the county; if found true, he was to stamp them with a seal, to be provided for the purpose; but if not in conformity to the standard, to seize and retain such weights or measures. Once in every five years, each county commissioner was to compare the county standards with those in the office of the secretary of state. The act prescribes a heavy fine for using weights or measures not tried and sealed by the State or county commissioners; the fees for sealing were to be established by the levy court of each county.

A supplement to the above act, passed February 14, 1845, authorizes the commissioners appointed to procure standards for each of the three counties to make them of any *form* that might seem to them most suitable, conforming only in the weight or measure of the standard, to those established by Congress.

They were also authorized to procure such scales or balances as might be necessary, to be deposited in the office of the secretary of state.

Another supplement to the act of 1837, passed February 27, 1849, enacts that "the standard weights and measures of the United States, now deposited in the office of the secretary of state, shall be, and the same are hereby, established and declared to be the true and legal standards of such weights and measures within this State; and the three several sets of weights and measures which have been deposited in the respective offices of the prothonotaries of the several counties, under the provisions of the act to which this is a supplement, shall be, and the same are hereby, established and declared to be true duplicate standards of such weights and measures, by which said duplicate standards all weights and measures used within this State shall be tried, tested, proved, and sealed or stamped, in the manner hereinafter provided." Each county commissioner, to be appointed by the governor for a definite term, was required to take an oath of a prescribed form, and to give bond for the faithful performance of his duty. Once in every two years, in the month of September, each commissioner was to appoint a time, in each hundred of the county, when he would attend for the purpose of testing the weights and measures in use. At least twenty days' public notice of this appointment was to be given.

The act defines the fees to be received by the commissioners for sealing, and the penalties for any use of weights or measures not thus tried and proved; it makes the secretary of state responsible for the safe-keeping of the originals in his office, and directs him to compare the county standards with them on the 1st of May, 1852, and on the same day every five years thereafter. The prothonotary of each county was to be responsible for the preservation of the county standards, and to allow the commissioner free access to them.

Chapter 66, "of weights and measures," of the "Revised Code" of Delaware, adopted in February, 1852, re-enacts the law of 1837, as thus amended by the above supplementary acts, with some modifications.

The title of "regulator of weights and measures" is given to the commissioner appointed by the governor for each county; and instead of fees for sealing weights and measures, each regulator is to receive a fixed salary, to be paid by the county; he is also made responsible for the safe-keeping of the county standards; and is also required to attend for inspecting weights and measures, in September or October, after due public notice, in three of the most public places in each hundred, instead of five in each hundred, as established by the former law.

The weight of a bushel of wheat is fixed at sixty pounds avoirdupois, and corn at fifty-six pounds.

No law since that of 1852 has been enacted in the State.

MARYLAND.

The whole history of the laws of Maryland upon weights and measures, including the detailed laws relating to particular sections and towns, is given in the valuable report of J. H. Alexander, esq., upon the weights and measures of Maryland, and the construction of the yard measures, made in 1845. Their history, up to 1817, is also given in the Hon. John Quincy Adams' report of 1821. It will, therefore, only be necessary to refer to the more important acts passed since 1821, the titles of the laws being given in the Appendix, (No. 12.)

Until the year 1825, the law of 1671, "for providing a standard with *English weights and measures* in the several and respective counties within this province," which had been renewed from time to time, and continued under different titles, remained in force. The standards from the exchequer, and particularly the *Winchester bushel*, were the standards of the State.

On the 8th of March, 1826, was passed "An act for regulating and inspecting weights and measures used in this State," which enacts:*

1st. That on or before the first of August, 1826, the governor and council should furnish the levy court of each county with a standard of each of the several kinds of weights and measures used at the custom-house in Baltimore.

2d. That the levy court, on or before the first of May in every year, shall appoint a keeper of the standards as furnished, taking a bond in the penalty of 500 dollars for malfeasance or damage to the standards.

3d. That the standard keeper shall, once a year, inspect, and stamp or brand with the letters M. S., (Maryland standard,) in the most effectual manner, all weights and measures used in the vending of articles within this State; the employment of weights and measures otherwise shall be under a penalty not exceeding twenty dollars.

The same penalty was imposed for using condemned weights and measures or scale-beams not inspected.

6th. That the keepers of the standards attend, at least once a year, at the different markets, towns, or villages of their county, and at the

---

* Report of J. H. Alexander, esq., upon weights and measures, in 1825, to the governor of Maryland.

public inspection warehouses at least twice a year, after giving public notice; they shall inspect and adjust all beams, weights, and measures, and shall enter such adjustment in a register, with the names of the parties, to be submitted to the levy court.

The law specifies the fines and penalties for refusing or neglecting to have weights and measures tried and sealed. The compensation of the keepers was to be such as the levy court should allow, and was probably intended to be a stated salary for each county, as in Delaware.

In March, 1828, passed " An act to regulate the gauging of casks, and the inspection of domestic distilled liquors in this State."

"It prescribes, among other things, that the gaugers to be appointed under it 'shall conform to the present Baltimore standard of wine measure,' using correct gauging instruments and Dycas' hydrometer, 85 degrees of which is the standard of proof spirit ; but whenever the government of the United States shall determine to employ a different hydrometer, the State gaugers shall procure and use hydrometers of the same description."*

Supplements to the act of 1825, passed in 1831, '32, and '33, made the offices of the commissioners of the counties of Harford, Allegany, and Anne Arundel, the depositories of the county standards, as there were no levy courts, by name, in those counties ; the fees for trying and sealing weights and measures were also fixed.

In 1842 passed a resolution of the legislature, as follows :

"*Resolved by the general assembly of Maryland*, That the governor be, and he is hereby, authorized and directed to distribute to the levy courts or commissioners, as the case may be, of the several counties of this State, each, one standard of the several kinds of weights and measures which shall be received by this State from the United States."

The following table shows the dimensions and proportionate capacities for tobacco hogsheads, as established at different times by the laws of Maryland :†

Date.	Stave, length.		Head, diam.		Bilge, diameter.	Sum of diameter.—Head and bilge.	Proportional capacity.	Remarks.
	Max.	Min.	Max.	Min.				
	Inches.	Inches.	Inches.	Inches.	Inches.	Inches.		
1658	43	42	27	26			100	
1692	44	43	31	30			136	Hogshead to weigh 90 lbs.
1694	48	46	32	31			156	Tare to be marked.
1704	48	46	32	30			161	Tare to be rated by purchaser at 40 lbs. to the barrel.
1711	48		30				145	Tare to be marked.
1715	48		32		37		201	Not to repeal preceding.
1747	48					70	204	Net weight, in hogshead, 950 pounds.
1828	50					76	250	

*Report of J. H. Alexander, esq., on weights and measures, in 1825.
† Report of J H. Alexander, esq., on weights and measures, in 1825.

The dimensions of white and red oak staves and headings are fixed by acts of 1841 and '42, as follows:

Staves, 28 inches long, 3 inches wide, ⅜ inch thick.

Headings, 18 inches long, 5 inches wide, ⅝ inch thick.

The hundred weight of 100 pounds, and ton of 2,000 pounds, were established by a law of 1818, " respecting hay and straw brought for sale to the city of Baltimore."

The last law enacted by the legislature was that approved in 1842.

VIRGINIA.

The act passed by the legislature of Virginia in 1792, and which re-enacted a previous law of 1734, entitled "An act for more effectually obliging persons to buy and sell by weights and measures according to the English standard," continued in force until after the establishment by Congress of standard weights and measures. Upon the receipt of the balances by the State of Virginia, in accordance with the act of Congress of June 14, 1836, the legislature, by an act entitled "An act providing for the preservation and use of the standard weights and measures received from the general government," passed March 19, 1847, directed that they be placed in a suitable room of the capitol, in the custody of the clerk of the council, who was to be the "superintendent of the standard weights and measures;" from whom each county and corporation court had power to obtain verified standards of the same; which, when so obtained, were to be kept in the clerk's office of each county or corporation, or any other place that the court might designate. A more detailed act was subsequently passed, and is contained in chapter 89, "of weights and measures," of the "Code of Virginia." It enacts that "the weights, measures, and balances, received by this State under a resolution of Congress, approved the 14th day of June, 1836, and an act of Congress, approved the 7th day of July, 1838, shall be kept in the capitol, in a room to be assigned by the governor and fitted up for the purpose; they shall be the public standards of weights and measures in this State;" that the clerk of the council shall be ex-officio superintendent of weights and measures, until the governor should appoint another superintendent; that the court of each county or corporation shall provide, within one year from the passage of the act, and ever after keep at the expense of the county, a set of weights and measures of the following denominations, viz: "of dry measure, one half bushel, one peck, and one half peck, made of copper, pewter, or wood; of wine measure, one gallon, one half gallon, one quart, one pint, one half pint, and one gill, made of copper or pewter; one set of brass weights to four pounds, computed at sixteen ounces to the pound, with suitable scales and steel-beam; one set of iron weights, from one pound to fifty pounds; also, of long measure, one yard, made of brass, copper, or steel; and a set of troy weights, from the lowest denomination to eight ounces;"—all to be strictly conformable to the State standards, and verified by the State superintendent of weights and measures. The county standards to be kept by such persons as may be designated by the court as "sealer of weights and measures," and to be re-compared with the State standards once in every ten years. Every sealer of weights and measures shall, at least once in every year, give public notice of the times and places at which he will attend for the purpose of trying and proving the weights and measures in use by the citizens; and once in every three years he shall go around to all the shops, stores, hay scales, and platform balances, and try such as have not been brought to him, or as he has not been requested to test. The court is authorized to appoint more than one sealer of weights and measures, for each of which a set of standards, as above, are to be provided. Suitable scales are to be provided by the superintendent and by the sealers of weights and measures. The act specifies the fees to be paid to each for trying and sealing, the penalty for any county or corporation refusing to provide the above standards, for neglect of duty on the part of the superintendent or any sealer of weights and measures, and for any person using, in buying or selling, any weights, measures, scales, balances, steelyards, &c., not properly tried and sealed.

No tender by any bank of gold weighed with weights not sealed is legal.

It does not appear that the standards for the counties were provided as contemplated in the above law, for another law was passed March 15, 1851, for this purpose. The act is entitled "An act authorizing the governor and superintendent of weights and measures to contract for, and have manufactured in Virginia, weights and measures for each county and corporation in the State." These standards were to be made of cast iron, brass, or composition, instead of copper, or pewter, or wood, as established by the previous act; a set of balances is to be added; all to be manufactured as applied for by the counties, &c., and to be first paid for by the State; the amount being reimbursed by the counties or corporations when received by them. All the other provisions of the previous act are continued in force.

"An act concerning the salaries of certain officers of government, compensation of the members and officers of the general assembly, mileage, and other allowances," passed June 5, 1852, fixes the salary of the superintendent of weights and measures at three hundred dollars.

"An act increasing the fees of the sealer of weights and measures for the city of Richmond," passed January 12, 1853, increases the fees from five to eight cents for each piece tried and proved; and also makes it the sealer's duty to go around to all the shops, stores, &c., once in every two years, instead of three years, as established by chapter 89 of the Code of Virginia. No subsequent act touching the matter of weights and measures has been passed by the legislature.

NORTH CAROLINA.

An old law of the State, enacted prior to the Revolution, during the administration of Governor Gabriel Johnson, was in force at the date of Mr. Adams' report, in 1821. This was subsequently revised, and adopted with the "Revised Statutes of North Carolina;" the standards established, however, were the same as by the terms of the old law, which were to be "according to the standard in the *Exchequer of England*, and which have been hitherto used in this State."

It required the justices of each county to provide for, and at the expense of the county, sealed weights of hundred, half hundred, quarters of hundred, half quarters of hundred, seven pounds, four, two, one, and a half pounds; yard and ell measures, of brass or copper; half bushel, peck, and *gallon*, dry measure; gallon, pottle, quart, and pint, of wine measure; also, a stamp for brass, tin, iron, lead, or pewter weights or measures; and a brand for wooden measures; all of which were to be kept at the court-house of the respective counties by a "standard keeper," to be elected by the justices of the county court. He was required to take an oath and give bond for the safe-keeping of the standards and the faithful performance of his duty. Every person using weights, measures, or steelyards, was required to bring them to the "standard keeper" for comparison, and to have them tried and sealed every two years; the standard keeper to seal such as were or could be made conformable to the standards; suitable penalties for using weights or measures for the purpose of buying or selling that have not been sealed are prescribed by the act.

The above act remained in force until the session of 1838–'39, when an act "concerning weights and measures" was passed, authorizing the governor "to procure for each of the counties of the State one complete set of all the weights and measures adopted as standards by resolution of Congress, approved the 14th of June, 1836, which shall correspond with the standards furnished for this State, by the Secretary of the Treasury of the United States, in pursuance of the said resolution," and take the most effective measures to have the above copies speedily and with little expense conveyed to the court-houses of the respective counties and delivered to the county clerks.

This was amended at the session of 1842–'43, by an act authorizing the governor to suspend the procuring of the *whole* sets of weights and measures for each of the counties, and to furnish only the following: a yard measure, to be made of substantial wood, to be stamped with the letters "N. C.," and to be placed in a secure wooden box; a half bushel, peck, gallon, half gallon, quart, pint, half pint, and gill, all to be stamped with the letters "N. C." Such of the other weights and measures, not in the foregoing list, as had been delivered to the clerk of one or more counties, were also to be furnished to the others.

Chapter 117 of the Revised Code adopts the standards of the United States, and provides for the distribution of copies thereof to the counties. Each person using weights or measures is required "to bring all his weights, or measures, or steelyards, to the standard keeper of the county where such person shall reside or trade, to be there tried by the standard;" and at least once in every two years thereafter shall have them re-examined and adjusted, under penalty for their use in default thereof of fifty dollars.

The measure of an acre of land is also fixed therein at one hundred and sixty square perches.

A copy of chapter 117 was furnished under seal, September 3, of the present year, by the executive, as containing the most recent legislation on the subject of weights and measures.

SOUTH CAROLINA.

The old laws of this State established the weights and measures in accordance with the "*London standards.*"

An act was passed December 8, 1840, "to provide weights and measures in each district," which directed that the clerk of the court of common pleas and general sessions of each judicial district should furnish and keep in his office the weights and measures established by law as the standards of the district; but the act does not define the standards.

After the receipt of the standards from the government, the legislature "*Resolved*, That his excellency the governor be, and he is hereby, requested to have duplicates of the weights and measures furnished to the State of South Carolina by the United States, and now in the town of Columbia, constructed out of some cheap and suitable materials, and sent to each of the clerks of the courts throughout the State, so that there may be accuracy and uniformity in weights and measures in the different districts."

Upon the receipt of the large balance intended for the State from the general government, the legislature, by a joint resolution, in December, 1845, requested the governor to receive it, and to have fitted up a suitable building in which it might be kept, together with the other balances to be received, and weights and measures.

An act was passed December 20, 1853, prescribing the mode to be adopted in measuring timber at Charleston, and another of the same date provides for supplying a set of the weights and measures established by law to the several judicial districts of the State not already furnished.

No recent enactments have been made by the legislature.

GEORGIA.

A law of this State, enacted on the 10th of December, 1803, which declared that the weights and measures established as standards by the cities of Augusta and Savannah should be the fixed standards of the State until the Congress of the United States should make provision on the subject, remained in force until 1839, at which time that portion of it relating to the *standards* was repealed by the following:

"'Act to amend an act passed December 10, 1803, entitled An act to make uniform a standard of weights and measures in this State,'" assented to December 23, 1839. It ordains that the standard of weights and measures adopted by the Congress of the United States shall be the standard weights and measures of the State.

It makes it the duty of the governor to procure immediately, in some cheap and economical way, one hundred copies of each of these standards, then at Milledgeville ; one of each to be given to each county, to be kept in the custody of the clerk of the "Inferior Court," and to issue his proclamation giving publicity to the fact, and calling upon all citizens to have their weights and measures tried and sealed by the standards. It prescribes the manner in which notice to the citizens shall be given by the justices of the inferior courts, and the penalties for using weights or measures not sealed, after the limited period had expired. The act to which this was amendatory specified the manner in which the comparisons with the standards should be made, and the fees to be charged.

An act was passed December 30, 1847, entitled "An act to abolish the allowance of ' tare' or gross weight on bales of unmanufactured cotton," which, as its title signifies, abolished the deduction which it had been customary, in some cases, to make from the actual weight of cotton, for the *tare* or draft ; and specifies the penalty or fine for each bale upon which such deduction should have been made.

With these, the legislation in this State upon the general subject of weights and measures seems to have ended.

An act to regulate the weighing of cotton, rice, indigo or other product, approved March 3, 1856,* prescribes a form of oath to be taken by "any salesman or other person in any of the cities, towns, villages, railroad stations or depots in this State," before declaring the weight of such commodities.

FLORIDA.

By a letter from the governor of the State, it appears that no laws upon weights and measures have been passed by the legislature.

ALABAMA.

The first law upon the subject of "weights and measures," known to have been passed since Alabama became a State, was in 1828, and authorizes the secretary of State to procure, at the expense of the State, a set of weights and measures of the best quality for each county in the State. Each set was to consist of the following : one weight of 50 pounds, one of 25, 14, 7, and two of 4 pounds, of 2, and of 1 pound avoirdupois, "according to the *standard of the United States*," with proper scales for weights ; also one foot, and one yard cloth measure ; one half-bushel, one peck, and one half-peck, "dry measure;" "one gallon, one-half gallon, one quart, one pint, one-half pint, and one gill, *wine measure.*"

A set was to be delivered to the clerk of the court of each county, by the secretary of State, as soon as they could be procured with convenience.

It prescribes the manner in which the county clerks shall give notice of the receipt of such standards ; their duty in regard to testing all weights and measures presented to them for that purpose, with the fees in each case : and the penalty for using weights and meas-

---

* To alter amendment to an act approved February 7, 1854.

ures not thus tested and sealed, in buying or selling, after the lapse of three months from the time of the county clerk's notice.

A subsequent act, passed after the direction by Congress for distribution of weights and measures, declares that there shall be but "one standard of measure of length and surface, one of weight, and one of capacity, throughout this State," which shall be in conformity to the standards established by Congress. All contracts were to be construed in accordance thereto.

Any counties that had not received their standards in accordance with the law of 1828 were directed to be supplied as soon as practicable by the secretary of State at the expense of the State. The "judges of probate of each county," when furnished with such standards, were to give proper notice by advertisement. The law prescribes the manner in which the judges shall test the weights and measures brought to them, the seal, the fees to be charged, and the penalties for buying or selling with weights or measures not thus sealed.

In 1852, an act was passed entitled "An act to provide for the preservation of the balances intended for the adjustment of the standard weights and measures," (approved February 9, 1852,) which authorizes the governor to have a suitable building erected, at the cost of the State, and not to exceed a certain sum, for the reception of the weights and measures furnished to the State by Congress. It specifies that it shall be erected on the grounds of the university at Tuscaloosa, and be under the supervision of some member of the faculty. This building has been completed, according to the plan and dimensions furnished by the superintendent of weights and measures, and evinces a proper appreciation of the elaborate standards furnished by the United States, as well as a proper feeling as regards the general importance of the subject.

Up to the present date no alterations have been made in the laws relative to weights and measures in this State.

MISSISSIPPI.

The first act in relation to weights and measures passed by the legislature, after Mississippi became a State, was in 1818, entitled "An act to provide for inspections and for other purposes," approved February 6. It confirms the previous acts of the territorial legislature in the years 1807 and 1815, as far as the standards established by them are concerned, the avoirdupois weights of which were to be "according to the standard of the United States if one was established, but if there were none such, according to the *standard of London*" with liquid *wine* measures. The standards thus confirmed by the above act of 1818 were to continue "until Congress shall fix a standard for the United States."

Congress having, by act of June 14, 1836, directed the distribution of standards to the States, the legislature, by "An act to furnish a uniform standard of weights and measures to the several counties in the State of Mississippi," approved March 4, 1846, directed the secretary of State to furnish to the several "clerks of probate," as soon as practicable, " a uniform standard of weights and measures according to the provisions of the act of Congress establishing a uniform standard of weights and measures for the United States." It is made the duty of each clerk to give notice of such standards, in at least five public places, requiring all millers, owners of cotton gins, grocers, and others vending by measures, and by weights, to have their weights and measures tried and proved by the above standards in his possession. The fines for refusal or neglect to comply with the above requirement, and the fees for trying and proving the weights and measures are defined. Each clerk has the power to appoint agents in different places in his county to aid in carrying out the provisions of the act.

The law of 1846 was re-enacted January 31, 1852, for the supply of standards to the counties.

General laws relative to weights and measures in this State remain unchanged up to the present time.

LOUISIANA.

Before Louisiana was admitted into the Union, the weights and measures used in the province were those of France.

By an act of the legislature of the 21st December, 1814, the governor of the State was required to procure, at the expense of the State, weights and measures corresponding with those used by the revenue officers of the United States, together with scales and a seal, to be deposited in the custody of the secretary of State, to serve as the general standard for the State.

By "An act supplementary to an act entitled 'an act to establish a uniform standard of weights and measures within this State,' approved December 21, 1814," (the act above referred to,) the sixth section of that act, specifying the penalties for keeping or using, for the purpose of buying and selling, weights, measures, or steelyards, not tried and sealed by a sealer of weights and measures, was re-enacted, but was restricted in its application to the parish of Orleans. This proviso was approved February 28, 1824.

The whole of the law of 1814 was re-enacted by an act approved June 1, 1846, entitled "An act to provide for the appointment of inspectors of weights and measures, to define their duties and for other purposes," with some modifications in regard to the appointment of "inspectors," their duties as regards the trial and proving of the weights and measures of the citizens, the sealing, &c.

It retains the "dry measure" to be known under the name of *barrel*, which shall contain three and a quarter bushels, *conformable to the American standard*, and be divided into half and quarter barrels. Coal is to be sold by the barrel or bushel; wheat, when sold by the bushel, shall be understood to mean 60 lbs., corn 56 lbs., oats 32 lbs., barley and rye 32 lbs. The above act, although it is a revival of the act of 1814, with slight modifications, yet contains a full adoption of the revenue standards in use at New Orleans.

No law appears to have been passed, in recognition or adoption, in express terms of the standards authorized to be distribnted to the States by the act of Congress of July 7, 1838.

The enactment of 1846 is the latest of which a copy is on file in this office relative to the subject of weights and measures.

TENNESSEE.

The first law on weights and measures in this State was passed in 1779, and is contained in chapter 11, of 1803, of the revised statutes. It does not establish *State* standards, but the first section directs the levying of a tax in all the *counties* of the State by the majority of the justices of the peace of each county, in order to procure the following standards, viz: "sealed weights of half hundreds, quarters of hundreds, seven pounds, four pounds, two pounds, one pound and half pound ; measures of ell and yard, of brass or copper; measures of half bushel, peck and half peck, of dry measure ; a gallon, *pottle,* quart, pint and half pint, of *wine measure;* stamps for brass, tin, iron, lead or pewter, and also brands for wooden measures." The standards are no more definitely described than that the gallon, pottle, &c., shall be of *wine measure;* but the wording of the act is very analogous to that of an act of the State of Virginia, passed August, 1734, and the standards described are identically the same, except that the law of Virginia declares in its first section that the standards shall be *"according to the standard of the exchequer in England."* As the people of this State mostly came from Virginia, there appears to be little cause to doubt that the law in question was derived from the Virginia act, and was intended also to establish the English exchequer standards.

The law of 1779 directs that standard keepers, to be elected for each county, shall have charge of the standards, and, if necessary, accompanied by a constable, examine the weights, measures and steelyards, in use for buying and selling in the county, and any person found with false or altered weights, measures or steelyards, to be arrested, brought before a justice and bound over for trial. The weights and measures found true are to be sealed ; the penalties for neglect to have such tried and sealed after due notice, for altering them after being once sealed, and for using weights and measures and steelyards that have not been tried and sealed, are defined.

Section 13 of the above law, prescribing heavy penalties for selling any kind of grain, salt, &c., in less measure than the standard, was repealed in 1831.

The act of March 1, 1856, adopts the United States standards furnished in 1854 as the legal units of weight and measure to be used throughout the State. This is the most recent act of legislation on the subject.

KENTUCKY.

By an act, approved February 1, 1839, the governor is authorized and requested to have made at the penitentiary one set of weights and measures for each county, "agreeably to the standards furnished by the general government of the United States, and now in posses sion of the governor of this State." The act directs that each county court shall, on or before the 1st of January, 1840, provide for the use of the county, at the expense of the county, a set of the standards thus directed to be made; under a penalty of five dollars for each member for every court suffered to pass before compliance with the act.

Chapter 34 of the revised statutes of Kentucky contains a law which directs, as above, that the governor shall have manufactured for each county, not furnished therewith, a set of "weights, measures *and balances,*" as duplicates of those furnished to the State by the United States; that each county court shall procure a set for the county, at the expense of the county, under a penalty for neglect, as above, by which standards any person desirous of having his weights and measures tested may have the same done by the person appointed to keep the standard, at a certain fee; that any person buying or selling by any weights, measures or balances, not thus tried and sealed, or who shall keep such for that purpose, shall pay a prescribed fine; that the *hundred weight* shall consist of 100 lbs., and the *ton* of 2,000; that a bushel of different substances shall consist, in weight, as follows:

Wheat	60	lbs. to the bushel.
Rye	56	" "
Indian corn	56	" "
Barley	48	" "
Bran	20	" "
Oats	$33\frac{1}{3}$	" "
Potatoes	60	" "
Beans	60	" "
Clover seed	60	" "
Timothy seed	45	" "
Flax seed	56	" "
Hemp seed	44	" "
Buckwheat	52	" "
Blue grass seed	14	" "
Cornmeal	50	" "
Onions	57	" "
Salt	50	" "

The weight of a bushel of potatoes was subsequently fixed at fifty-six pounds, of clover seed at fifty-six, bituminous coal at eighty pounds and of cannel coal at seventy pounds. Since the adoption of these regulations no laws have been passed on the subject.

OHIO.

The only law passed by this State previous to 1817, as appears from the report of Mr. Adams in 1821, was one in January, 1811, which merely directed the county commissioners of each county to cause to be made one half-bushel measure, to contain 1075.2 solid inches, which was to be kept in the county seat, and to be called the standard. This dimension is in exact proportion to the Winchester bushel.

This law was repealed by "An act regulating weights and measures," passed March 5, 1835, (modelled upon the law enacted in New York in 1826, as reported by Professor James Renwick, of Columbia College.) In nearly the whole it was a literal copy of that law, which was drawn with much care, ability, and scientific knowledge.

The standards established were—

1st. As *standard of length*, the *yard*, as used in the State of New York on the fourth of July, 1776, which had been found, by experiments with a brass rod, at Columbia College, in the city of New York, latitude 40° 42' 43" north, to bear to the pendulum at that place vibrating seconds in a vacuum, at the temperature of melting ice*, the proportion of one million (1,000,000) to one million eighty-six thousand one hundred and forty-one, (1,086,141.) The actual standard to be measured in a straight line between two points, engraven upon golden disks inserted into a straight brass rod.

2d. The standard of weight to be the *pound* of such magnitude that the weight of a cubic foot of distilled water, at its maximum density, weighed in a vacuum with brass weights, should be equal to 62½ pounds.

3d. The standard of *capacity* to be the *gallon*, of which there should be two kinds: one for liquids, to contain, at the mean pressure of the atmosphere at the level of the sea, *eight pounds* of distilled water, at its maximum density; the other, for *dry measure*, to contain *ten pounds* of distilled water under the same circumstances.

4th. The *bushel* was to contain 80 pounds of distilled water, or eight *gallons for dry* measure.

The unity of standards designed to be established, for length, weight, and measure, was thus in Ohio, as in New York, destroyed by introducing *two kinds* of gallons, one of which, the gallon for dry measure, should have been denominated a half-peck, and thus have avoided the confusion of having two standards of the same name, but of different capacities.

This law was amended by an act passed February 3, 1844, which specified that whenever *clover seed* should be sold by the bushel, and no special agreement made as to the measure or weight, the bushel should consist of *sixty pounds*.

The law of March 5, 1835, was repealed by "An act to provide for a uniform standard of weights and measures," passed February 21, 1846. It enacts "that there shall be but one standard of measure of length and surface, one of weight, and one measure of capacity, and also a standard hydrometer for ascertaining the strength of spirituous liquors throughout this State."

"That the standard of weights and measures furnished the State of Ohio, by the Secretary of the Treasury of the United States, under a resolution of Congress, approved June fourteenth, one thousand eight hundred and thirty-six, shall hereafter be the legal standard of weights and measures in this State." That they shall be deposited in the office of the secretary of State, who is *ex officio* "State sealer of weights and measures," and shall be kept in the boxes which were

---

* 39.10158 inches.

furnished by the general government, and only opened for the purpose of comparing the county standards, except by joint resolution of both houses of the general assembly, or upon the call of either house for information, or by order of the governor for scientific purposes. The State sealer was required to provide copies of the original standards, for the use of each county, of the following materials, viz: one half-bushel measure of $\frac{1}{8}$th inch copper, with brass rim; one gallon measure of $\frac{1}{16}$th inch copper, with brass rim and handle; one half-gallon, one quart, one pint, and one half-pint, to be made in the same manner; fifty, twenty-five, twenty, ten, five, four, three, two, and one pound weights, avoirdupois, to be made of cast-iron, turned, polished, and tinned; and one half-pound, one quarter-pound, two ounce, one ounce, half-ounce, and quarter-ounce weights, troy, to be made of brass; one brass yard measure, graduated into feet, inches, and tenths. The State sealer to furnish copies of them before December 7, 1846, to each of the counties; the standards being marked with the letter "O," (Ohio,) and an appropriate device for each county, which device should be recorded and a copy of the record furnished with the standards.

The town sealers were to be furnished in the same manner, by the State sealer, with copies of the original standards, at the expense of the towns.

The act specifies the duties of the county and town sealers of weights and measures, the fees to be received, the penalties for neglect or non-performance of duty, the action in case of death, resignation, or removal from office, and the penalties for using weights or measures not tried and sealed, almost identical with the corresponding sections of the law of 1835.

The last two sections of the act establish the hydrometer constructed by Elisha and Charles Dwelle as the standard hydrometer for determining the strength of spirituous liquors, and declares the strength of proof, as designated by it, should be of the specific gravity of 93.67, at 60° of Fahrenheit, distilled water at the same temperature being reckoned 10,000.

It was also made the duty of the governor to appoint, every five years, one or more adjusters of hydrometers for the use of inspectors and others, in the State.

An amendment to this act, February 8, 1847, established the weight of a bushel of different substances, as follows:

Wheat...............60 pounds to the bushel.
Indian corn.........56   "   "   "
Rye or flax-seed...56   "   "   "
Barley..............48   "   "   "
Clover-seed.........64   "   "   "
Oats................32   "   "   "

"An act to establish the standard measure of stone coal, coke, and unslacked lime," passed February 14, 1848, established the bushel of stone coal, coke, and unslacked lime, to be equal to 2,688 cubic inches, the lawful measure for these substances to contain two bushels, and to be 24 inches diameter at the top, 20 inches at the bottom, and 14.1 inches deep.

An act was passed February 24, 1848, entitled "An act to *amend* the 'Act to provide for a uniform standard of weights and measures,' passed February 21, 1846." This specifies the damages to be recovered in a suit against any persons who have used in buying or selling, any weights, measures or beams, which have not been tried and sealed, by any person so defrauded.

The amendment of February 8, 1847, was still further amended by an act passed February 25, 1848, which merely changed the weight of a bushel of clover-seed from 64 pounds to 60 pounds.

March 23, 1850, a law was passed, entitled "An act supplementary to 'An act to provide for a uniform standard of weights and measures,' passed February 21, 1846," which supplies an omission in that law, by providing for furnishing each of the counties with a balance, with which to make the comparison of the weights.

These were to be made by contract, at the expense of the State, under the direction of the State sealer of weights and measures.

The act of 1850 was the last adopted by the legislature in reference to the subject of weights and measures.

MICHIGAN.

A territorial act of Michigan, " to regulate weights and measures," approved April 12, 1827, declares "That there shall be kept at the treasury office, to be in the custody, and under the care of the treasurer of the Territory for the time being, one just beam, one certain measure for distance, and capacity, that is to say, avoirdupois and troy weights; bushels, half-bushels, pecks, half-pecks, and quarts; and gallons, half-gallons, quarts, pints, half pints, and gills; and one certain rod for long measure; and that the standard of weights and measures, now in use in the *State of New York*, shall be the standard for ascertaining all beams, weights, and measures, throughout this Territory, until the Congress of the United States shall establish the standard of weights and measures for the United States."

The standards in use in New York, at that time, were derived from those in the English exchequer. The act provides for supplying the counties and townships with standards, and declares, that the territorial standards shall be of iron, brass or copper, as the treasurer shall direct; that those for the counties and townships, shall be of such materials as the supervisors of each county shall direct; that the clerk of each county and township shall be ex-officio sealer of weights and measures for the county or township; that the clerk of the county shall compare the county with the territorial standards once every three years, and that the clerks of the towns shall examine, try, and prove, the weights, measures, and steelyards, in use by the citizens. The act prescribes the fees to be received by the sealers of weights and measures, the penalties for using weights and measures not sealed, and for neglect, or refusal to comply with its requirements.

The whole of the above law is revived in Chapter 31, "Of Weights and Measures" of the "Revised Statutes of Michigan," adopted

May 18, 1846, with some additions, among which are the legal weights of a bushel of the following grains, &c.:

Wheat or clover-seed......60 pounds to the bushel.
Rye or Indian corn.........56 " " "
Oats...........................32 " " ".
Barley........................48 " " "
Buckwheat...................42 " " "
Dried apples or peaches..28 " " "

No law appears to have been passed adopting the United States standards, although they were all furnished to the State previous to 1842.

The last enactment relative to weights or measures is that referred to as having been made in 1846.

INDIANA.

The act of January 21, 1818, entitled "An act regulating weights and measures," was only a revival of the territorial act of 7th December, 1807. It authorized and required the several boards of county commissioners to provide for their several counties, at the expense of the same, a set of the following weights and measures, viz: "one measure of one foot, or twelve inches, *English measure*, so called; also, one measure of three feet, or thirty-six inches, as aforesaid; also, one half bushel measure for dry measure, which shall contain one thousand and seventy-five and one-fifth solid inches; also, one gallon measure which shall contain two hundred and thirty-one solid inches; which measures shall be of wood or any metal the court may think proper; also, one set of weights commonly called avoirdupois weights." These were to have the name or initial letter of the county stamped upon them, and were to be kept by the clerk of the circuit court of each county. The act specifies the manner and limit of the notice to be given to the citizens by the county commissioners as soon as they should have provided the standards; the manner in which the weights and measures of the citizens shall be tested by the clerks of the circuit courts, and the seal to be attached.

The law of 1818, with its amendments, was re-enacted June 9, 1852, by "An act for the regulation of weights and measures," contained in chapter 117 of the Revised Statutes. It recites the same description of the standards as before recognized by the State. In addition, the legal weight of a bushel of different kinds of grains is given in this act, and in an amendment approved March, 1, 1853, as follows:

Shelled corn................... 56 lbs. avoirdupois to a bushel.
Indian corn, (on the cob)... 68 " "
Wheat............................ 60 " "
Buckwheat..................... 50 " "
Corn meal...................... 50 " "
Beans............................ 60 " "
Potatoes........................ 60 " "
Oats.............................. 32 " "
Clover seed.................... 60 " "

Hemp seed............	44 lbs.	avoirdupois to a bushel.
Blue grass seed......	14 "	"
Castor beans..........	46 "	"
Dried peaches........	33 "	"
Dried apples..........	25 "	"
Onions..................	57 "	"
Salt.......................	50 "	"
Mineral coal...........	70 "	"
Timothy seed.........	45 "	"
Rye.......................	56 "	"
Flax seed...............	56 "	"
Barley...................	48 "	"

It will be observed that the United States standards have not been formally recognized by law in this State; although the defined contents of the *gallon* for liquid measures, (231 cubic inches,) and that of dry measure, (1075.2 cubic inches,) are exactly the same as the standard contents of the United States standards.

The act of 1852 was amended February 28, 1855, by changing the standard weight for onions from fifty-seven to forty-eight pounds the bushel, and fixing the weight of a ton of hay at two thousand pounds.

ILLINOIS.

Illinois was originally a part of the territory of Indiana, and retained the territorial act of the latter in relation to weights and measures until the 22d of March, 1819, when an act was passed, modelled upon the law of 21st January, 1818, but having the peculiarity of departure from the English standard weights by fixing the avoirdupois pound at 7,020 grains troy, instead of 7,000.

This act was repealed by "An act regulating weights and measures," approved March 4, 1843, which declares that "there shall be but one standard of measure, of length, and surface, one of weight, and one of capacity, throughout the State, which shall be in conformity with the standard of measures, length, surface, and weight, established by Congress," and directs that the secretary of State, who is to be ex-officio "State sealer of weights and measures," shall procure standards for the State in conformity thereto, as follows, viz: a yard, a pound, a liquid gallon, and a half bushel. These are to be considered as original standards, and deposited in his office in a chest, which is only to be opened for the purpose of making comparisons with the county standards, except by a joint resolution of both houses of the legislature, or on a call of either house for information, or by the order of the governor for scientific purposes.

Copies of these are to be made of such materials as the State sealer shall direct, and deposited in the office of the clerk of the commissioner's court of each county, who is to be responsible for their preservation.

The State standards are to be sealed with the letter "I," and the county standards with the same, and an additional device for each particular county. These devices were to be recorded in the State sealer's office, and copies also delivered with the county standards.

WEIGHTS AND MEASURES. 75

The law makes it the duty of the county sealer to test all weights and measures brought to him for that purpose, and seal those which are found to be in conformity with the standards; and in order that the sellers and all persons who use them, shall have their weights and measures so tested, it declares that any purchaser who is defrauded in consequence of a neglect on the part of the seller to do so, can obtain, by action for damage, five times its amount, with costs of suit. The county sealer of weights and measures is also to compare the standards in his possession once in every ten years with those in the State sealer's office, and is made liable to a heavy fine in case of a failure to do so.

The following is established as the weight of a bushel of the different kinds of grain usually bought and sold in the State, in case of no special agreement as to weight or measurement being made between the buyer and seller, viz:

Sixty	pounds of	Wheat	to constitute a	*bushel.*
Fifty-four	"	Rye	"	"
Fifty-two	"	Indian corn	"	"
Forty-four	"	Barley	"	"
Forty	"	Buckwheat	"	"
Thirty-two	"	Oats	"	"

The "hundred weight" is to be understood to consist of one hundred pounds, and *twenty* such *hundreds* to make *one ton.*

All commodities sold by *heaped measure* are to be heaped up as high as the articles will admit in the form of a *cone*, the outside rim of the measure being the *base* of the cone. The dry commodities not heaped were to be stricken by a straight rod or a roller, which should be of the same diameter from end to end.

The above law as re-enacted March 3, 1845, is contained in chapter 108 "of weights and measures" of the revised statutes of the State.

It was amended by an act approved February 15, 1851, fixing the weight of a bushel of corn at fifty-six pounds, and that of February 17, 1851, which simply established the weight of a bushel of "castor beans" at 46 lbs. avoirdupois, and again, February 10, 1853, establishing the weight of a bushel of the following products, viz:

Field beans..........................	56 lbs.	to the bushel.
Castor beans	46 "	"
Clover seed.........................	60 "	"
Flax seed	54 "	"
Timothy seed......................	42 "	"
Hemp seed..........................	40 "	"
Stone coal...........................	80 "	"

An act approved February 14, 1855, fixed the weight of a bushel of each of the following commodities and repealed all laws inconsistent therewith:

Shelled corn.........................	56 lbs.	to the bushel.
Corn in the ear....	70 "	"
Wheat...................................	60 "	"
Rye.......................................	56 "	"

WEIGHTS AND MEASURES.

Oats	32	lbs.	to the bushel.
Barley	48	"	"
Irish potatoes	60	"	"
Sweet potatoes	55	"	"
White beans	60	"	"
Castor beans	46	"	"
Clover seed	60	"	"
Timothy seed	45	"	"
Flax seed	56	"	"
Hemp seed	44	"	"
Blue grass seed	14	"	"
Buckwheat	52	"	"
Dried peaches	33	"	"
Dried apples	24	"	"
Onions	57	"	"
Salt	50	"	"
Stone coal	80	"	"
Malt	38	"	"
Bran	20	"	"
Turnips	55	"	"
Plastering hair	8	"	"
Unslacked lime	80	"	"
Corn meal	48	"	"
Fine salt	55	"	"

No subsequent action has been taken on the subject of weights and measures in this State.

IOWA.

It appears by communications from the secretary of State, that the law contained in chapter 56, of "weights and measures" of the code of Iowa, is the only one in regard to weights and measures in force in that State. This law makes it the duty of the State treasurer to procure, at the expense of the State, a set of the following weights and measures, to be kept in the treasurer's office, and to be the State standards, viz:

One yard and one foot measure; one half bushel, peck, and half peck, the half bushel to contain 1,075⅕ cubic inches; one gallon, (231 cubic inches,) one quart, one pint, and one gill; a set of avoirdupois weights, consisting of a pound, a half pound, a quarter pound, an ounce and a ten pound weight.

The "perch" of mason's work or stone is declared to be 25 cubic feet.

All contracts in which there is no special agreement as to the weights or measures, are to be understood as above, with the exception of the measure of wheat, oats and all kinds of grain and seeds. The number of pounds of each which was to constitute a bushel is prescribed as follows:

Of wheat	60 lbs.	avoirdupois	to the bushel.
Of shelled corn	56	"	"
Of corn in the cob	70	"	"

Of rye.............................	56 lbs.	avoirdupois to the bushel.
Of oats...........................	35 "	"
Of barley	48 "	"
Of potatoes..................	60 "	"
Of beans.........................	60 "	"
Of bran..........................	20 "	"
Of clover seed	60 "	"
Of timothy seed...........	45 "	"
Of flax seed	56 "	"
Of hemp seed................	44 "	"
Of buckwheat...............	52 "	"
Of blue grass seed.........	14 "	"
Of castor beans.............	46 "	"
Of dried peaches	33 "	"
Of dried apples.............	24 "	"
Of onions	57 "	"
Of salt..........................	50 "	"

As soon as the standards are procured, the treasurer is to give notice in a newspaper, upon which it is made the duty of the county judge of each county to obtain a set of weights and measures exactly corresponding to the State standards, and deposit them in the office of the county treasurer, to be there kept and to constitute the *county standards*.

The county treasurer shall "from time to time cause them to be tested by the State standards and made to agree therewith."

It authorizes any person wishing to have his weights or measures tested to call on the county treasurer for that purpose, and prescribes the fees to be paid the treasurer, who was to seal them if found true, or destroy them if not conformable to the standards.

The law does not, however, in order to force a compliance with its requisition, prescribe penalties for the use of weights and measures not thus sealed.

The standards thus established are identical in dimensions with the United States standards, although the latter, as such, are not recognized. The troy weights are not adopted.

The legislature of this State has made no subsequent enactment in regard to weights and measures.

WISCONSIN.

The "revised statutes" of 1839 contain an act passed while Wisconsin was a Territory, entitled, "An act to regulate weights and measures," which was evidently modeled upon the act of the State of New York of 1826. It declares that "there shall be but one standard of measure of length and surface, one of weight, and one of capacity in this Territory;" and establishes the following standards, all of which were to be according to those in legal use in the State of New York. 1st, the *yard*, as standard of length and surface; 2d, the unit or standard of the capacity measures to be the *gallon;* of which there were to be *two kinds*, one for *liquids* and one for *dry measure;* 3d, the standard of weight to be the *pound*, divided into 16 ounces; no troy weights being established. It specifies the divisions and multiples of the above standards, and the dimensions of measures for the sale of articles by heaped measure, which are the same as those of New York. The above standards were to be procured by the treasurer of the Territory, who was ex-officio "sealer of weights and measures," and to be kept in his office. County standards, copies of the foregoing, were to be procured by the treasurer of each county, who was to be county sealer of weights and measures. These were to be sealed with the word "Wisconsin," and such other device as the treasurer should direct; and re-compared and sealed by the territorial standards once in every five years

As soon as the standards were procured, public notice was to be given by the county sealer for all persons to have their weights, measures and steelyards tried and sealed.

The act provides for the transfer of the standards upon the death, resignation, or removal from office of the county sealer, to his successor, and for action in case of neglect or refusal to do so.

The fees are also defined, and the liabilities in case of any person being injured or defrauded by the use by any persons of weights, measures or steelyards not tried and sealed.

The hundred weight was to consist of 100 lbs., and the ton of 2,000 lbs.

The legal weight of a bushel of different kinds of grain, &c., was fixed as follows:

Wheat............	60 lbs.	to the bushel.
Rye...............	56 "	"
Indian corn......	56 "	"
Barley............	45 "	"
Oats..............	32 "	"

The above act was renewed under the State organization, in an act contained in the revised statutes of the State A. D. 1849, chapter 42d "of weights and measures." The State treasurer was to be the "State sealer," and "the county treasurer the county sealer of weights and measures." The county standards, such as were not already provided, were to be procured by the "county supervisors," at the expense of each county, exactly conformable to the State standards, but of such material as the supervisors might direct; to be sealed with the letters "Wis.," and certified by the State sealer, and deposited in the county treasurer's office. They were to be re-compared and sealed every five years, from the 1st of January, 1850. The county sealer was to procure a seal with which to seal the town standards. The penalties for neglect of the board of supervisors to procure county standards, for neglect of duty on the part of any sealer of weights and measures, and the fees for sealing are specified.

The vibrating steelyards are to be allowed, when tried and proved by a sealer. The hundred weight is to consist of one hundred pounds avoirdupois.

The legal weight of a bushel of different kinds of grains, &c., is fixed as follows:

Wheat.....................................	60 lbs.	to a bushel.
Clover seed............................	60 "	"
Rye..	56 "	"
Indian corn............................	56 "	"
Oats.......................................	32 "	"
Barley...................................	48 "	"
Buckwheat.............................	42 "	"
Dried apples..........................	28 "	"
Dried peaches........................	28 "	"

In heaped measures, the substances measured are to be heaped as high as can be without effort.

The above act, in the revised statutes of 1849, declares in its first section that "the weights and measures, together with the scales and beams * * * * which are now or may hereafter be deposited in the treasury of this State, shall be preserved by the treasurer and be the *public standards.*" In this light the following act may be considered an adoption of the United States standards, viz: "An act to provide for the receiving and safekeeping of the set of standard weights and measures, and to appropriate money to defray expenses," approved April 17, 1852; which, as its title indicates, merely authorizes the governor to provide for the receiving and safekeeping of the set of weights and measures in the United States treasury, subject to the order of the State. These have since been delivered and set up at the State capitol.

The last act of legislation (published March 31, 1854,) fixes the weight of a bushel of potatoes at sixty pounds, of flax seed at fifty-six pounds, and of timothy seed at forty-six pounds.

MISSOURI.

The territorial act of July 28, 1813, was re-enacted in December 18, 1824, and directed the several tribunals established for transacting county business within the State to provide for, and at the expense of, the respective counties, one foot, and one yard, English measures; one half-bushel, to contain $1,075\frac{1}{5}$ cubic inches, for dry measure; one gallon, to contain 231 cubic inches, and smaller measures in proportion; to be of wood or any metal the court should think proper; also one set of avoirdupois weights, and one seal, with the initial of the county inscribed thereon, all to be kept by the clerks of said tribunals for the purpose of trying and sealing the measures and weights used in the counties.

The use, or keeping to buy or sell, of weights and measures, not corresponding with these standards, after due notice, was prohibited under penalties by the same act; but with a proviso that all contracts or obligations made previous to the taking effect of the act should be settled, paid and executed agreeably to the weights and measures in common use when the contracts or obligations were made or entered into.

All persons wishing their weights and measures tried by the county standards are to apply to the clerk of the county, who, if he finds them to correspond with the standards, shall seal them with the seal to be provided for that purpose.

The above act was renewed December 8, 1834, that portion defining the standards, and the duties of the county sealers, being verbatim the same as the old law. The penalties for knowingly using or keeping any measures or weights not conforming to the standards, after due notice has been given of their having been provided, is defined, but with a provision in another section that it shall not apply to the use of any weight or measure which may be to the advantage of the purchaser. Each constable is required, from time to time, to inspect the measures and weights used by millers, merchants, grocers, pedlers and other dealers within his township, and to report to some justice of the peace any violation of the act.

An act of February 13, 1841, declares, that hereafter, in the sales of hemp, 100 lbs. shall constitute the hundred weight.

A joint resolution of the senate and house of representatives, approved February 22, 1843, directs, that the weights and measures received by the State from the general government be deposited with the secretary of State for safe keeping, and that he shall correspond with the Secretary of the Treasury of the United States to ascertain if any more measures are to be furnished, and if so, to keep the same safely, and to report at the next session of the general assembly.

It does not, however, appear that any further action was taken with a view to their adoption by the State, for on the 17th of March, 1845, the old law of 1813, as renewed in 1834, was re-enacted almost verbatim, the only addition being a section fixing the weight of a bushel of different grains ; wheat being fixed at 60 lbs., rye at 56 lbs., and Indian corn at 52 lbs. to the bushel. No troy weights were ever recognized by the State.

The act approved November 27, 1855, provides as follows :

Section 1. "The clerk of each county court shall provide, at the expense of the county, one measure of one foot, or twelve inches, English measure ; one measure of three feet, or thirty-six inches, English measure, denominated one yard; one half-bushel measure, which shall contain one thousand seventy-five and one-fifth cubic inches, denominated dry measure ; one gallon measure, which shall contain two hundred and thirty-one cubic inches ; one half-gallon measure, which shall contain one hundred and fifteen and one-half cubic inches ; one quart measure, which shall contain fifty-seven and three-fourths cubic inches ; also one set of weights called avoirdupois weights, and one seal with initials of the county inscribed thereon ; which measures, weights and seal shall be kept by the clerk of the county court of each county."

Section 4. "The hundred weight shall consist of one hundred pounds avoirdupois, and twenty such hundreds shall constitute a ton."

The fifth section of the same act fixes the weight of articles offered for sale by the bushel as follows :

Wheat, beans, clover seed or potatoes, sixty pounds to the bushel ; rye, corn, or flaxseed, fifty-six pounds; barley, forty-eight pounds; oats, thirty-five pounds; bran, twenty pounds; onions, fifty-seven pounds ; dried peaches, thirty-three pounds ; dried apples, twenty-four pounds; buckwheat, fifty-two pounds; castor beans, forty-six pounds; hemp seed, forty-four pounds; blue grass seed, fourteen pounds; salt, fifty pounds; mineral coal, eighty pounds.

The measure for charcoal is fixed at twenty-six hundred cubic inches per bushel.

ARKANSAS.

The only law of the State upon the subject is that of February 12, 1838, in force by the proclamation of the governor, of March 20, 1839, which is founded upon the law of Missouri of 1834, of which it is an almost literal copy. It establishes as standards the foot and the yard, English measure; the half bushel to contain $1,075\frac{1}{5}$ cubic inches for dry measure; the gallon to contain 231 cubic inches, and smaller measures in proportion for liquid or *wine measure;* a set of avoirdupois weights, made of iron or brass; all of which it requires the clerk of each county to procure for, and at the expense of, the respective counties, together with a seal with the initials of the county; which are to be securely kept by each clerk, who is to seal with the seal all weights and measures brought to him for that purpose which correspond with the above standards.

No legislative action has adopted the United States standards which have been furnished to the State, nor has the troy weight been established.

The most recent act relative to weights and measures is that passed in 1838.

TEXAS.

The only law on weights and measures in this State was enacted in 1846, and approved May 7, and authorizes the governor to procure, at the expense of the State, a set of weights and measures, in conformity with the standard adopted and in use by the government of the United States, which was declared to be the legal standard of the State; and to cause correct copies of the above standards, when procured, to be made, and after being properly inspected and sealed with an appropriate seal, to deliver a full set of such weights and measures, upon application, to the chief justice of each county, at the expense of the county. The county courts of the several counties are authorized to grant licenses to a suitable person or persons to make and vend weights and measures, under prescribed regulations, who are, however, not allowed to sell or distribute them until they have been inspected by some authorized person to see that they correspond with the State standard. No penalties are prescribed for using false weights and measures.

Inquiries made in 1853, and within the present year, have elicited no further information respecting the regulations which may be now in force.

CALIFORNIA.

By "An act to establish a standard of weights and measures," passed March 30, 1850, it is declared that there shall be but one standard of measure of length and surface, one of weights, and one of measure of capacity, throughout the State, which shall be in conformity with those established by Congress. It was made the duty of the secretary of state, who was to be ex-officio "State sealer of weights and measures," to procure, in conformity with the above, the following original standards, viz: a yard, a pound, a liquid gallon, and a half bushel; and to deposite them in a box or case in his office, which was only to be opened for the purpose of testing the county standards, except on the call of either house of the legislature, or by a joint resolution, or by the order of the governor, for scientific purposes; copies of the above original standards for and at the expense of each county, to be made of such materials as the State sealer might direct, were to be procured and deposited with the clerk of each county court, who was to be ex-officio county sealer of weights and measures; each of the copies being impressed by the State sealer with the letter "C," and such additional device for each county as the State sealer might direct, which was to be recorded in the State sealer's office, and a copy delivered to the county sealer with the standards.

All contracts for any work to be done or anything to be sold thereafter to be executed, were to be understood to be made according to the above standards. The hundred weight was to consist of 100 lbs. and the ton of 2,000 lbs.; articles sold by heaped measure were to be heaped in the form of a cone as high as the articles would permit, the outside of the measure being the base of the cone; and all articles not heaped, to be stricken with a straight stick or roller of the same diameter from end to end. The law directs the county sealers to compare the copies in their possession with the State standards once in every ten years under pain of a heavy fine, and to compare all weights and measures that may be brought to him for that purpose with the county standards; and if he finds them true, to seal them. The fees for sealing, as well as the liabilities for any person using any measures, weights, or beams, whereby any purchaser shall be injured or defrauded, are defined. The act fixes the weight of several kinds of grain which shall be taken for a bushel, as follows: wheat, 60 lbs.; rye, 54 lbs.; Indian corn, 52 lbs.; barley, 50 lbs.; buckwheat, 40 lbs.; and oats, 32 lbs.

The above act was amended by an act approved April 30, 1853, so as to make it the duty of the county sealer to procure, in addition to the standards enumerated in the act of 1850, the usual subdivisions of such weights and measures which were to be certified by the weigher and measurer of the United States custom house, and deposited in the office of the county sealer. They were to be sealed with the seal of the county court, and a certificate under the affidavit of the county sealer was to be entered upon the minutes of the court, a copy of which was to be transmitted to the secretary of state, and filed by him in his office. Each person using weights and measures is required by this amendment to have such tried and sealed by the county sealer *every year*, and is prohibited using unsealed weights, measures, or beams, under a heavy fine.

By "An act to provide for the appointment of a gauger for the port of San Francisco," approved May 3, 1852, the gauger, to be appointed by the governor, is required, after taking oath and giving bonds for the faithful discharge of his duties, to gauge and inspect all liquors and wines which are, or shall arrive, in that city; the fees for which, as well as the fine for any person in the city selling or offering for sale any wines or liquors without the inspector's mark thereon, is prescribed.

The law of 1853 is the latest enacted in this State.

MINNESOTA TERRITORY.

The law in force in this Territory is the old territorial law of Wisconsin, and was adopted here in 1849. The standards established by it, as stated under the head of Wisconsin, are the *yard*, the *gallon*—of which there were to be two kinds, one for liquid and the other for dry measure—and the *pound*, all of which were to be according to the same as then in legal use in the State of New York.

The Revised Statutes of 1851 fix the hundred weight at one hundred pounds avoirdupois, and the weights of commodities sold by the bushel as follows:

Wheat at............	60 pounds.	Buckwheat.........	42	pounds.
Clover seed............	60 "	Barley..............	48	"
Rye.	56 "	Dried apples........	28	"
Indian corn............	56 "	Dried peaches......	28	"
Oats.....................	32			

Section 12 of the Revised Statutes provides that the half bushel and parts shall be the standard measure for charcoal, fruits, and commodities usually sold by heaped measure, and that "in measuring such commodities, the half bushel or other smaller measure shall be heaped as high as may be without special effort or design."

Since 1851 no legislation has occurred bearing on the subject of weights or measures.

TERRITORY OF NEW MEXICO.

By the act of January 12, 1852, the United States standards are adopted and legalized as the weights and measures to be used in the Territory. The same act legalized the use of the *fanega, half fanega, almud, vara*, and the *cuartilla*, as measures of capacity; the *half fanega* to contain two thousand four hundred and seventy-six and a fourth cubic inches; the *almud*, as a measure of capacity, to be one-sixth part thereof; and the *cuartilla* to be equal to the United States standard pint measure. It was made the duty of the treasurer of the Territory to procure the standards authorized, and thereafter to approve and seal the weights and measures used by purchasers and venders, who were required to present the same for comparison yearly within sixty days from the expiration of thirty days' notice given by the treasurer, under a penalty, for using in default of such approval and seal, not to exceed one thousand dollars.

The act of February 8, 1853, repeals the general provision just recited, and directs that the judges of probate, in their respective counties, shall, on being informed that the treasurer of the Territory has procured standards, apply for sealed and approved copies thereof to serve as standards in the several counties; and the inhabitants of each county are to present to the probate judge their weights and measures for comparison within thirty days from the publication of notice to that effect. A fee of twenty-five cents is allowed to the treasurer of the Territory and judges of probate for each measure compared, and penalties attach of not less than twenty nor more than one hundred dollars for non-compliance with the provision relative to comparisons. The judges of probate every third year are to have the standards in their respective keeping compared with the weights and measures in the care of the treasurer of the Territory.

WASHINGTON TERRITORY.

AN ACT relative to weights and measures.

SECTION 1. *Be it enacted by the legislative assembly of the Territory of Washington,* That the weights and measures, together with the scales and beams, and those made in conformity therewith, which are now or may be hereafter deposited in the treasury of this Territory, shall be preserved by the treasurer and be the public standard in this Territory.

SEC. 2. The treasurer of the Territory shall be the sealer of weights and measures, and he shall have and keep a seal which shall be so formed as to impress the letters W. T. upon the weights and measures, scales and beams, to be sealed by him, with which he shall seal all such authorized public standards of weights and measures, and all the weights and measures, scales and beams to be provided by the several counties, when examined by said treasurer, and found to be in conformity with the standard weights and measures, scales and beams aforesaid; and the treasurer of each county shall be the sealer of weights and measures for said county, and he shall provide a suitable seal, and seal all weights and measures brought to him for that purpose when the same are found to be in conformity with the legal standards.

SEC. 3. When any commodity shall be sold by the hundred weight, it shall be understood to mean the net weight of one hundred pounds avoirdupois; and all contracts concerning goods and commodities sold by weight, shall be construed accordingly, unless such construction would be manifestly inconsistent with the special agreement of the parties contracting.

SEC. 4. Whenever wheat, rye, Indian corn, oats, barley, clover seed, buckwheat, dried apples, dried peaches, potatoes, or onions shall be sold by the bushel, and no special agreement as to the measure or weight thereof shall be made by the parties, the measure thereof shall be ascertained by weight, and shall be computed as follows:

Sixty pounds for a bushel of wheat or clover seed;
Fifty-six pounds for a bushel of rye or Indian corn;
Thirty-six pounds for a bushel of oats;

Forty-five pounds for a bushel of barley;
Forty-two pounds for a bushel of buckwheat;
Twenty-eight pounds for a bushel of dried apples or dried peaches;
Sixty pounds for a bushel of potatoes;
Fifty pounds for a bushel of onions, turnips, beets, and other vegetable roots.

SEC. 5. Two thousand one hundred and fifty and forty-two one-hundredths cubic inches shall be the contents of the legal bushel within the meaning of this act, and the half bushel and parts thereof shall be the standard measure for charcoal, fruits, and other commodities customarily sold by heaped measure; and in measuring such commodities the half bushel or other smaller measure shall be heaped as high as may be without special effort or design.

To the laws recited above, was appended the certificate of the secretary of the Territory, Charges H. Mason, esq., under date December 17, 1856; and the letter of the governor forwarding them intimates that no other laws have been passed in relation to weights and measures.

Many kinds of grains, seeds, and other substances, which have been bought and sold by measure, are now usually exchanged by weight; and most of the States have established by law the number of pounds avoirdupois which shall be understood to constitute a bushel, unless there be some special agreement as to the measure between the buyer and seller. Of some grains, &c., the legal weight of the bushel in different States is not always the same, which, no doubt, arises from the variety of the weight of the product in different soils. The table (see Appendix No. 14) of the legal weights of these different products in the respective States will illustrate this.

The following States have enacted that one hundred avoirdupois pounds shall be the legal hundred weight, and two thousand pounds the legal ton:

California, Connecticut, Iowa, Illinois, Indiana, Kentucky, Maine, Maryland, Missouri, New Hampshire, New York, New Jersey, Ohio, Rhode Island, Vermont, Wisconsin, and Massachusetts.

In Michigan, and Minnesota and Washington Territories, the hundred weight, by law, is fixed at one hundred pounds.

From the foregoing abstract of the laws of the several States, it may be seen that a great advance has been made towards uniformity of law; and from the well known action of several States in the matter, the uniformity of fact seems to have received a large share of public attention.

The two parts of the plan submitted by the Hon. John Q. Adams, for the action of Congress, were—1st. To fix the standard, with the partial uniformity of which it is susceptible, for the present, excluding all innovations. 2d. To consult with foreign nations for the future and ultimate establishment of universal and permanent uniformity

In regard to the first part of the plan, the essential principle was laid down by Mr. Adams that, in the establishment of the standards for the Union, no innovations should be allowed in the system then recognized in the country, no trifling or partial attempts at change should be permitted, and all attempts at either should be steadily rejected by Congress as unworthy of the high purposes of the subject, as not only not leading to uniformity, but as tending to the reverse, namely: to increase diversity and confusion. Mr. Hassler, whose conclusions on this matter agreed in the main with Mr. Adams, examined the weights and measures from the custom-houses of the United States and determined those which, in the midst of much diversity, were in most general use.

It has always appeared to me matter of regret that this opportunity was not taken so far to simplify the actual standards as to use but one pound as the unit of weight, and one measure of capacity, deciding between the avoirdupois and troy pounds and the dry and liquid measures. Such a reform would, I think, have been gladly accepted.

Another most desirable one, in my estimation, would have been the introduction of the decimal subdivision, similar to those in our coinage—a change which would have been very difficult to effect while old usages and old weights and measures were so generally diffused among the States. This reform might, possibly, have jeoparded the other. When made—and it will one day assuredly be made—this reform will require the exercise by Congress of its constitutional prerogative. The material standards, too, must be withdrawn and the new ones be diffused. One generation would nearly suffice to effect this change if, as in Holland, the new weights and measures were introduced through the schools. The children of the country becoming familiar with them in the primary schools, seeing the actual material standards of length, capacity, and weight, at frequent and stated times in early youth, and retaining that familiarity as they passed into the higher schools, would be readily prepared for their universal use when reaching mature life. But the old material standards must disappear, and not, as in our coinage, be tolerated by usage alongside of the lawful standards, destroying which Mr. Adams has so well called the uniformity of fact.

A third desirable change, in my judgment, would have been to establish simple relations between the length and capacity unit, and to connect them with the unit of weight. This could have been done without altering practically the standards in use.

Such changes were, in general, avoided, and probably upon the principle laid down by Mr. Adams. Coming into the charge of an unfinished work, I conformed as far as I could to the plans already in part executed by my predecessor, Mr. Hassler, as I could co-operate heartily in the endeavor to produce that uniformity of fact which was the basis of the system. I have not failed, from time to time, to press forward the second part of this established system, namely, the endeavor at universal uniformity.

The same principle was carried out in the action of Congress, in June, 1836, establishing the present standards, and providing for their distribution to each of the States. The importance was fully felt by those entrusted with procuring accurate copies of the English original, and in constructing the elaborate copies for the States and custom-houses; and it has so far been carried out by the States in a manner very gratifying to those interested in the subject.

The first part of Mr. Adams' plan has (as far as legal standards are concerned, and in a great degree) been accomplished, but the second part, that which recommends the consultation with foreign nations for the ultimate establishment of universal uniformity, remains yet to be acted on. The importance of the subject cannot but be deeply felt by every one truly interested in the universal brotherhood and substantial improvement of the human race. France was the first to take an important step in the matter, in the projection and final accomplishment of the great work of the measurement of an arc of the meridian passing through her territory, thus giving an ultimate natural standard to which all measures of extension might be referred. To this work she gave the important and universal character which it deserved by inviting the co-operation of all nations. The subsequent adoption of the metrical system with the metre, the forty millionth part of the circumference of the earth as the unit of linear measurement, was a great era in the progress of uniformity.

True, the progress of science has shown that this metre is not really the forty millionth part of the meridian, as supposed; true, that Great Britain has developed an opposition to this national standard which seems almost insuperable, and has been followed by the continental nations in this opposition.

The first fact does not necessarily imply the change of unit, though it does point to the failure to realize its true extent; but the second seems conclusive in regard to the necessity for new efforts at international uniformity.

In these remarks, as well as in my former reports, I have purposely avoided the subject of the coinage, though the same general principles apply obviously to it, partly, that under the law it is in a very different condition from that of weights and measures, but more from the reserve which I think executive officers in different branches of the government should have in touching upon subjects confided by law to others. As a citizen, I take a deep interest in the subject of international coinage, but, as an officer of the Treasury Department, look to the United States mint for suggestions in regard to its alteration.

By reference to the interesting account of the metrical system, in the letter of M. Silbermann, (Appendix No. 17,) it will be seen that it has extended widely beyond the boundaries of France, and has been adopted by law in Spain, Belgium, Greece, Holland, Lombardy, Poland, and Switzerland, in Europe; and Chili, Columbia, and Mexico, on this continent.

This shows great interest and progress in the establishment of the metrical system. The system of England has likewise been improved, and is now formed upon a sound basis. Both it and the system of the United States are now well established and clearly defined; those of other countries are more or less so, and thus will be endured easier the work of ascertaining the relations of these partial systems of the different nations, and of combining them all in one permanent and universal system for all nations.

The troubles in Europe, subsequent to my report of 1847–'48, were unfavorable to action in accordance with the suggestions in relation to this matter contained in it; and although similar indications appear at the present time, a movement is yet perceptible there in regard to the subject of universal uniformity, which is highly favorable to the action proposed. And has not the time arrived, in the general progress of commercial and international intercourse, and the rapid advance of our own country in science, wealth, and power, when her voice should be heard in an important matter like this? Should not Congress make the proposition to all nations to meet, by their representatives, and consult for the purpose of establishing permanent and universal uniformity of weights and measures? Such action could not fail to meet with a response due to the greatness of the subject, and, if the great object be attained, to lead to results productive of vast and lasting benefit to the human race.

Very respectfully submitted.

A. D. BACHE,
Superintendent of Weights and Measures.

Hon. JAMES GUTHRIE,
Secretary of the Treasury.

APPENDIX No. 1.

Resolution of Congress providing for the distribution of weights and measures.

From the acts of the twenty-fourth Congress of the United States.

Resolved by the Senate and House of Representatives of the United States of America in Congress assembled, That the Secretary of the Treasury be, and he hereby is, directed to cause a complete set of all the weights and measures adopted as standards, and now either made, or in progress of manufacture, for the use of the several custom-houses, and for other purposes, to be delivered to the governor of each State in the Union, or such person as he may appoint, for the use of the States respectively, to the end that a uniform standard of weights and measures may be established thoughout the United States.

Approved June 14, 1836.

DEPARTMENT OF STATE,
June 15, 1836.

A true copy, compared with the roll in this office.
ASBURY DICKINS.
Chief Clerk.

See "United States Statute at Large," Vol. 5, page 133.

APPENDIX No. 2.

Act of Congress of 1799, directing a semi-yearly comparison of weights and measures used in custom-houses.

By a law of Congress, passed in 1799, 5th Congress, 2d session, it was ordered that "the surveyor [of each port of the United States] shall, from time to time, and particularly on the first Monday in January and July in each year, examine and try the weights, measures and other instruments used in ascertaining the duties on imports, with standards to be provided by each collector, at the public expense, for that purpose; and when disagreements and errors are discovered, he shall report the same to the collector, and obey and execute such directions as he may receive for the correction thereof, agreeably to the standards aforesaid."—(Statutes at Large, Vol 1, page 643.)

APPENDIX No. 3.

Act of Congress of 1825, authorizing the Secretary of the Treasury to adopt a new hydrometer for ascertaining the proof of liquors in the custom-houses.

From the acts of the eighteenth Congress of the United States.

CHAPTER IV. *An act authorizing the Secretary of the Treasury to adopt a new hydrometer for ascertaining the proof of liquors.*

Be it enacted by the Senate and House of Representatives of the United States of America in Congress assembled, That the Secretary of the Treasury be, and he is hereby, authorized, under the direction of the President of the United States, to adopt and substitute such hydrometer as he may deem best calculated to promote the public interest, in lieu of that now prescribed by law, for the purpose of ascertaining the proof of liquors; and that after such adoption and substitution, the duties imposed by law upon distilled spirits shall be levied, collected and paid according to the proof ascertained by any hydrometer so substituted and adopted.

Approved January 12, 1853.

See "United States Statutes at Large," Vol. 4, page 79.

APPENDIX No. 4.

Circular to the governors of States in regard to balances.

OFFICE OF WEIGHTS AND MEASURES,
Washington, September 13, 1853.

SIR: I have the honor to inform you that a set of balances, intended for the adjustment of standard weights and capacity measures, and furnished to your State under act of Congress, is now ready for delivery, and would respectfully ask your directions as to the time and place of delivery, and as to the person who may be duly authorized by you to receive it. The balances are of three different sizes, for the adjustment of heavy, medium and light weights, or of large, medium and small capacity measures. The balance of the largest size is contained, with its appendages, in five boxes about $5\frac{1}{2}$ feet long, and from about $3\frac{1}{2}$ feet to 10 inches wide, and 20 to 10 inches deep. It will require a space of about 6 by 8 feet to set it up properly. The balance of the medium size will require a space of 6 feet by 6; and that of the smallest size of 3 feet by 6. They should be placed upon a firm foundation, on a ground floor or partition-wall built of brick or other masonry.

I append a drawing of a small building, which would be appropriate for the preservation and use of the standards of weights and measures, which have been or are to be distributed to your State, and would respectfully recommend that such a one may be provided for these elaborate and costly standards. They should at least be preserved in a fire-proof building, and placed upon a very firm floor. When you are prepared to receive the balances, which are now ready for delivery to you, the assistant of weights and measures will be sent to set it up and explain its construction and use to the agent in whose charge you may place it. It would be desirable that a scientific gentlemen, connected with some institution of learning in your State, should have the charge of the standards of weights and measures, and of the balances, and that they should only be used under his direction for the adjustment or verification of county or other standards.

By an answer addressed to me at this office, under cover to the Secretary of the Treasury, you will oblige yours, very respectfully,

A. D. BACHE,
Superintendent of Weights and Measures.

His Excellency the GOVERNOR *of the State of* ———.

APPENDIX No. 6.

Reports in relation to the analysis of sugars, molasses, &c., and hydrometers for the custom-houses.

1. A report of chemical analysis of sugars, molasses, &c., and of researches on hydrometers made under the superintendence of Professor A. D. Bache, by Professor R. S. McCulloh, February 17, 1845.—(Senate document 165, 28th Congress, 2d session.)
2. A report of scientific investigations relative to the chemical nature of saccharine substances, and the art of manufacturing sugar, made under the direction of Professor A. D. Bache, by Professor R. S. McCulloh, February 27, 1847.—(Senate 209, 29th Congress, 2d session.)
3. Second report on inquiries and researches relative to hydrometers, &c., made under the superintendence of Professor A. D. Bache, by Professor R. S. McCulloh, May 29, 1848.
4. Report upon the preparation of the hydrometers and manual of tables to be used in testing the strength of spirituous liquors in the custom-houses, under the superintendence of Professor A. D. Bache, by Professor R. S. McCulloh, February 26, 1849.
5. Report upon the delivery of the hydrometers and manual of tables to the collectors of the ports east of Richmond, and the condition of the standard weights and measures furnished to the custom-houses, made June 28, 1851.

There are two reports from the Treasury Department, dated June 15, 1844, and July 31, 1846, relating to this subject. The first communicating copies of regulations in relation to the importation of foreign sugar and molasses.—(Senate document 12, 28th Congress, 2d session.) The second relative to frauds in recent importations of sugar and molasses from the West India islands, and the measures necessary to prevent their recurrence.—(Senate No. 467, 29th Congress, 1st session.)

APPENDIX No. 7.

Report of Woods Baker, esq., upon the delivery of the hydrometers and the condition of the standard weights and measures furnished to the custom-houses.

OFFICE OF WEIGHTS AND MEASURES,
Washington, June 28, 1851.

SIR: In pursuance of an appointment of the Secretary of the Treasury, dated August 27, 1850, I received your instructions directing me to perform the following duties:

1st. To deliver to the collectors of customs of certain named ports between Portland, Maine, and Alexandria, Virginia, the hydrometers, or spirit test, made by J. G. Greiner, jr., of Berlin, and the manual of tables accompanying them, which were to be furnished to me by Professor R. S. McCulloh, of the college of New Jersey, Princeton.

2d. To receive from the several collectors of the ports above alluded to all the old hydrometers of Dycas' patent, and others heretofore authorized, or which had been or were then in use, and to subject them to a comparative examination in order to determine their reliability.

3d. To ascertain the condition of the standard weights and measures furnished to the several custom-houses, above alluded to, by the Treasury Department, and to ascertain whether the verification of the weights and measures in common use is made as directed by the law of 1799.

4th. To make inquiries into the modes of estimating the quantity of spirits and other liquids contained in casks, by gauging or otherwise. These duties having been severally performed as required, I respectfully submit the following report in relation to them respectively:

1st. The delivery of hydrometers and manuals.

Having received the requisite number of hydrometers and manuals from Professor R. S. McCulloh, who had previously verified them, with my assistance under your superintendence, by comparison with standard instruments, (see Senate document No. 28, 31st Congress, 2d session, page 19,) I proceeded directly to the first point of delivery, Portland, Maine, and then visited each of the custom-houses successively, and in the order stated in the following table, No. 1. To each collector a circular was delivered, authorizing me to act in the matter, of which the following is the form:

(CIRCULAR—NEW SERIES—No. 41.)

TREASURY DEPARTMENT,
August 12, 1850.

SIR: By authority of an act of Congress approved January 12, 1825, and under the direction of the President of the United States, I have adopted and do hereby substitute the centesimal alcoholometer of Tralles for the hydrometer of Dycas, to be used hereafter for ascertaining the proof of liquors and levying duties thereon.

This letter will be handed to you by Woods Baker, esq., who will receive from you all the hydrometers in your possession belonging to the United States, and which you are hereby directed to deliver to him, taking his receipt therefor; in return, he will deliver to you and take your receipt for whatever number of spirit proofs and manuals of tables he may have been instructed to leave with you.

In using the Treasury spirit proof and the tables, the directions given in the latter, as well as those in the instruction herein enclosed, drawn up by Professor R. S. McCulloh, approved by Professor A. D. Bache, and adopted by this department, must be closely followed.

The bearer is instructed to show to you and to your subordinates the manner of using said spirit proof and tables; and you are referred to Senate document No. 50, 1st session 30th Congress, for much detailed information.

In the event of accidental fracture of the instruments entrusted to you, you will not attempt to replace them by purchasing others, (which is hereby prohibited,) but will promptly apply to this department and be furnished with such as shall have been verified by comparison with the standards provided for the purpose.

Very respectfully, your obedient,
THOMAS CORWIN,
Secretary of the Treasury.

To COLLECTOR *of port of* ———.

In delivering the hydrometers, or spirit proofs and manuals, I endeavored to explain fully and clearly to the collectors and their subordinate officers, and especially to the *"provers,"* the principle upon which the instrument was founded, and the mode of using it, referring them, for more detailed information, to the document mentioned in the above circular. They were also particularly charged to abandon the use of the terms "first proof," "second proof," &c., which, by the adoption of the new instrument, had become obsolete, and, instead of the old practice, to mark upon casks the strength as given by the table of true per cents. of the manual. They were also directed to apply to the Treasury Department for other instruments in case of fracture of those given them, and not to supply themselves from the nearest shop, as the practice was when the old hydrometers were used, thus incurring the risk of obtaining an inaccurate instrument. To avoid breakages, they were advised to conform strictly to the directions given in the following printed copy of instructions, which accompanied each hydrometer:

INSTRUCTIONS TO THE UNITED STATES REVENUE OFFICERS.

1st. The hydrometer or spirit proof of Tralles, as made of glass by J. G. Greiner, jr., and adopted by the United States government, consists of a bulb containing an accurate Fahrenheit thermometer, and an attached stem enclosing a scale graduated to show the apparent per cents. by volume of alcohol contained in spirituous liquors. The instrument is packed with a glass cylinder in a morocco case.

2d. To use said spirit proof, pour a portion of the spirits to be inspected into the glass cylinder, immerse the instrument in it, with its bulb downwards, and allow the whole to stand a few moments to attain uniformity of temperature; then observe the indication, or that per cent. upon the graduated stem which is in the plane of the surface of the liquor, and the temperature shown by the thermometer, and refer to the manual of tables to obtain the true per cent. or commercial value corresponding to the observed data, as therein explained.

3d. Indications should not be read by looking down upon the stem or graduated scale of the instrument, and upon the top of the liquor, but from below upwards through the side of the glass cylinder, and the liquor itself if sufficiently clear, or in the plane of the surface if otherwise. The reason of this is, that the small portion of the liquor which is drawn up by capillarity upon the stem may cause error if the indication is read from above.

4th. Gauging and proving of liquors must in all instances be performed simultaneously, and not separately or at different temperatures.

5th. All gauging of alcoholic liquors are hereafter to be reduced (table 1 of the manual) to the volumes they would have at the mean or standard temperature of 60° Fahrenheit, to which temperature their strengths are also referred.

6th. In describing the strengths of liquors, and marking cases therewith, the *true per cent.* by volume (table 1 of the manual) will hereafter be always substituted for the obsolete terms "first proof," "second proof," &c.

7th. When instruments have been used they should not be put back wet into their cases, but be first gently and carefully wiped dry with a soft cloth.

8th. To avoid frequent accidents, the instruments should always be handled with extreme care, by its bulb rather than by its delicate stem, and it should not be laid down on hard tables, or other bodies.

9th. Never attempt to remove the glass cylinder and the spirit proof both together from their case, or hold them in contact in one hand.

10th. Careless handling of these delicate instruments by curious persons should never be permitted, and it should always be borne in mind by those entrusted with them that their fragility demands constant care and attention.

RICHARD S. McCULLOH, *Assistant, &c.*

Approved by

A. D. BACHE,
Superintendent of Weights and Measures.

It may be well to remark here, that section 4 of the above instructions was introduced for the purpose of facilitating the computation, by means of table 3 of the manual, of the quantity of absolute alcohol contained in a cask of spirits, should Congress at any future time pass a law directing specific duties to be levied upon spirits. The value of the coarse liquors, as whiskey, rum, gin, alcohol, inferior wines and brandies, Jamaica spirits, &c., depending chiefly upon their strength or the amount of absolute alcohol contained in them, the quantity of absolute alcohol would naturally furnish the basis for the duty upon such liquors; while in the case of the finer wines and brandies, flavor being the chief element of their value, an *ad valorem* duty would be required in order to render the tariff of charges perfectly just. Under the existing *ad valorem* tariff, the direction above alluded to need not be carried into effect, as the strength marked upon a cask of spirits is not combined with its contents to determine the duty upon it. Indeed, it is doubtful whether it is expedient to require conformity to it at any time, especially at the larger ports. The offices of "proving" and "marking" and of gauging at these ports are separate and distinct; and it is found in practice that both operations cannot at all times be carried on together consistently with as rapid a discharge of business. Performing the two operations sepa-

WEIGHTS AND MEASURES.

rately would incur a little more computation only, in case the temperature of the two determinations differed.

It was also found that practical difficulties would be encountered in enforcing the regulation embraced in section 5 of the above instructions. You were duly informed of the obstacles in this case, and it was deemed advisable to suspend its execution until the practice of gauging, as practised in the United States custom-houses, was investigated, and a uniform system adopted by the Treasury Department.

At the more important ports, as Boston and New York, I not only explained the manner of using the hydrometers and manuals in the offices of the "provers," but accompanied them to the wharves and instructed them practically. They found no difficulty in comprehending and applying the new instrument, and in nearly every instance they expressed themselves pleased with its simplicity and general superiority to the old one, and made no objection to resign the use of the old ones and deliver them to me, as directed by the circular.

The following table contains a list of the custom-houses at which I delivered, in person, the number of instruments stated, together with those sent to the western coast by other means of conveyance. It presents a complete schedule of the distribution up to this date.

No. 1.

Hydrometers and manuals delivered to the custom-houses.

Where delivered.	Receipted for by whom.	No. of hyrd.	No. of man.	When delivered.	By whom delivered.	Remarks.
				1850.		
San Francisco	J. S. Westcott, ag't.	1	1	Sep. 7	J. S. Westcott..	Delivered by Mr. Baker in Philadelphia to Mr. Westcott to take to the western coast.
Astoria, O. T.	......do............	1	1	7	......do.........	
Portland, Me.	B. Cushman, surv'r.	1	1	27	Woods Baker..	
Portsmouth, N. H.	Lory Odell, coll'r..	1	1	28	......do.........	
Newburyport, Mass	H.W. Kinsman, coll.	1	1	20	......do.........	
Salem, Mass.	J. L. Waters, d. coll.	2	2	Oct. 1	......do.........	
Boston, Mass	P. Greely, jr., coll'r.	6	6	2	......do.........	
Barnstable, Mass.	L. N. Small, d. coll.	2	2	7	......do.........	
New Bedford, Mass.	W. T. Russell, coll.	1	1	9	......do.........	
Providence, R. I.	W. P. Greene, sur'r.	1	1	10	......do.........	
New Haven, Conn.	J. Donogh, collector	2	2	12	......do.........	
New York, N. Y.	H. Maxwell, coll'r..	10	10	16	......do.	
Philadelphia, Pa	W. B. Norris, coll'r.	6	6	26	......do.........	
Wilmington, Del.	Chas. Polk, coll'r...	1	1	28	......do.........	
Baltimore, Md.	E. T. Griffin, sur'r..	4	4	29	......do.........	
Alexandria, Va.	Jos. Eaches, coll...	1	1	31	......do.........	
Monterey, Cal	J. H. C. Mudd, ag't.	1	1	Dec. 7	J. H. C. Mudd.	Delivered in Washington to Mr. Mudd to take to the western coast.
San Diego, Cal	......do............	1	1	...do...	......do.........	
Benicia, Cal.	......do............	1	1	...do...	......do.........	Removed from Benicia to San Francisco. (See letter of J. H. Clay Mudd, dated San Francisco, March 13, 1851.)
				1851.		
Puget's Sound, O. T.	S. P. Moses, coll'r...	2	2	Jan. 21	S. P. Moses....	
San Francisco, Cal.	Adams & Co.'s Express.	3	3	24	Adams & Co.'s Express.	To replace those lost by fire when the custom-house was burned.
				1852.		
Norfolk, Va.	Collector	3	3	Au. 13	Woods Baker.	
Richmond, Va.	....	1	1	June	Woods Baker.	
Petersburg, Va.	....	1	1	June	Woods Baker.	

Of the 100 hydrometers purchased from Greiner, 49 have been distributed, as shown in the preceding table; the remainder have been disposed of as follows:
3 deposited in the Treasury Department.
2 delivered to Hackenrath & Van Damme, of New York, by authority of Treasury Department, to be replaced.
1 presented to the British Excise Department.
1 presented to the Smithsonian Institution.
3 retained by Professor R. S. McCulloh.
42 are herewith returned to the office of weights and measures.

NOTE.—*The following supplementary table shows the distribution made of hydrometers since the death of Mr. Baker, in* 1852:

Where delivered.	By whom receipted for.	No. of hydrs.	No. of man.	When delivered.	By whom delivered.
Charleston, S. C.	Surveyor of port.	1	1	Dec'r, 1852	C. O. Boutelle.
Savannah, Ga.	Deputy collector.	1	1	Ap'l 26, 1853	Prof. A. D. Bache.
Georgetown, S. C.	Collector	1	1	Ap'l 29, 1853	Prof. A. D. Bache.
Wilmington, N. C.	Surveyor of port.	1	1	May 7, 1853	Prof. A. D. Bache.
New York		1		May 23, 1853	Adams & Co.'s Exp.
Bureau of Provisions and Clothing*		1	1	Feb. 23, 1854	
Boston		4		Mar. 30, 1854	Adams & Co.'s Exp.
Boston		6		Jan. 7, 1856	Adams & Co.'s Exp.
New Haven, Conn.		2		Feb. 7, 1856	Adams & Co.'s Exp.
New Orleans, La.	Collector	3	3	Feb. 25, 1856	Dr. B. A. Gould, jr.
New York		6		Ap'l 26, 1856	Adams & Co.'s Exp.

Twenty-five of these instruments were procured of Greiner & Son in the past summer. The number now on hand for distribution to the custom-houses is thirty-four.

2. OLD HYDROMETERS RECEIVED AND COMPARED.

The old hydrometers collected at the several custom-houses visited were of various constructions, though chiefly of Dycas' patent, and, with but few exceptions, in a most dilapidated condition, as the following detailed statement will show:

Portland, Maine, 1. No. 5,222, Dycas' patent, new kind. A new instrument. Glass cylinder lost; with this exception, in perfect order.

Portland, Maine, 2. No. 4,719, Dycas' patent, new kind; box badly broken. Thermometer broken; bulb dinged slightly; three brass weights lost; glass cylinder lost.

Portsmouth, New Hampshire. No. 8, Dycas' patent, old kind; without glass cylinder; 14 brass weights lost.

Portsmouth, New Hampshire. Two extra scales and a lot of extra weights.

Newburyport, Massachusetts, 1. (Without number,) no thermometer; very roughly constructed.

---

* Delivered to Purser Sinclair.

WEIGHTS AND MEASURES. 97

Newburyport, Massachusetts, 2. No. 1,069, Dycas' patent; thermometer lost; bulb dinted badly; 8 weights lost; the whole in very dirty condition.

Salem, Massachusetts, 1. (Without number,) Dycas' old kind, without thermometer; bulb dinted, and stem bent; scale lost and 10 weights lost.

Salem, Massachusetts, 2. No. 1,045, Dycas' patent; thermometer lost; bulb very badly dinted; 1 weight lost.

Salem, Massachusetts. No. 4,849, Dycas' patent; thermometer lost; glass cylinder lost; imperfect stem; one weight lost.

Boston, Massachusetts, 1. No. 4,812, Dycas' old kind; without thermometer; scale lost; bulb dinted; some of the weights belong to a different bulb; 1 lost.

Boston, Massachusetts. No. 2, (without number,) no thermometer; bulb dinted; scale lost; one weight lost.

Boston, Massachusetts, 3. No. 5,334, made by Thomas Barnett, London; without thermometer; large box-wood scale; a heavy stem attached to bulb; letters of the alphabet on stem indicating divisions; only four weights belong to it.

Boston, Massachusetts. No. 3,926, Dycas' patent, a new instrument, in good condition, except four weights lost.

Boston, Massachusetts. Four extra scales, extra weights, and one bulb without box.

Barnstable, Massachusetts. A rough old instrument, by Christopher Colles, of New York, with hollow cylindrical stem; 11 weights to be screwed on to correct for temperature, marked, respectively, 30 ex. cold; 35 very cold; 40 cold; 45 cool; 50 temperate; 55 warmth; 60 warm; 65 very warm; 70 hot; 75 very hot; 80 ex. hot.

New Bedford, Massachusetts. An old instrument like that at Barnstable.

Providence, Rhode Island, 1. No. 75, Dycas, made by Fisher & Son, Philadelphia, in good order.

Providence, Rhode Island, 2. No. 2,676, A Dycas saccharometer in good order, except the thermometer, lost.

Providence, Rhode Island, 3. Christopher Colles, like the one at Barnstable.

New Haven, Connecticut, 1. No. 9, Dycas, made by Fisher & Son. Thermometer broken; scale broken; bulb dinted.

New Haven, Connecticut, 2. No. 2,078, Dycas; bulb dinted, one weight lost.

New Haven, Connecticut, 3. No. 2,068, Dycas; bulb dinted; thermometer having been broken, replaced by another, one weight lost.

New Haven, Connecticut, 4. No. 361, Dycas; bulb dinted; one weight lost.

New Haven, Connecticut, 5. One extra bulb and broken scale, no box.

New York, N. Y., 1. No. 6,338, Dycas; bulb badly dinted; thermometer lost; ten weights lost; all in dirty condition.

New York, N. Y., 2. No. 200, Dycas; bulb badly dinted; stem broken; weights, thermometer and glass cylinder lost.

New York, N. Y., 3. No. 6,342, Dycas; bulb slightly dinted; thermometer, cylinder, and 19 weights lost.

Ex. Doc. 27——7

New York, N. Y., 4. No. 6,343, Dycas; bulb dinted, thermometer broken; glass cylinder and seven weights lost.
New York, N. Y., 5. No. 6,341, Dycas; bulb dinted; stem broken; thermometer, cylinder, and two weights lost.
New York, N. Y., 6. No. 6,340, Dycas; bulb dinted; thermometer cylinder, and nine weights lost; dirty.
New York, N. Y., 7. No. 852, Dycas, by Fisher & Son; bulb dinted; seven weights lost.
New York, N. Y., 8. No. 456, Dycas, by Fisher & Son; bulb dinted and dirty; thermometer, scale, and 13 weights lost.
New York, N. Y., 9. No. 200, Dycas, by Fisher & Son; nothing remaining but the box and most of the weights.
New York, N. Y., 10. No. 514, Dycas, by Pike & Son; bulb dinted; thermometer and 20 weights lost.
New York, N. Y., 11. No. 579, Dycas, by Fisher & Son; bulb reduced by dinting to one-half its original size; thermometer out of order, 13 weights lost. *This instrument was in actual use.*
New York, N. Y., 12 & 13. Two Sykes' which had never been used; no thermometer.
New York, N. Y., 14. A lot of extra weights.
Philadelphia, Pa., 1. No. 336, Dycas, by Fisher & Son; bulb dinted; one weight lost; key of box lost.
Philadelphia, Pa., 2. No. 703, Dycas, by Fisher & Son; bulb deeply dinted; in dirty condition.
Wilmington, Del. No. 20, Dycas, by Fisher & Son; bulb dinted; thermometer broken; in dirty condition.
Baltimore, Md., 1. No. 5,841, Dycas, by Gammage; glass cylinder lost; otherwise in good condition.
Baltimore, Md., 2. No. 4,654, Dycas, by Arstall; bulb slightly dinted; glass cylinder and two weights lost.
Alexandria, Va., 1. Dycas, old kind; without thermometer.
Alexandria, Va., 2. No. 1,060, Dycas, by Fisher & Son; bulb dinted; thermometer lost, in dirty condition.
Alexandria, Va., 3. A lot of extra weights and old boxwood scale.
New Orleans, La., 1. Dycas, by Fisher & Son; in good order.
New Orleans, La., 2. Two of same kind, incomplete and worthless. Most of the weights wanting.

The above instruments, when they were collected, were deposited in the office of weights and measures, where they now are. They were subjected to an examination and comparison with each other, to test the accuracy with which they would furnish results, and for this purpose, alcohol of the respective strengths of 80, 50, and 24 per cent. was employed. A large proportion of them it was impossible to examine in this manner, in consequence of lost weights, or some other radical deficiency. Had it been attempted to compare the uncondemned ones, at indications intermediate to those given, it would have failed in many cases, by reason of loss of weights.

The following table exhibits the result of the comparison, showing conclusively the unreliability of the instruments collectively, and the great necessity of withdrawing them from use and substituting for them instruments simple in principle and less likely to become deranged.

WEIGHTS AND MEASURES.

No. 2.

Comparison of old custom-house hydrometers, (Dycas'.)

Custom-house, received at.	Mark of hydrom.	80 per cent. alcohol.		50 per cent. alcohol.		24 per cent. alcohol.	
		Temp.	Ind'n.	Temp.	Ind'n.	Temp.	Ind'n.
Portland, Maine	5222	70	262	72	128	74	58
Do	4719	68	261	72	125	74	54
Portsmouth, New Hampshire	8	Weights lost.		72	125	72	52
Newburyport, Massachusetts	--------	67	262	72	130	72	60
Do	1069	Weights lost.		72	119	72	59
Salem, Massachusetts	--------	Weights lost.		71	112	71	44
Do	1045	67	324	71	177	71	107
Do	4849	67	260	71	123	71	55
Boston, Massachusetts	4812	67	256	71	120	71	49
Do	--------	67	281	70	146	70	74
Do	3926	67	262	70	126	70	56
Providence, Rhode Island	75	67	265	70	128	70	56
New Haven, Connecticut	9	67	253	70	122	70	54
Do	2078	67	260	70	125	70	55
Do	2068	67	258	70	125	70	49
Do	361	67	261	70	125	70	55
New York, New York	6343	67	263	68	127	68	57
Do	6340	67	254	68	124	68	53
Do	852	67	258	68	129	68	59
Do	456	67	273	68	129	Weights lost.	
Philadelphia, Pennsylvania	336	67	261	70	125	70	55
Do	703	67	262	70	125	70	55
Wilmington, Delaware	20	67	257	68	126	68	56
Baltimore, Maryland	5841	67	262	68	126	68	56
Do	4654	67	261	68	126	68	55
Alexandria, Virginia	--------	67	262	68	120	68	60
Do	1060	67	264	Weights lost.		68	57

NOTE.—To have rendered the above table more complete, I should have had the means of reducing the indications to the standard temperature of 60°, and then found from table XL of McCulloh's last report on hydrometers, (see Sen. Doc. No. 50, 1st session 30th Congress, page 531,) by interpolation, the corresponding values in per cents of alcohol. But as the reduction referred to was not in my power for want of proper tables, the results are presented precisely as obtained. In their present form their want of harmony is readily seen.

3*d. Condition of standard weights and measures and their comparison with those in common use.*

Sets of standard weights were delivered to the custom-houses in 1836, by the Treasury Department, consisting of the following pieces.

$$\left.\begin{array}{l}\text{One 1 lb. Troy}\\\text{`` 1 `` Avoirdupois.}\\\text{`` 2 `` \quad ``}\\\text{`` 3 `` \quad ``}\\\text{`` 4 `` \quad ``}\\\text{`` 5 `` \quad ``}\\\text{`` 10 `` \quad ``}\\\text{`` 20 `` \quad ``}\end{array}\right\}\text{Arranged in one box.}$$

$$\left.\begin{array}{l}\text{One 25 lbs. Avoirdupois}\\\text{`` 50 ``}\end{array}\right\}\text{Arranged in one box.}$$

The boxes containing the above weights were provided with fittings for each weight, thus securing them from being misplaced and injured during transportation; the lids being fastened on by nuts and screws. The two boxes were suitably packed together in a strong outer box provided with a lock. With each set was sent a printed copy of the following.

Instructions relating to the use of the standard weights.

1st. Never touch the weight with the hand in any case whatever.

2d. The weights are to be lifted out and in their places, on being moved, by means of the fork or hook, covered with leather, which are added to the boxes for that purpose, and fitting the different weights.

3d. When the weights are taken out of the boxes, they must always be placed upon clean white paper, that they may not become scratched or soiled, as well when placed on the balance as otherwise.

4th. The whole collection must be kept in a safe and dry place, free from all disturbances or danger of damage.

5th. They must never be moved away from under the care of the officer under whose charge they are to any other building or place to make comparisons, but any weights to be compared must be brought to the place of deposit of the standards, to undergo the comparison.

6th. To make a good comparison, the standard weight must be placed in one of the basins of the scales, and in the other must be put any heavy bodies to make exact counterpoise to the same; when thus an exact equilibrium is obtained, the standard weight is removed, and in its stead the weight to be compared is to be placed. Whatever may have *to be added to the weight compared* by so much is it too light; whatever may be needed to *add* to the *counterpoise*, will indicate the weight compared so much too heavy.

7th. That the utmost caution is to be observed in the use of the weights will be self-evident. In all cases the weights must not be left exposed to the open air, when not absolutely necessary.

8th. As the standard weights have all their proper legal weights, it is proper to observe, that in comparing rough weights for common mercantile use there ought always to be a certain allowance made, for the wear of such weights in their use, by an over weight proportioned to the magnitude, the kind of use the weight is intended for, and the usage it may have to withstand, as, after a while, such weights would otherwise too soon become too light and deviate too much from the accuracy that may be wished in them ; by this allowance they remain longer near enough to the desired accuracy, before needing new adjustment.

9th. The value of each weight is marked upon a paper fastened to the bottom of its place in the box, (in preference to stamping it upon the weights,) so that the removal of the weights can never disturb them, the fitting of the weights not admitting of their being misplaced. It is only to be observed that these papers must never be removed.

10th. The boxes are expressly made without locks ; the cover must be lifted up straight, as the brass bars at the sides direct. When the weights are in, the cover must be screwed down tight to its place by means of the four finger-screw knobs.

F.R. HASSLER, *Supt.*

Standard yards were sent to the principal custom-houses in 1840, with proper instructions for their safe-keeping, and mode of use in comparisons. The following are the directions relating to their preservation:

"1st. The standard shall never be touched with the naked hand warm, or in any way damp from perspiration, or otherwise. It is proper not to suffer any dust to collect upon it which could occasion hard rubbing ; any dust is to be removed, in any case, by wings or feathers of a *wild bird*, because they will not occasion any scratches, like the wings of fowls, ducks, &c., would do.

2d. It must not be removed from its place in the box, except for the most important comparisons of metallic measures."

Standard liquid measures were sent to the principal custom-houses in 1842, the following pieces comprising a set:

One gallon, with a glass cover.
" half gallon, "
" quart.
" pint.
" half pint.

To some of the custom-houses of less importance it was deemed unnecessary to furnish more than the one gallon standard. The one gallon was packed in a mahogany box by itself ; the parts of a gallon were arranged together, and provided against rubbing and shifting, by a velvet lining and separate fittings. The two boxes were enclosed together in a strong packing case.

The standard half bushels were adjusted and reported ready for distribution in your report of 1846, but they have not yet been ordered by the Treasury Department to be sent to their destination, with one exception, which is at New York, forwarded by special request of the collector of the port.

By a law passed in 1799, 5th Congress, 2d session, it was ordered, that the surveyor (of each port of the United States) "shall, from time to time, and particularly on the first Mondays in January and July, in each year, examine and try the weights, measures, and other instruments used in ascertaining the duties on imports, with standards to be provided by each collector, at the public expense, for that purpose; and when disagreements or errors are discovered, he shall report the same to the collector, and obey and execute such directions as he may receive for the correction thereof, agreeably to the standards aforesaid."—(Statutes at Large, vol. 1, p. 643.)

Your instructions rendered it my duty to ascertain the condition of the standards at the custom-houses visited; also, whether the comparisons required by the law just quoted were regularly made. As the existing tariff does not require any measurements by the yard measure, there was no necessity for making comparisons with the standard yard.

Portland, Maine. The standards at the custom-house at this place were in a good condition generally, a few pieces only having slight finger marks, or inconsiderable indentations. The comparisons required by law were made, according to the statement of the surveyor, regularly at the periods presented.

Portsmouth, New Hampshire. The standards here were also in tolerably good order, but no comparisons were made with the weights, as there was rarely any occasion to use the common scales.

Newburyport, Massachusetts. Considering the dampness of the room in which the standards are by necessity kept here, they are in better order than could have been expected. The comparisons are said to be regularly made.

Salem, Massachusetts. With the exception of the gallon, the standards are in good order, and the comparisons are made as required.

Boston, Massachusetts. The yard was found to be very much tarnished, the marks on it being scarcely legible. The other standards were in very good condition. The common scales were adjusted, when necessary, by the maker, who attended to the comparison.

Barnstable, Massachusetts. They were all, excepting the gallon, in perfect order. The business transactions here did not require comparisons to be made.

New Bedford, Massachusetts. The gallon was somewhat corroded; all the other standards were in perfect order. Comparisons are not made, as the scales in use are fitted up once a year in Boston.

Providence, Rhode Island. All the standards here are nearly as perfect as when sent from the office. The comparisons are said to be made.

New Haven, Connecticut. The standards here are, in most cases, in good order, and the comparisons are made as required.

New York, N. Y. The half bushel and the small capacity measures were in perfect order, but the other standards had suffered considerably from rough usage. The comparisons were made twice a year, or as much oftener as was found necessary.

Philadelphia, Pennsylvania. The standards here were in excellent condition, and the comparisons were made very carefully at the times prescribed.

Wilmington, Delaware. Some of the standards here were slightly tarnished, but they were generally in good condition. Comparisons are not made, as there is no necessity for so doing.

Baltimore, Maryland. The weights here are in bad order. The other standards do not require remark. The comparison is made more frequently than the regulation requires.

Alexandria, Virginia. All the standards here are in very bad condition, and require to be re-adjusted before reliable comparisons can be made. The comparison required by law is not made.

GAUGING.

On inquiring into the methods pursued at the different custom-houses, for estimating the capacity and contents of casks containing imported liquors, oil, molasses, &c., I found a great want of uniformity among them, the same process not being followed by the gaugers at any three custom-houses. No allowance is made for differences of temperature, and other irregularities are found. The Treasury Department has accordingly authorized you to investigate the subject, with the view of introducing a uniform system in all the custom-houses of the United States.

Respectfully submitted by your obedient servant,
WOODS BAKER.
Prof. A. D. BACHE,
Superintendent Weights and Measures.

OFFICE OF WEIGHTS AND MEASURES,
December 13, 1851.

SIR: In compliance with your verbal instructions, I visited the custom-houses at Portland, Salem, Boston, New Haven, New York, and Philadelphia, to inquire into the practical working of the hydrometer, recently introduced by the Treasury Department, and have the honor respectfully to report as follows:

At the ports of Portland, Portsmouth and Salem no liquors had been received, and the officers had no occasion to use the hydrometers even once. Of course the instruments were in perfect order.

I was informed by the surveyors, as well as by the subordinate officers using the instruments, at the Boston, New Haven, New York and Philadelphia custom-houses, that the new hydrometers are considered greatly superior to the old ones in point of simplicity, and the only objection which could be urged against them is their fragility, which requires great care in handling; but this was more than counterbalanced by the greater rapidity with which they performed their work. Only two of the instruments left at the above ports have been broken: one at Boston, and one at New York. This is good evidence of the care taken of them. The "markers" at all these places are well instructed in their use, and perform the operations properly.

The merchants at first complained of the change of system, which no longer admitted of the use of the conventional terms "proof," "second proof," &c., and of the substitution of "per cent.," which confused them in their mixing operations; but they are now generally becoming reconciled to the new system, and the new hydrometers are greatly in demand by the liquor dealers at the large ports.

Very respectfully, yours, &c.,

WOODS BAKER.

Prof. A. D. BACHE, L. L. D.,
Superintendent of Weights and Measures.

APPENDIX No. 8.

Table showing the States, foreign governments, &c., to which balances have been delivered, with those on hand ready for delivery.

| | States, &c. | BALANCES | | | When delivered. | By whom delivered. | Remarks. |
		Large.	Medium.	Small.			
1	California	1	1	1	Dec., 1850		Shipped per cutter Polk.
2	Connecticut	1	1	1	Nov. 30, 1854	E. Liomin	Set up at Hartford.
3	Delaware	1	1	1	April, 1847	Jos. Saxton	Set up in State House.
4	Iowa	1	1	1	Dec. 13, 1855	E. Liomin	Set up at State House, Iowa City.
5	Kentucky	1	1	1	Oct. 28, 1853	By request of Gov'r.	Sent to Capt. N. Craig, Louisville.
6	Maine	1	1	1	Nov., 1850	Prof. A. D. Bache..	
7	Maryland	1	1	1	Mar., 1848	Jos. Saxton	Set up at Annapolis.
8	Massachusetts	1	1	1	Dec., 1846	......do............	Set up at State House in '47.
9	New Jersey	1	1	1	April, 1845	......do............	Set up in State House.
10	New York	1	1	1	...do...1846	......do............	Do.
11	Ohio	1	1	1	July, 1847	......do............	Do.
12	Oregon	1			April, 1850		Shipped for Astoria.
13	Pennsylvania	1	1	1	Aug., 1850	......do............	Set up in State House.
14	South Carolina	1	1	1	July, 1848	......do............	Set up in building provided at Columbia.
15	Tennessee	1	1	1	July 10, 1854		Delivered to John Heriges, superintendent.
16	Texas	1	1	1	June, 1848	R. H. Fauntleroy...	Since returned to office.
17	Virginia	1	1	1	Nov., 1850	Jos. Saxton	Set up at State House.
18	Wisconsin	1	1	1	Nov. 11, 1854	E. Liomin	Set up at Madison.
	U. S. Mint at Philadelphia..	1	...	...	July, 1849		Of extra size, new pattern.
	Branch mint at N. Orleans..	1	...	...	June, 1848		Do.
	U. S. Treasury Department.	1	...	...	——, 1843		Formerly used in the office of weights and measures.
	Naval Academy, Annapolis.	...	...	1			Not made in the office.

WEIGHTS AND MEASURES.

Balances presented to foreign governments.

Names.	BALANCES			When delivered.	By whom.	Remarks.
	Large.	Medium.	Small.			
Great Britain	1	...	...	July 4, 1843	Mr. Everett, U. S. minister at London.	In conformity with a resolution of both Houses of Congress.
France	1	...	1	Nov., 1850	M. Vattemare	In conformity with a joint resolution of both Houses of Congress, approved June 30, 1848.
Government of Siam	1	1	...	—, 1853	Com. Perry, Japan Expedition.	By authority of the Treasury Department.
Government of Japan	1	1	...	—, 1853	......do............	Do.
Total to foreign governments	4	2	1			

Balances in use in the office of weights and measures.

Description.	When constructed.	Use made of them.
One balance, very large size, 67 inches between the knife edges.	Previous to 1844.	For the adjustment of the bushel and half bushel measures.
Two balances, with the beam, 42 inches between the knife edges.	......do..........	For adjusting weights from 20 to 50 pounds.
Two balances, 30 inches between knife edges.	......do..........	For adjusting weights from 2 to 10 pounds.
Two balances, 15 inches between knife edges.	......do..........	For adjusting small weights.
One small balance, with conical beam	Made in Boston.	

Summary of the work on balances for the States.

	Balances.		
	Large size.	Medium.	Small size.
Whole number of balances of the kind constructed for the States completed up to January 1, 1857, inclusive of those presented to foreign governments, loaned, &c.	31	31	35
Of which number there have been delivered to States, &c., (exclusive of Texas, from which the balances were returned,) including one to Oregon	20	16	16
Presented to foreign governments by authority of Congress or Treasury Department.	4	2	1
Total delivered[*]	24	18	17
On hand in the office, ready for delivery upon application to the States, including those loaned by authority, and to be returned	7	13	18
Sum of those on hand and delivered	31	31	35
Number yet to be constructed to complete the 35 sets for the States ordered by Treasury Department, and to replace those presented to foreign governments.	7	4	....

[*] Including two for the Mint, and one deposited at the Treasury.

APPENDIX No. 9.

List of States and custom-houses to which standard weights, measures, and balances have been delivered, December 31, 1856.

A indicates the set of weights allowed to States.
B indicates the set of weights for custom-houses.
G indicates the gallon measures.
P indicates the parts of the gallon.
H indicates the half bushel.
Y indicates the yard measure.

DECEMBER 31, 1856.

Where delivered.	Weights.	Capacity measures.	Length measures.	Balances.	When delivered.	Remarks.
State of Maine	aA	G P H	Y	b3	July 31, 1841	a Including both avoirdupois and troy ounce weights.
Custom-house at Passamaquoddy.	B	G			Previous to Apr. 5, 1842.	b Balances shipped in November, '1850, and delivered at Augusta in May, 1851.
Machias	B	G			.... do	
Frenchman's Bay	B	G			.... do	
Penobscot	B	G			.... do	
Belfast	B	G			.... do	
Waldoborough	B	G			.... do	
Bangor	*					
Wiscasset	B	G			.... do	
Bath	B	G			.... do	
Portland and Falmouth	B	G P	Y		.... do	
Saco	B	G			.... do	
Kennebunk	B	G			.... do	
York	B	G			.... do	
State of New Hampshire	A	G P H	Y		.... do	With avoirdupois and troy ounce weights.
Custom-house at Portsmouth	B	G	Y		.... do	
State of Massachusetts	cA	G P H		d3	.... do	c Including avoirdupois and troy ounce weights.
Custom-house at Newburyport.	B	G P			.... do	d Balances delivered at Cambridge in December, 1846.
Gloucester	B	G			.... do	
Boston and Charlestown	B	G P	Y		.... do	
Salem	B	G P	Y		.... do	
Marblehead	B	G			.... do	
Plymouth	B	G			.... do	
Fall River	B	G			.... do	
Barnstable	B	G			.... do	
New Bedford	B	G P	Y		.... do	
Edgartown	B	G			.... do	
Ipswich e	B	G			.... do	e Not now a custom-house.
Nantucket	B	G			.... do	
State of Rhode Island	A	G P H	Y		.... do	
Custom-house at Providence	B	G P	Y		.... do	
Bristol, (Bristol and Warren)	B	G			.... do	
Newport	B	G			.... do	
State of Connecticut	A	G P H	Y	f3	.... do	f Balances delivered at Hartford, November 30, 1854.
Custom-house at Middletown	B	G			.... do	
New London	B	G	Y		.... do	
New Haven	B	G P			.... do	
Fairfield	B	G			.... do	
Stonington	*					
State of Vermont	A	G P H	Y		.... do	
Custom-house at Burlington	B	G			.... do	
Alburg	*					

* At Treasury Department.

APPENDIX No. 9—Continued.

Where delivered.	Weights.	Capacity measures.	Length measures.	Balances.	When delivered.	Remarks.
State of New York	aA	bG P H	†Y	c3	1838–'46–'50.	a Including both avoirdupois and troy ounce weights.
Custom-house at Champlain.	B	G			Previous to Apr. 5, 1842.	b Sent June 18, 1846.
Oswegatchie, (Ogdensburg)	B	G			..... do	
Cape Vincent	B	G			..... do	c Balances delivered at Albany in April, 1846.
Sackett's Harbor	B	G			..... do	
Oswego	B	G			..... do	
Niagara, (Lewiston)	B	G			..... do	
Buffalo Creek, (Buffalo) d	B	G			..... do	d This is the name on the list of custom-houses.
Genesee	B	G			..... do	
Sag Harbor	B	G			..... do	
New York	B	G P He	Y		..... do	e Sent September 3, 1849.
State of New Jersey	fA	G P H	Y	g3	... do	f Including avoirdupois and troy ounce weights.
Custom-house at Perth Amboy.	B	G			..... do	g Balances delivered at Trenton in April, 1845.
Bridgeton	B	G			..... do	
Burlington	B	G			..... do	
Great Egg Harbor	B	G			..... do	
Little Egg Harbor	B	G			..... do	
Newark	B	G P			..... do	
Camden	*	G			October, 1853	
State of Pennsylvania	hA	G P H	Y	i3	Previous to April 5, 1842.	h Including avoirdupois and troy ounce weights.
Custom-house at Presqu'Isle, (Erie.)	B	G			..... do	i Balances delivered at Harrisburg, Aug.,'50. Y delivered October, 1846.
Philadelphia	B	G P H	Y		..... do	
Pittsburg	*	G			October, 1853	
State of Delaware	jA	G P H	Y	k3	Previous to Apr. 5, 1842.	j Including avoirdupois and troy ounce weights.
Custom-house at Wilmington	B	G P	Y		..... do	k Balances delivered at Dover in 1847.
State of Maryland	lA	†G P H	Y	m3	March, 1848.	l Including avoirdupois and troy ounce weights.
Custom-house at Baltimore	B	G P Hn	Y		Previous to Apr. 5, 1842.	m Balances delivered at Annapolis in March, 1848.
Annapolis	B	G			..... do	n H at Treasury Department.
Oxford	B	G			..... do	o Not on the list of custom-houses.
Vienna	B	G			..... do	
Snow Hill o	B	G			..... do	
St. Mary's o	B	G			..... do	
Town Creek	*					
District of Columbia, (at Washington.)	pA	G P H	Y	q3	..... do	p Including avoirdupois and troy ounce weights.
						q Balances ordered and ready to be delivered at once.
Custom-house at Georgetown	B	rG			..... do	r Delivered in October, 1853.
State of Virginia	sA	G P H	Y	t3	Previous to 1843.	s Including avoirdupois and troy ounce weights. Set replaced in Sept., 1853.
Custom-house at Alexandria	B	G P H	Y		Sept. 25, 1853	t Balances delivered at Richmond in November, 1850.
Richmond	B	G P	Y		Previous to Apr. 5, 1842.	
Norfolk	B	G P	Y		..... do	
Tappahannock	B				..... do	
Cherrystone, (Eastville)	B	G			B previous to 1843; G in Oct., 1853.	
Yorktown	B	G			G in Oct.,'53	
Petersburg	B	G			..... do	
East River u	B				Previous to Apr. 5, 1842.	u Not custom-houses at present time
Folly Landing u	B				..... do	
Wheeling	*	G			October, 1853	
Yeocomico	*	G			..... do	
State of North Carolina	A	G P H	Y		Previous to 1843.	
Custom-house at Elizabeth City.	B	G			Previous to Apr. 5, 1842.	

* At Treasury Department.
† Sent March 23, 1850.
‡ Delivered April 26, 1843.

APPENDIX No. 9—Continued.

Where delivered.	Weights.	Capacity measures.	Length measures.	Balances.	When delivered.	Remarks.
Edenton	B	a G			Previous to Apr. 5, 1842.	a Delivered in October, 1853.
Plymouth	B				......do.....	
Washington	B				......do.....	
Newbern	B	a G	Y		......do.....	
Ocracoke	B	G			......do.....	
Beaufort	B	b G			......do.....	b Delivered in October, 1853.
Wilmington	B	G P			......do.....	
State of South Carolina	c A	G P H	Y	d 3	......do.....	c Including avoirdupois and troy ounce weights.
Custom-house at Charleston	B	G P	Y		......do.....	
Georgetown	B				......do.....	d Balances delivered at Columbia in July, 1848.
Beaufort	B	e G			......do.....	e Delivered in October, 1853.
State of Georgia	A	G P H	Y		......do.....	
Custom-house at Savannah	B	G P	Y		......do.....	
St. Mary's	B				......do.....	
Brunswick, (Darien)	B	G			......do.....	
Sunbury f	B				......do.....	f Not custom-houses.
Hardwicke f	B					
State of Alabama	g A	G P H	Y		......do.....	g Including avoirdupois and troy ounce weights.†
Custom-house at Mobile	B	G P	Y		......do.....	
State of Florida	A	G P H	Y		......do.....	At Treasury Department.
Custom-house at Pensacola	B				......do.....	
St. Augustine	B				......do.....	
Key West	B	G P			......do.....	
St. Mark's, (Port Leon)	B				......do.....	
St. John's, (Jacksonville)	B				......do.....	
Apalachicola	B	G P			......do.....	
State of Louisiana	§A	G P H	Y		Nov'r, 1849	§ Including avoirdupois and troy ounce weights.
Custom-house at New Orleans	B	G P	Y		Previous to Ap'l 5, 1842.	
Teche, (Franklin)	B				......do.....	
State of Texas	h A	G P H	Y	i 3	Previous to 1847.	h Including avoirdupois and troy ounce weights.
Custom-house at Galveston	*					i Balances delivered at Galveston in June, 1848, subsequently returned to office.
Brazos de Santiago	*					
Saluria, (La Salle)	°					
State of Mississippi	A	G P H	Y		Previous to 1842	At Treasury Department.
Custom-house at Pearl river	B					
Natchez	*					
Vicksburg	*					
State of Tennessee	A	G P H	Y	3	July 10, 1854	
Custom-house at Nashville	*					
Memphis	*					
State of Kentucky	j A	G P H	Y	k 3	1843	j Including avoirdupois and troy ounce weights.
Custom-house at Louisville	*					k The balances were delivered in Nov. 1853.
State of Ohio	l A	G P H	Y	m 3	Previous to Ap'l 5, 1842	l Including avoirdupois and troy ounce weights.
Custom-house at Miami, (Toledo.)	B				......do......	m Balances were delivered at Columbusi July, 1847.
Sandusky	B	G			......do......	
Cuyahoga, (Cleveland)	B				......do......	
Cincinnati	*					
State of Michigan	A	G P H	Y		......do......	
Custom-house at Detroit	B				......do....?	
Michilimackinac	B				......do......	
State of Illinois	A	G P H	Y		......do......	
Custom-house at Chicago	*					

* At Treasury Department.
† All the standards were destroyed by fire in 1849 and replaced in April, 1852.

APPENDIX No. 9—Continued.

Where delivered.	Weights.	Capacity measure.	Length measures.	Balances.	When delivered.	Remarks.
State of Wisconsin	A	G P H	Y	3	Nov. 11, 1854	
Custom-house at Milwaukie	*					
State of Missouri	A	G P H	Y		do	
Custom-house at St. Louis	*					
State of Arkansas	A	G P H	Y		do	
State of Iowa	A	G P H	Y	a 3	Nov. 6, 1856	a Balances sent December 12, 1855.
Burlington	*					
State of Indiana	A	G P H			Oct., 1847	
Evansville	*					
New Albany	*					
State of California	b A	G P H	Y	c 3		b Including avoirdupois and troy ounce weights.
Custom-house at San Francisco	B	G P H	Y		Dec., 1849	c Balances, weights, and measures were shipped in December, 1849.
Monterey	B	G H			Feb., 1851	
San Diego	B	G H			do	
Sacramento	*					
San Joaquin, (Stockton)	*					
Sonoma, (Benicia & Vallejo)	B	G H			do	
Minnesota Territory						
Custom-house at Minnesota, (Pembina.)	*					
Washington Territory			Y		May, 1853	Delivered to Gov. I. I. Stevens.
Custom-house at Olympia, (Puget's Sound.)	B	G H	Y		April, 1851	
Oregon Territory				1	April, 1850	
Custom-house at Astoria,	B	G P H	Y		April, 1851	Shipped.
Umpquah, (Scottsville.)	B	G H	Y		do	Shipped.

* At Treasury Department.

APPENDIX No. 10.

Miscellaneous distribution of standard weights and measures.

How disposed of.	Sets of large weights.	Sets of small weights.	Yard measure.	Sets of liquid measures.	Half bushel measure.	Balances.	When delivered.	Remarks.
Deposited in the office of the Secretary of the Treasury.	1	1	1	1	1	....	Previous to April 5, 1842.	
Applied to use of the sub-treasury..	2	2	....	......	....	....	...do......	
Deposited in the Patent Office.....	1	1	1	1	1	....	...do......	
Deposited in the War Department.	1	....	....	......	....	....	...do......	
Mint at Philadelphia	....	2	....	......	....	....	...do......	
Branch mints, (delivered to the mint at Philadelphia.)	....	6	....	......	....	1*	...do......	* Large balance delivered in 1849.
Mint at New Orleans	....	1*	....	......	....	1†	....	* Delivered in Jan., 1848. † Large balance delivered in May, 1848.
Navy yard at Brooklyn, N. Y... ..	....	....	1	......	....	....	...do......	
Use of Coast Survey................	....	....	2	......	....	....	...do......	
Use of General Land Office	....	....	1	......	....	....	...do......	
Delivered to Mr. Hassler to be sent to England.	1	1	1	1	1	1*	July 24, 1843	* Large balance.
Presented to France	1	1	1	§1	1	2*	Oct., 1850	* Large and small balance.
Chilian Astronomical Expedition ..	....	....	....	......	....	1*	June 26, 1849	* Small balance and foot measure, (returned in 1853.)
Sent to Japan by Com. Perry......	1	1	1	Gall.	1	1*	June, 1852	* Medium sized balance.
Sent to Siam by Com. Perry.......	1	1	1	Gall.	1	1*	....do......	* Do. do.
Land office in California , ...	....	...	1	......	....	....	Dec. 20, 1851	
Land office in Oregon.............	....	....	1	......	....	....	...do......	
Land office in Iowa, Minnesota, and Wisconsin.	....	....	1	......	....	....	May, 1851	
Gov. Stevens, Washington Territ'y	....	....	1	......	....	....	May, 1853	
Engineer Bureau	....	....	1	......	....	....	Jan'ry, 1848	
Topographical Engineer Bureau...	....	....	1	......	....	....	Feb'ry, 1853	
Bureau of Ord., Hyd'y, U. S. N....	1	1	1	Gall.	1	....	Mar. 2, 1850	With two sets of troy grains weights, from 4000 grains to .01 of a grain.
Naval Academy at Annapolis......	....	1*	....	......	....	1†	March, 1852	* Delivered March, 1852. † Delivered small balance November, 1850.
Post Office Department	....	*	....	......	....	....	Dec'r, 1853	* Delivered 3 oz. and 3 half oz. weights.
Prof. Henry, Smithsonian Institution.	....	1*	....	......	....	1†	Nov. 18, 1851	* Loaned to be returned. † Small balance.
Prof. Alexander, Baltimore........	....	1*	....	......	....	1*	Nov., 1853	* Ounce weights and medium sized balance loaned and to be returned.
Commodore Shubrick.............	1*	....	....	1*	....	1*	May 13, 1852	* Loaned and to be returned.

§ Shipped April 11, 1852.

APPENDIX No. 11.

Circulars to Governors of States asking for copies of laws.

[Circular.]

OFFICE OF WEIGHTS AND MEASURES.
Washington, D. C., July 29, 1853.

SIR: It is very desirable to obtain for the files of this office copies of all laws enacted by the several States of the Union, in relation to standard weights, measures, and the gauging of casks; I have therefore the honor to request that you will favor me by causing copies of all such laws as have been enacted by the State of ———, since March, 1819, together with the laws and regulations now in force, to be sent, addressed to me at this office, under cover to the Hon. James Guthrie, Secretary of the Treasury.

Any other information in relation to the subject, which it may be in your power to furnish, will be received with pleasure.

Yours, very respectfully,

A. D. BACHE,
Superintendent of Weights and Measures.

His Excellency the GOVERNOR
of the State of ———.

[Circular.]

OFFICE OF WEIGHTS AND MEASURES,
Washington, D. C., June 12, 1856.

SIR: To complete the files of this office, it is desirable to obtain verified copies of laws which may have been passed by the legislatures of the several States of the Union, and approved in relation to standard weights, measures of length and capacity, and the gauging of casks.

The records now contain copies of acts relative to weights and measures and gauging, passed in the legislature of ———, prior to and including that approved ——— 18—, which were transmitted to this office by the executive, on my application therefor, in 1853.

Yours, very respectfully,

——— ———,
Superintendent of Weights and Measures.

His Excellency the GOVERNOR
of the State of ———.

[Circular.]

OFFICE OF UNITED STATES WEIGHTS AND MEASURES,
Washington, D. C., September 26, 1856.

SIR: Since the issue of the circular letter which I had the honor to address to your Excellency in June, requesting copies of recent laws relative to weights and measures which may have been passed by the legislature of the State of ———, a resolution was adopted in the Senate of the United States calling for a detailed report from the Superintendent of United States Weights and Measures, to be presented in December next. The resolution referred to requires a statement of the substance of all laws enacted in relation to weights and measures, by the several States of the Union; and I would therefore respectfully request to be furnished with verified copies of any acts which may have been approved by the executive of ———, since ——— 18—. The legislation bearing on the subject of weights and measures, and that relative to gauging, prior to that date, is now on file in this office.

Very respectfully, yours,

A. D. BACHE,
Superintendent U. S. Weights and Measures.

His Excellency the GOVERNOR OF ———

APPENDIX No. 12.

Titles of laws passed by the several States of the Union in relation to weights and measures during the period intervening between the years 1819 and 1854, with a statement showing their authenticity.

MAINE.

[A copy of the laws on the subject subsequent to 1841 was received from Governor W. G. Crosby, with letter dated Belfast, Maine, November 16, 1853. The laws previous to that date and subsequent to 1820 were copied in the libraries of Congress and of the State Department, both copies being at the expense of this office.]

Laws regulating weights and measures, approved February 5, 1821. Revised Statutes, chapter 131.	1821
Of tobacco and onions, approved February 24, 1821; chapter 56.	1821
Of nails, approved February 28, 1821; chapter 55.	1821
Of fire-wood, bark and coal, approved March 8, 1821; chapter 60.	1821
Of flaxseed, approved March 8, 1821; chapter 57.	1821
Of pot and pearl ashes, approved March 10, 1821; chapter 52.	1821
Of lime casks, approved March 15, 1821; chapter 98.	1821
Of lime and lime casks, approved March 15, 1821; chapter 213.	1821
Of butter and lard, approved March 19, 1821; chapter 53.	1821
Of hogshead hoops; chapter 100.	
Of fish, approved March 22, 1821; chapter 54.	1821
Of shingles, clapboards and staves, approved March 26, 1821.	1821

WEIGHTS AND MEASURES.

Resolve authorizing the State treasurer to suspend the purchase of a standard of weights and measures. Passed February 6, 1822; chapter 27.	1822
Of shingles, clapboards and staves, approved February 12, 1824; chapter 66.	1824
An act regulating the weight of hoops, staves, and other articles, approved February 25, 1828; chapter 404.	1828
Resolve authorizing the State treasurer to purchase a standard of weights and measures. Approved March 22, 1831; chapter 47.	1831
Of beef and pork, approved February 27, 1832; chapter 50.	1832
Of potatoes, approved March 23, 1835; chapter 101.	1835
Of measures of salt, corn and grain, approved March 4, 1836; chapter 71.	1836
Of the standard weights of ruta baga, sugar beets, mangle wurzel, and rye, and Indian meal, approved April 2, 1836 and February 24, 1838; chapter 72.	1836 1838
An act additional to an act for the due regulation of weights and measures, approved March 2, 1839; chapter 375.	1839
Of lime and lime casks, approved March 22, 1839; chapter 184.	1839
An act to regulate the sale of oats, chapter 228.	
Of fish, approved March 22, 1839; chapter 91.	1839
Of hair, chapter 46.	
Of weights and measures, act of July 31, 1841; chapter 73.	1841

NEW HAMPSHIRE.

[A bound volume of the compiled statutes of the State was received, accompanied by a letter from the Hon. John L. Hadley, Secretary of State, and dated Concord, N. H., September 22, 1853. Manuscript copies of the original laws of 1828, 1840, and 1848 were obtained at the Congressional and State Department libraries.]

An act regulating the weighing of merchandise and other commodities, approved July 6, 1827; Rev. Stat. chapter 1.	1827
An act in addition to an act entitled "An act regulating scale beams, steelyards, weights and measures." Approved December 29, 1828; chapter 2.	1828
Resolution by the senate and house of representatives in general court convened in relation to the United States standard weights. Approved December 17, 1840; chapter 591.	1840
An act in amendment of chapter 110 of the Revised Statutes relating to weights and measures, approved in 1848.	1848
Measurers of grain, how chosen, their duty and their fees; sealed measures to be used; penalties for fraud of measures and selling without measures.	
Standard weight of oats and of potatoes; mode of measuring; bread to be sold by weight; weight of bread regulated; penalty for unlawful sale of bread.	
Standard weights and measures for the State, how kept; county sealers, how appointed; their duties and fees. Each	1849

Ex. Doc. 27——8

town to be provided with a set of standard weights and measures; town sealer of weights, &c., how chosen; his duties and fees; size of measures for charcoal, and articles sold by heaped measure. Penalty for using weights and measures not sealed or unjust. Penalty on selectmen for not providing a set of standard weights, &c., for town. Weights and measures, how sealed. "Hundred weight" means one hundred pounds. Weighers to weigh accordingly. Penalty for weighing illegally. Suits not to be commenced until notices. Laws of 1848, chapter 702. Approved January 1, 1849. — 1849

VERMONT.

[A copy of chapter 73, of the compiled statutes of Vermont, was forwarded to this office by the Hon. Pliny H. White, Secretary of State, with a letter dated St. Johnsbury, Vermont, September 20, 1853. Copies of additional laws, passed by the State in 1816, 1824, 1828, 1830, 1831, and 1842, were obtained from the above mentioned libraries.]

Acts in relation to weights and measures. Passed November 6, 1816. — 1816

The above is repealed by the second section of the act passed October 27, 1828. — 1828

Act in relation to weights and measures. Passed November 18, 1824. — 1824

An act in addition to an act relating to weights and measures; passed March 8, 1797. Passed November 9, 1831. — 1831

An act in addition to chapter 69 of the Revised Statutes. Approved November 1, 1842. — 1842

An act adopting as state standards the United States standard weights and measures. Chapter 73, of compiled statutes of Vermont.

An act relating to the standard weight of potatoes, passed in 1852. — 1852

An act prescribing the standard measurement of wood and bark, passed in 1855.* — 1855

MASSACHUSETTS.

[Manuscript copies from the revised statutes of November, 1835, were received from the secretary of State. These copies included, besides extracts from chapters 28 and 30 of the above statutes, resolves on the subject of weights and measures, approved April 20, 1847, and acts passed in 1847 and 1851, respectively. Copies of laws passed in 1835, '37, '43, '46, '52 and '53, were obtained from the libraries of Congress, and of the State Department.]

Resolve concerning the standard weights and measures in the Treasury, October 30, 1835. Chapter 117. — 1835

Of charcoal boxes and baskets. — 1835

From the revised statutes of 1835. Chapter 28. — 1835

Of weights and measures. Chapter 30, of the revised statutes of November, 1835. — 1835

Resolve in relation to weights and measures. March 4, 1837. — 1837

---

* Certified copy sealed June 25, 1856.

WEIGHTS AND MEASURES. 115

Resolve concerning standard weights and measures. Approved March 22, 1843. Chapter 46. — 1843
Resolve for the reception and safe keeping of the standards of weights and measures. Approved March 13, 1846. Chapter 49. — 1846
Resolves concerning the standard weights, measures, and balances. Approved April 20, 1847. — 1847
An act concerning weights, measures, and balances. Approved April 23, 1847. From the laws and resolves of 1847. — 1847
An act in further addition to an act concerning weights, measures, and balances. Approved April 24, 1851. From the laws and resolves of 1851. — 1851
An act to regulate the measurement of charcoal. Approved May 21, 1852. — 1852
An act to regulate the measurement of charcoal. Approved May 4, 1853. — 1853
An act regulating the sale of anthracite, bituminous or mineral coal. Approved April 14, 1855.* — 1855
An act to regulate the sale of wheat, corn and other grain, and meal. Approved April 26, 1855.* — 1855
An act concerning the sale of onions. Approved June 4, 1856.* — 1856

RHODE ISLAND.

[Complete copies of all the laws passed by that State since 1819, were received from E. R. Potter, esq., commissioner of public schools, with a letter dated Providence, R. I., November 14, 1853. See appendix, No. 13, for letter of E. R. Potter, esq.]

An act explanatory of an act, establishing a uniform method of gauging throughout this State. Passed January, 1820. — 1820
An act establishing a just and equal method of gauging in and throughout the State. Digest of 1822. — 1822
An act to prevent fraud in fire-wood and charcoal exposed to sale. Digest of 1822. — 1822
An act ascertaining the weight of a bushel of Indian and rye meal. Digest of 1822. — 1822
An act regulating the sale of onions sold by the rope or bunch. Digest of 1822. — 1822
An act to regulate the weight of a bushel of potatoes. Passed October 1823., — 1823
An act substituting net weight for gross weight in sales and contracts relating to articles of merchandise. Passed June 1825. — 1825
An act in addition to an act entitled "An act substituting net weight for gross weight in sales and contracts relating to articles of merchandise." Passed January, 1830. — 1830
An act explanatory and in amendment of an act entitled "An act to prevent fraud in fire-wood and charcoal exposed to sale." Passed October, 1830. — 1830
An act in amendment of an act entitled "An act ascertaining the weight of a bushel of Indian and rye meal." Passed October, 1836. — 1836

* Copies certified June 19, 1856.

An act in amendment of an act entitled "An act to regulate the weight of a bushel of potatoes." Passed January, 1838. 1838
An act to regulate the weight of a bushel of onions. Passed January, 1838. 1838
An act establishing a method of gauging. Digest of 1844. 1844
An act to prevent fraud in fire-wood and charcoal exposed for sale. Digest of 1844. 1844
An act substituting net weight for gross weight and ascertaining the weight of certain articles. Digest of 1844. 1844
An act in relation to gauging and for the appointment of gaugers. Passed June, 1847. 1847
An act in amendment of an act, entitled "An act in relation to gauging and for the appointment of gaugers." Passed January, 1848. 1848

CONNECTICUT.

[A manuscript copy of title 58 of the revised statutes of the State of Connecticut, and of acts concerning weights and measures passed in 1850, was received from Hon. John P. C. Mather, Secretary of State, with a letter dated Hartford, Connecticut, August 17, 1853. The correctness of the copy was certified to by the same gentlemen, and the seal of State attached. Copies of laws passed in 1827 and 1838 were procured from the Congressional and State Department Libraries.]

An act relating to weights and measures. Passed 1827. 1827
An act in addition to, and alteration of, an act entitled "An act relating to weights and measures." Enacted 1827. 1827
An act in addition to an act regulating weights and measures." Enacted 1838. 1838
An act relating to weights and measures. Passed in 1850. Title 58 of Revised Statutes. 1850
An act in addition to "An act concerning weights and measures." Approved June 22, 1850. 1850
An act authorizing the sale of potatoes by weight. Approved June 22, 1850. 1850

NEW YORK.

[John Patterson, esq., superintendent of weights and measures for the State of New York, forwarded with a letter dated Albany, October 4, 1853, a printed copy of the only law then in force in that State, which was passed April 11, 1851. A manuscript copy of all the other laws passed since 1819 on the same subject was sent by him with a letter dated Albany, October 24, 1853.]

An act authorizing the election of measurers in the counties of Kings, Queens, and Richmond. Passed February 9, 1821. 1821
An act respecting the sealers and inspectors of weights and measures in the city of New York. Passed March 27, 1821. 1821
An act for the payment of the officers of government therein mentioned. Passed April 3, 1821. 1821
An act directing certain counties to be supplied with standard brass yard measures. Passed March 22, 1822. 1822

WEIGHTS AND MEASURES. 117

An act concerning standard measures of capacity. Passed April 23, 1822. — 1822

An act to provide for the purchase of standard weights and measures for the assistant State sealer in the city of Albany. Passed April 18, 1826. — 1826

An act concerning the territorial limits and divisions, the civil policy and the internal administration of this State. Of the computation of time, of weights and measures, and the money of account. Of weights and measures. Part I, title II, chapter 19, of Revised Statutes of the State of New York. Passed December 3, 1827. — 1827

An act to repeal a certain section of the Revised Statutes relative to the measurement of dry commodities. Passed April 20, 1830. — 1830

An act directing the mode in which the expenses for furnishing standard weights and measures are to be defrayed. Passed February 4, 1831. — 1831

An act authorizing the appointment of measurers of grain, wood, and stone, for the villages of Port Schuyler and West Troy, in the town of Watervliet, in the county of Albany. Passed March 14, 1831. — 1831

An act providing for the appointment of an assistant State sealer of weights and measures. Passed April 26, 1831. — 1831

An act regulating the measuring of grain in the city of New York. Passed April 14, 1832. — 1832

An act to amend an act entitled "An act to authorize the appointment of a measurer of stone in and for the city of Albany." Passed March 28, 1833. — 1833

An act authorizing the several towns in the county of Suffolk to elect measurers of wood. Passed April 26, 1833. — 1833

An act authorizing the appointment of a weigher and measurer for the town of Greenbush, in the county of Rensselaer. Passed April 6, 1833. — 1833

An act amending the act entitled "An act regulating the measuring of grain in the city of New York," passed April 14, 1832. Passed April 18, 1834. — 1834

An act respecting inspectors and sealers of weights and measures in the city of New York. Passed April 22, 1834. — 1834

An act regulating the weighing of merchandise in the city of New York. Passed May 1, 1835. — 1835

An act to amend the Revised Statutes in relation to the sale of pressed hay. Passed May 6, 1835. — 1835

An act to create and regulate a standard for measuring bran and shorts. Passed May 11, 1835. — 1835

An act to amend an act entitled "An act regulating the weighing of merchandise in the city of New York," passed May 1, 1835. Passed May 16, 1836. — 1836

An act to regulate the selling of grain. Passed May 19, 1836. — 1836

An act to authorize the appointment of measurers of grain 1837
in the counties of Duchess and Orange. Passed March 14,
1837.
An act concerning the inspection laws. Passed May 14, 1840
1840.
An act in relation to measurers, weigh-masters, and harbor- 1840
masters in the city of Brooklyn and village of Williamsburg.
Passed May 14, 1840.
An act to amend the inspection laws. Passed April 18, 1843
1843.
An act to replace and repair certain State standards of 1844
weights and measures which had been destroyed or injured by
fire. Passed March 25, 1844.
An act to compel the town of Ossian to pay certain moneys 1844
equitably due to the town of Burns. Passed April 5, 1844.
An act to regulate the weight of sack salt. Passed April 1848
5, 1848.
An act in relation to weights and measures. Passed April 1851
11, 1851.
An act to amend the act entitled " An act in relation to 1854
weights and measures," passed April 11, 1851. Passed April
15, 1854.*

NEW JERSEY.

[A certified manuscript copy, with the seal of the State attached, of "An act to establish a uniform standard of weights and measures in this State," approved April 17, 1846, was received from the Hon. Thomas S. Allison, Secretary of State, with a letter, dated Trenton, N. J., August 10, 1853. Manuscript copies of acts passed in 1844 and 1846, were procured from the Congressional and State Department libraries.]

An act to establish a uniform standard of weights and meas- 1844
ures in this State. Approved March 13, 1844.
An act to establish a uniform standard of weights and meas- 1846
ures in this State. Approved April 17, 1846.
An act supplemental to the act entitled " An act to establish 1846
a uniform standard of weights and measures in the State of
New Jersey." Approved March 12, 1846.
An act to establish a uniform standard of weights and meas- 1855
ures. Approved April 17, 1846. (Revised Statutes, 1057.)
Act of 1855.† Pam. Laws, 288.

PENNSYLVANIA.

[A manuscript copy of an act passed April 15, 1834, and entitled "An act to fix the standards and denominations of measures and weights in the Commonwealth of Pennsylvania," was certified to, provided with the State seal, and sent to this office, by E. S. Goodrich, Esq., Deputy Secretary of the Commonwealth, with a letter, dated Harrisburg, Pa., September 19, 1853. Manuscript copies of acts passed in 1818, '22, '27, '30, '38, '40,' 43, '44, '45, '46, '47 '48, '49, '50, and '51, were obtained from the libraries before mentioned.]

An act establishing a standard weight for grain and foreign 1818
salt. Passed March 10, 1818.

---

* Certified copy sealed June 21, 1856.
† Certified copy sealed June 17, 1856.

WEIGHTS AND MEASURES.

An act prescribing the duties of a sealer of dry measures of the city and county of Philadelphia. Passed April 2, 1822. — 1822

An act to regulate the inspection of flour in the borough of York, and for other purposes. Passed April 12, 1823. — 1823

An act concerning weights and measures. Passed February 17, 1827. — 1827

An act concerning weights and measures. Passed April 5, 1830. — 1830

An act to fix the standards and denominations of measures and weights in the commonwealth of Pennsylvania. Passed April 15, 1834. — 1834

An act granting certain powers to the cities of Lancaster and Philadelphia, and for other purposes. Passed April 16, 1838. — 1838

An act supplementary to an act granting certain powers to the cities of Lancaster and Philadelphia, and for other purposes. Passed March 11, 1840. — 1840

An act to provide for the ordinary expenses of government, and for other purposes. Passed September 29, 1843. — 1843

An act authorizing the governor to appoint a sealer of weights and measures for the county of Wayne. Passed March 14, 1844. — 1844

An act authorizing the secretary of the commonwealth to distribute copies of the standard weights and measures, and for the appointment of sealers. Passed April 15, 1845. — 1845

An act to regulate the standard weight of Indian corn. Passed April 16, 1845. — 1845

A supplement to an act entitled "An act authorizing the secretary of the commonwealth to distribute copies of the standard weights and measures, and for the appointment of sealers." Act of 21st April, 1846. — 1846

An act to regulate the standard weight of charcoal. Passed January 22, 1847. — 1847

An act regulating the sale of corn meal in the counties of Bucks, Montgomery, Delaware, and the city and county of Philadelphia, and for other purposes. Act of 8th April, 1848. — 1848

An act to establish a uniform standard for the measure of bituminous coal, and authorizing the appointment of a wood inspector for the borough of Lewistown. Act of 23d March, 1849. — 1849

An act supplementary to an act entitled "An act to establish a uniform standard for the measure of bituminous coal, &c." Act of 6th April, 1850. — 1850

An act authorizing the appointment of an auctioneer, or auctioneers, in the borough of Easton, and relative to short measure and weight in the sale of dry goods, groceries, &c. Act of 11th April, 1850. — 1850

An act to provide for the establishment of true meridian lines, and of standard measure for surveyors' chains, and to regulate the practice of surveyors in the commonwealth. Act of 26th April, 1850. — 1850

An act changing the law in Tioga county relating to weights, beams, and measures, and for other purposes. Act of 3d April, 1851.   1851

An act relating to the measurement of coal in Alleghany county, and for other purposes. Act of 12th April, 1851.   1851

DELAWARE.

[A letter was received from Hon. Alfred P. Robinson, secretary of State, dated Georgetown, Delaware, August 30, 1853, forwarding to this office a volume of laws. This volume, however, has not come to hand, all inquiries concerning it having proved fruitless. All the laws regulating weights and measures in this State, and passed severally in 1837, 1845, 1849, and 1852, were copied from the statutes on file in the library of Congress, or in that of the State Department.]

An act fixing the standard of weights and measures, and regulating the same within this State. Passed February 18, 1837.   1837

A supplement to the act fixing the standard of weights and measures, and regulating the same within this State. Passed February 14, 1845.   1845

A supplement to the act entitled "An act fixing the standard of weights and measures, and regulating the same within this State." Passed February 27, 1849. Revised Statutes, chapter 406.   1849

Of weights and measures. Adopted Febuary, 1852. Revised Statutes, chapter 66.   1852

An act regulating the weight of a bushel of wheat and Indian corn. Adopted February, 1852. Revised Code, chapter 67.   1852

MARYLAND.

[Professor Alexander's "Report on standard of weight and measure," prepared by authority of the general assembly of the State, was received for examination from Hon. John Randolph Quin, Secretary of State, with letter dated Annapolis, Maryland, September 15, 1853. A copy of the laws on weights and measures, passed in 1826 and 1828, as well as a resolution of the session of 1842, "in relation to distribution of the United States standards," were procured from the above cited libraries.]

An act for regulating and inspecting weights and measures used in this State. Passed March 8, 1826. Chapter 206.   1826

An act to regulate the gauging of casks and the inspection of domestic distilled liquors in this State. Passed March 13, 1828. Chapter 181.   1828

Resolution directing the distribution to the several counties of this State of United States standard weights and measures. Resolution of the session of 1842.   1842

VIRGINIA.

[A manuscript copy of all the acts passed by the State of Virginia since the year 1819 was received from Hon. George W. Munford, Secretary of the Commonwealth, with letter dated Richmond, Virginia, August 19, 1853.]

An act providing for the preservation and use of the standard weights and measures received from the general government. Passed March 19, 1847.   1847

WEIGHTS AND MEASURES.

Of weights and measures. Code of Virginia, chapter 89.

An act authorizing the governor, and superintendent of weights and measures to contract for, and have manufactured, copies of the standard weights and measures for distribution to the several counties and corporations within the State, and for other purposes, in relation to weights and measures. Passed March 15, 1851. Chapter 14. — 1851

An act concerning the salaries of certain officers of government, compensation of the members and officers of the general assembly, mileage, and other allowances. Passed June 5, 1852. Chapter 23. — 1852

An act increasing the fees of the sealer of weights and measures for the city of Richmond. Passed January 12, 1853. — 1853

NORTH CAROLINA.

[From this State was received a manuscript copy of all the laws now in force, copied from the Revised Statutes, chapters 40, 55, and 120.]

An act concerning weights and measures. Chapter 120, Revised Statutes of North Carolina.

Acts of assembly in relation to weights and measures, passed in 1838, 1839. Chapter 40, Revised Statutes. — 1838

Acts of assembly, 1842, 1843, amending acts of 1838, 1839, in relation to weights and measures. Chapter 55, Revised Statutes. — 1842

An act concerning weights and measures. Chapter 117, Revised Code of North Carolina.*

SOUTH CAROLINA.

[A copy of a report and resolutions, proposed by the committee on agriculture and internal improvements, and adopted by the legislature of the State in 1845, was prepared at the expense of this office, certified to and forwarded by W. F. Arthur, esq., librarian, with a letter dated Columbia, South Carolina, November 14, 1853. An act to provide weights and measures in each district, passed in 1840, and a resolution requiring the governor to furnish duplicates of the United States standards to the clerks of the several courts, were copied from the libraries of Congress and the State Department.]

An act to provide weights and measures in each district. Passed December 8, 1840. — 1840

Resolution requesting the governor to have constructed duplicates of the weights and measures furnished to the State by the federal government, and to have such duplicates sent to the clerks of the courts throughout the State. — 1845

Report of the committee on agriculture and internal improvements, to whom it was referred to inquire and report as to the propriety of designating a person to receive, and a place to deposit, a large balance to be furnished to this State under an act of Congress. — 1845

---

* Certified copy sealed September 3, 1856.

Resolutions proposed by the committee on agriculture and internal improvements, requiring the governor to receive, on the part of the State, the large United States balances for the adjustment of weights and measures, and that he cause to be fitted up at Columbia a suitable building for their use and preservation. Agreed to in the Senate December 5, 1845, and in the House of Representatives December 15, 1845.	1845
An act to provide for the measuring of timber in the city of Charleston, and to create the office of inspector and surveyor thereof. Passed December 20, 1853.*	1853
An act to amend the law in relation to weights and measures. Passed December 20, 1853.*	1853

GEORGIA.

[A bound volume, containing a digest of the laws of the State, was received from the executive, through W. W. Payne, esq., with letter dated Milledgeville, Georgia, August 11, 1853.]

An act to regulate weights and measures in this State. Approved December 10, 1803. Vol. II, 134.	1803
An act to regulate the weighing of cotton and other commodities in this State. Approved December 8, 1806. Vol. II, 346.	1806
An act to regulate the manner of weighing with scales or steelyards throughout the State of Georgia. Approved December 16, 1815. Vol. III, 1,076.	1815
An act to amend an act passed December 10, 1803, entitled "An act to regulate weights and measures in this State." Assented to December 23, 1839. Pam. 224.	1839
An act to abolish the allowance of tare or gross weight on bales of unmanufactured cotton. Approved December 10, 1847. Pam. 294.	1847
An act to alter an act to amend an act to regulate the weighing of cotton and other commodities, approved February 7, 1854, and for other purposes. Approved March 3, 1856.	1856

ALABAMA.

[Three volumes of statutes were received from the governor of the State.]

Weights and measures. Acts of 1828.	1828
Acts in relation to weights and measures. Chapter 7. Revised Statutes brought down to 1852.	1852
An act to provide for the preservation of the balances intended for the adjustment of standard weights and measures, No 25. Approved February 9, 1852.	1852

MISSISSIPPI.

[Copies of the laws enacted by the State were procured from the statute books on file in the department libraries.]

An act concerning weights and measures. Approved December 23, 1815.	1815

---

* Certified copies sealed June 23, 1856.

WEIGHTS AND MEASURES.

An act to furnish a uniform standard of weights and measures to the several counties of the State of Mississippi. Approved March 4, 1846. Chapter 42. — 1846

An act to amend the laws in regard to weights and measures. Approved January 31, 1852. — 1852

LOUISIANA.

[By direction of his Excellency P. O. Hebert, Governor of Louisiana, this office was furnished by his private secretary, Thomas B. R. Hatch, esq., with a copy of the only law now in force in the State on weights and measures, passed in 1846, with a letter dated Baton Rouge, Louisiana, October 3, 1853. Copies of acts passed previous to 1846 were obtained from the Congressional library.]

An act to establish a uniform standard of weights and measures within this State. Approved December 21, 1814. — 1814

An act supplementary to an act entitled "An act to establish a uniform standard of weights and measures within this State," approved December 21, 1814. Approved February 28, 1824. — 1824

An act to provide for the appointment of inspectors of weights and measures, to define their duties, and for other purposes. Approved June 1, 1846. — 1846

TEXAS.

[A certified manuscript copy of the only legislative enactment of this State, consisting of an act approved May 7, 1846, authorizing the governor to have copies of the United States standards made and distributed to the several counties, was received from the Secretary of State, Hon. Thomas H. Duvall, with his letter dated Austin, Texas, August 20, 1853.]

An act to authorize the governor to procure, and have copied for the benefit of the several counties of this State, a full set of weights and measures in conformity to the standard now used and adopted by the government of the United States, and providing for the distribution of the same. Approved May 7, 1846. — 1846

OHIO.

[Received from Hon. William Trevitt, Secretary of State, with letter dated Columbus, Ohio, August 13, 1853, a certified manuscript copy with the seal of the State attached, of all the laws on the subject of weights and measures passed by the State.]

An act regulating weights and measures. Passed March 5, 1835. — 1835

An act to amend the act entitled "An act regulating weights and measures," passed March 5, 1835. Passed February 3, 1844. — 1844

An act to provide for a uniform standard of weights and measures. Passed February 21, 1846. — 1846

An act to amend an act entitled "An act to provide for a uniform standard of weights and measures," passed February 21, 1846. Passed February 8, 1847. — 1847

An act to establish the standard measure of stone coal, coke, and unslacked lime. Passed February 14, 1848. — 1848

An act to amend the "Act to provide for a uniform standard 1848 of weights and measures," passed February 21, 1846. Passed February 24, 1848.

An act to amend an act entitled "An act to provide for a 1848 uniform standard of weights and measures," passed February 21, 1846; passed February 8, 1847. Passed February 25, 1848.

An act supplementary to "An act to provide for a uniform 1850 standard of weights and measures," passed February 21, 1846. Passed March 23, 1850.

KENTUCKY.

[A volume of laws, containing the revised statutes adopted at the last session of the legislature, was sent to this office by Governor L. W. Powell, with a letter from his excellency, dated Frankfort, Kentucky, September 19, 1853.]

An act to provide a standard of weights and measures for the 1839 several counties of this State. Approved February 1, 1839. Chapter 1,093.

Weights and measures, chapter 34.

TENNESSEE.

[A copy of the only act passed by the State on the subject of weights and measures, as early as 1803, was obtained from the Revised Statutes on file in the State Department]

Acts in relation to weights and measures. Chapter 11, 1803 1803.

An act repealing the thirteenth section of an act passed 1779. 1831 Chapter 10. Passed December 15, 1831. Chapter 110.

An act to regulate weights and measures. Passed March 1, 1856 1856.*

INDIANA.

[Two volumes of the laws of the State, containing all the enactments on weights and measures, were transmitted by Hon. N. Hayden, Secretary of State, with letter dated Indianapolis, August 8, 1853.]

An act regulating weights and measures. Approved January 1818 ary 21, 1818. Chapter 110.

An act prescribing a uniform mode of ascertaining by weight 1845 the quantity of the different kinds of grain that shall pass for a standard bushel in this State. Approved January 13, 1845. Chapter 53.

An act for the regulation of weights and measures. Approved June 9, 1852. Chapter 117. 1852

An act to amend section 3 of an act entitled "An act for the 1853 regulation of weights and measures," approved June 9, 1852. Approved March 1, 1853.

An act to amend section 3 of an act entitled "An act for the 1855 regulation of weights and measures," approved June 9, 1852. Approved February 28, 1855.†

---

* Contained in bound volume, chapter 73.
† Printed leaf forwarded by the Governor December 26, 1856.

ILLINOIS.

[A manuscript copy of the existing laws on weights and measures was received, with the seal of the State attached, and certificate by the Secretary of State, Hon. Alexander Starne. Copies of other acts, passed since 1819, but not in force at the present time, were obtained from the Congressional and State Department libraries.]

An act regulating weights and measures. Approved March 22, 1819. — 1819

An act to regulate weights and measures. Approved March 4, 1843. — 1843

Weights and measures. Approved March 3, 1845. Chapter 108. — 1845

An act prescribing the standard weight of a bushel of Indian corn. Approved February 15, 1851. — 1851

An act prescribing the standard weight of a bushel of castor beans. Approved February 17, 1851. — 1851

An act regulating the standard weight of a bushel of field beans, castor beans, clover seed, flax seed, timothy, hemp seed, and stone coal. Approved February 10, 1853. — 1853

An act to amend an act concerning weights and measures. Approved February 14, 1855.* — 1855

MISSOURI.

[A volume of the laws of the State was received with a letter dated Jefferson City, Mo., November 11, 1853, from Hon. John M. Richardson, Secretary of State.]

An act regulating weights and measures. Passed July 28, 1813. — 1813

An act regulating and establishing weights and measures. Approved December 18, 1824. — 1824

An act to regulate weights and measures. Approved December 8, 1834. — 1834

An act to regulate the weight of hemp. Approved February 13, 1841. — 1841

Joint resolution respecting weights and measures. Approved February 22, 1843. — 1843

An act to regulate weights and measures. Approved March 17, 1845. Chapter 184, Revised Statutes. — 1845

An act to regulate weights and measures. Approved November 27, 1855.† — 1855

ARKANSAS.

[A printed copy of the digest of the laws of Arkansas, containing all the law on weights and measures, was forwarded from Little Rock, Arkansas, October 10, 1853, with letter of that date, by Hon. D. B. Green, Secretary of State.]

Weights and measures: Laws in relation to weights and measures passed by the State of Arkansas, chapter 168, Revised Statutes. Approved February 12, 1838. In force by proclamation of governor March 20, 1839. — 1838

---

* Certified copy sealed October 6, 1856.
† Certified copy sealed October 27, 1856.

126   WEIGHTS AND MEASURES.

MICHIGAN.

[A manuscript copy was received of chapter 31 of the Revised Statutes of Michigan, being an act on weights and measures, approved May 18, 1846. The seal of the State was attached, and the copy certified to by Rod. R. Gibson, esq , deputy Secretary of State. A copy of an act on the same subject, approved April 12, 1827, was obtained from the State Department library.]

An act to regulate weights and measures. Approved April 12, 1827.   1827

Of weights and measures. Approved May 18, 1846. Revised Statutes of Michigan, chapter 31.   1846

WISCONSIN.

[A certified manuscript copy of an act on weights and measures, taken from the Revised Statutes of 1849, title 12, chapter 42, was received from Hon. Charles D. Robinson, Secretary of State, with his letter, dated Madison, Wisconsin, August 18, 1853 Extracts from the revised statutes of 1839 were procured by the office from the laws on file in the State Department.]

An act to regulate weights and measures. From Revised Statutes of 1839.   1839

Of weights and measures. Title 12, chapter 42, of Revised Statutes of 1849.   1849

An act to provide for the receiving and safe keeping of the set of standard weights and measures, and to appropriate money to defray expenses. Approved April 17, 1852; chapter 404, Revised Statutes.   1852

An act to regulate the weight and measure of flax seed, timothy seed, and potatoes. Approved March 25, 1854.   1854

IOWA.

[A leaf from the Code of State Laws was received, containing all the law relating to weights and measures in force in the State, as certified to by Hon. George W. McCleary, Secretary of State.]

Weights and measures. Title 13. Regulations pertaining to trade. Chapter 56 of the Revised Code of Iowa.

CALIFORNIA.

[A letter was received from Charles H. Hempstead, esq., private secretary to Governor Bigler, dated October 26, 1853, enclosing a manuscript copy of all the laws of California on weights, measures, and gauging.]

An act to establish a standard of weights and measures. Passed March 30, 1850.   1850

An act to provide for the appointment of a gauger for the port of San Francisco. Approved May 3, 1852.   1852

An act entitled " An act to amend an act to establish a standard of weights and measures, passed March 30, 1850." Approved April 30, 1853.   1853

MINNESOTA TERRITORY.

[A copy of chapter 58 of the Laws of the Territory on weights and measures was obtained from the Congressional library.]

An act to regulate weights and measures. Passed in 1849; chapter 58.   1849

Law regulating weights and measures. From the Revised Statutes passed 1851.*   1851

NOTE.—All the copies of laws obtained from the volumes on file in the libraries of Congress and the State Department have been at the expense of this office.

TERRITORY OF NEW MEXICO.

An act relative to weights and measures. Passed by the legislative assembly of the Territory of New Mexico January 12, 1852.†   1852

An act relative to weights and measures. Passed February 8, 1853.†   1853

TERRITORY OF WASHINGTON.

An act relative to weights and measures.‡

APPENDIX No. 13.

Letter of E. R. Potter, esq., of Providence, Rhode Island, giving a brief account of the legislation of that State prior to 1819.

OFFICE OF COMMISSIONER OF PUBLIC SCHOOLS,
Providence, R. I., November 14, 1853.

SIR: The governor referred to me your letter requesting information as to the laws of the State of Rhode Island upon the subject of weights and measures and gauging since 1819. Herewith I send copies of all of them.

As Mr. Adams' report on weights and measures contains no information as to the laws of Rhode Island upon these subjects, the following memoranda may be interesting:

In the code of laws of 1647 it is enacted that "the measure shall be one and the weight one throughout the whole colony, and that every town shall have a common balance and weights and a common measure that every person may measure and weigh thereat, 12 H. 7, 5, see 9. H. 3, 26; and that every town be careful in the observance thereof. Furthermore it is agreed that whosoever shall use false weights and measures which are not according to the standard shall forfeit, &c., &c., 1 H. 7, 4," The references are intended to refer to the statutes of England.

---

* Certified copy sealed October 7, 1856.
† Certified copies sealed November 28, 1856.
‡ Certified copy sealed December 17, 1856.

By an act of March 1, 1663, it was enacted that a general sealer, &c., should be annually chosen, who should procure, at the colony's charge, a half bushel, peck, half-peck, ale quart, wine quart, wine pint, wine half pint, a yard and weights, which shall be according to the standard of his Majesty's exchequer in the kingdom of England. Towns were also to procure suitable standards.

An act was passed May, 1698, providing penalties on such towns as did not procure standards and have them sealed by the general sealer.

In February, 1728, the act of 1663 was substantially re-enacted.

By act of June, 1731, the assize of barrels was fixed at thirty-one gallons and a half.

The digest of 1767 contains an act fixing the measure of fire-wood the same as at present.

By an act of June, 1751, re-enacted in 1767, the subject of gauging was regulated. It was to be done "by Gunter." And by the act of 1767 the rule for finding the mean diameter is established "by multiplying the difference between the head and bung diameter with 0.65, and adding the product to the head diameter, or, which is the same otherwise expressed, by adding sixth-tenths and a half of the difference between the bung and head to the diameter at the head."

By an act of October, 1784, it is recited that Indian meal has been heretofore sold at fifty pounds to a bushel, and it is ordered to be sold hereafter at fifty-four pounds. Re-enacted in 1798.

The laws regulating the assize of lime casks and beef barrels I have passed over. There are among the ancient laws some regulating the assize of bread.

Very respectfully, your obedient servant,

E. R. POTTER.

Professor A. D. BACHE.
Superintendent of Weights and Measures.

APPENDIX No. 14.

Table showing the weight of a bushel of different grains and other substances, as established by law, in the different States—in pounds, avoirdupois.

States.	Rye.	Wheat.	Indian corn.	Buckwheat.	Barley.	Oats.	Flax seed.	Clover seed.	Bran.	Potatoes.	Beans.	Timothy seed.	Hemp seed.	Blue grass seed.	Corn meal.	Onions.	Salt.	Dried apples.	Dried peaches.	Castor beans.	Mineral coal.	Stone coal.	Corn on cob.	Hair.	Rye meal.	Ruta-baga.	Sugar beet.	Mangel wurzel.
Maine						30									50									11	50			64
New Hampshire	56	60	56		46	30				60																	64	
Vermont	56	60	56	46	48	32				60																64		
Massachusetts						32										52									50			
Rhode Island			56	45		28				60					50	50									50			
Connecticut	56	56	56	50	48																							
New York	56	60	56		48	32																						
New Jersey						30																						
Pennsylvania	56	60	56	48	47	32												~{80 / †70 / 62}	~{28}				~{80 / 70}					
Delaware						32																						
Louisiana	32				32	33½																						
Kentucky	56	60	56	52	48	33	56	56	20	56	60	45	44	14	50	57	50		28	46	70							
Ohio	56	60	56		48	33	56	60		60		45			45	48		25	33	46		80						
Michigan		60	56	42	48	32	55	60		60		45	44	14	50	57	~{50 / †55}	24	24				70					
North Carolina, ¶	56	60	54	50	48	30	56		20	60	60	46	44	14														
Indiana		60	56	50	48	32		60		60	60	45	44	14	48													
Illinois	56	60	56	52	48	32	56	60	20	60	60	45	44															
Wisconsin	56	60	56	42	48	32	56	60	20	60	60					57	~{50 / 50}	28	28	46		80	70					
Iowa	56	60	56	52	48	35	56	60	20	60	60					57	50	24	33	46								
Missouri	54	60	52	40	50	32	56			60								24	33									
California	56	60	56	42	48	32		60																8				
Minnesota Territory	56	60	56	42	45	36		60		60					50	50		28	28									
Washington Territory																												

* Coarse.   † Ground.   ‡ Fine.   § Bituminous.   ‖ Camel.   ¶ Not officially communicated.

NOTE.—No laws specifying the weight to the bushel of grain or other commodities have been passed by the States of Maryland, Virginia, South Carolina, Georgia, Florida, Alabama, Mississippi, Tennessee, Arkansas, or Texas.

APPENDIX No. 15.

Circular to the Ministers of the United States to England, France, the Netherlands, Prussia, and Belgium, asking for information in regard to the methods of gauging officially practiced in those countries, and correspondence in relation thereto.

OFFICE OF WEIGHTS AND MEASURES,
Washington, February 7, 1851.

SIR: It has been rendered my duty, by the Secretary of the Treasury of the United States, to prepare a report as a preliminary step to the introduction of a uniform system of gauging in the custom-houses of the United States. To render the report thorough, it is necessary to give a sketch of the history of the art, to give an account of the different processes which have been used, and are now in use in foreign governments, and the scientific bases upon which they are founded. As the readiest and most effective mode of acquiring the requisite information, I have thought it best to apply to the representatives of the United States at the different European courts, and through them to the authorities having the system of gauging under their control.

I would be much obliged to you if you will procure and forward, addressed to the Superintendent of Weights and Measures, at Washington city, at your earliest convenience, and by the speediest conveyance, copies of such laws and regulations in relation to the measurement of the capacity of casks, and the determination of their contents, as may be now in force in the government to which you are a representative, together with descriptions of the processes which have been and are now used, and whatever books and instruments are used by the gaugers employed by the government.

Any other information which it may be in your power to procure in relation to the matter would be most thankfully received. The Treasury Department has authorized a reasonable expenditure for the object, and payments not exceeding fifty dollars made for books or instruments will be refunded.

Very respectfully, yours, &c.,

A. D. BACHE,
Superintendent Weights and Measures.

Hon. ABBOTT LAWRENCE, *London, England.*
Hon. WILLIAM C. RIVES, *Paris, France.*
Hon. GEORGE FOLSOM, *Hague, Netherlands.*
Hon. D. D. BARNARD, *Berlin, Prussia.*
Hon. T. G. CLEMSON, *Brussels Belgium.*

APPENDIX No. 15. (1.)

Papers received from the Hon. Abbott Lawrence, United States minister at London: 1. *Letter of Thomas Memanter, esq., of the board of customs, London;* 2. *Memorandum by R. Troughton, esq., chief officer of the gauging department of the customs.*

BOARD OF CUSTOMS,
London, March 26, 1851.

DEAR SIR: I enclose a memorandum by the chief officer of the gauging department in the customs which will afford some information to Mr. Lawrence in reply to his enquiry. I send also a copy of the instructions placed in the hands of our gauging officers on their appointment. Mr. Troughton refers to a work, "Symond's Practical Gauger," which Mr. Lawrence will be able to procure, and he can also obtain a set of gauging instruments if he desires it.

But as gauging is an art as well as a science, the mysteries thereof can only be learned by practical experience, and I can only offer, if Mr. Lawrence should think it worth while to direct one of his officers to come over from the United States to London, to have him placed under instructions, and formally instructed in the mode adopted in this department for ascertaining and recording the quantities of casks and the strength of spirits liable to duty.

I am yours, very faithfully,

THOS. MEMANTER.
W. H. STEPHENSON, Esq.

The present English gallon is fixed by act of Parliament to be equal in bulk to 10 lbs. of distilled water at 62° Fah., and contains 277,274 cubic inches, (353.03 cylindrical inches.)

Our method of ascertaining the capacity of a cask by gauging, founded upon this data, is, first to reduce it to a cylinder, by finding the difference between the head and the bung diameters, which difference is multiplied by 0.7, upon the principle that a spheroid occupies two-thirds of its surrounding square, and that product, added to the head diameter, gives the mean diameter of a cylinder of the same capacity as the cask. The square of this mean diameter multiplied by the length of the cask, and the product divided by the circular divisor 353.03, gives the capacity, or full contents in gallons.

To ascertain the dimensions, we make use of rules or gauging instruments, viz: the long callipers, to find the internal length of the cask; the cross callipers, to find the internal horizontal diameter; the bung-rod, to find the perpendicular diameter; and the head rod, to find the diameter of the two heads. The last rule is also made use of to reduce the cask to a cylinder, and to find its full and ullage contents; and prevents the necessity of working them out by figures.

The first operation in gauging is to take the diameter of the two heads with the slide on the head rod, and the mean of the two is marked down as the head diameter. The bung diameter is next ascertained by taking the mean of the horizontal and perpendicular diameter for the true bung diameter, and the length is then taken and marked down. These three dimensions—length, head, and bung diameters—being thus found, the reduction of the cask and the casting out of its capacity by the head rod are the next operations.

Upon the upper part of the face of the head rod is inscribed a Gunter logarithmic line ranging from 25 to 400, and upon the upper line of the slide is a corresponding line of square roots, commencing at 18.79, which is termed the "gauge point," being the square root of the cylinder divisor 353.03, and implies that a cylindrical vessel one inch deep and 18.79 inches in diameter holds exactly one gallon. In the middle of the slide, to the left, is a line called the spheroid line, so divided as to take two-thirds of the difference between the head and bung diameters as the mean difference. The bottom lines of the slide and face are lines of inches.

The upright piece of brass upon the slide is to be placed to the head diameter, in the lower line of the rule; and the number on the spheroid line directly over the bung diameter, also on the lower line, shows the number to be added to the head diameter for the mean diameter of the cylinder required. The gauge point on the slide is then to be placed to the length, upon the upper line of the rule, and upon the same line, directly over the mean diameter, on the top line of the slide, is the full contents or capacity of the cask in gallons and fractional parts of a gallon, which fractional parts of a gallon, by our regulation, are not carried to account.

The spheroid line is calculated for the middle frustrum of the finest mathematical figure of an elliptical form, and, as almost all casks vary from this both in figure and thickness, it is necessary to make allowances upon the length to meet the deviations from the spheroid; otherwise, the result would be very erroneous, and, as no fixed rules or laws can be laid down for such allowances, the art of gauging is thereby rendered difficult, and can only be acquired by constant practice and a perfect knowledge of the various forms of casks imported from different countries. It would therefore be advisable, to obtain a correct judgment in gauging, that a competent person should be placed in communication with our gaugers, to be fully instructed in the use of the rules and the more abstruse parts of gauging, such as the method of ascertaining the mean bung and length dimensions, upon which accuracy so much depends.

The next process in gauging is to ascertain the ullage quantity in the cask. This is done by fixing the brass upon the bung rod to the mean or true bung diameter and dropping it perpendicularly into the bung-hole. The number of wet inches will be shown upon the rule when the perpendicular diameter exceeds the horizontal; but should it be the reverse, the same number of tenths of an inch must be added to the wet shown upon the rule as when added to the perpendicular diameter to make the mean bung diameter. Then upon the back of the head rod, which has three lines cut upon it: one on the top, marked A, and two on the side, marked B and C; also upon the bottom of the rule is a line, termed the segment line, *lying*. The first three lines are a double range of a Gunter logarithmic line from 1 to 100.

To cast the ullage, place the bung diameter on the lower line of the slide marked C to the 100 on the segment line, and under the wet inches and tenths upon the bottom line of the slide will be given the segment for the same segment line. Place the segment number thus found upon the top line of the slide marked B to the 1,000 on the top line of the rule marked A, and under the full contents of the cask, on the same line, will be given the ullage quantity required on the line B.

The duty upon spirits is charged at proof, which is fixed, by act of Parliament, to be of the specific gravity of 92.30 at 57° Fah., or twelve thirteenth parts in weight of an equal bulk of distilled water at that temperature. The actual strength of spirits is ascertained by an instrument termed Sike's hydrometer, which consists of a float and nine weights, giving a range of strengths from 70 per cent. over proof to water, and subdividing it into 500 equal parts; a thermometer, and a table book of concentrated strengths calculated from 30° to 80° of temperature.

Gauging being an art, there are no custom laws regulating it except the two acts before mentioned fixing the size of the gallon and the specific gravity of proof spirit, and also an act prohibiting the importation of spirits in casks of less capacity than twenty gallons.

The gauging rules and spirit hydrometer can be had of Messrs. Dring & Fage, who make for the customs; or of most other opticians; and the last edition of W. Symond's Practical Gauger is a very useful book upon the subject.

R. TROUGHTON, *Inspr.*

CUSTOMS, *March* 4, 1851,
London.

NOTE.—With the above papers came a set of gauging instruments, described above; a copy of the "Excise Officer's Manual;" a copy of "Instructions for the Gaugers;" "Directions for Gauging and Tabulating Distilling Utensils;" "An act for ascertaining and establishing uniformity of weights and measures, 17th June, 1824;" "Table of the areas of circles in imperial gallons to all diameters," &c.; and an octavo volume of Laws Regulating the Excise.

APPENDIX No. 15. (2.)

Letter received from the Hon. George Folsom, Chargé d'Affaires at the Hague, enclosing one to him from M. Van Borp, Minister of Finance of the Netherlands.

LEGATION OF THE UNITED STATES TO THE NETHERLANDS,
The Hague, June 24, 1851.

SIR: I had the honor to recieve your letter of February 7th last, requesting me to make inquiries relative to the system of gauging practised here. Having taken an early opportunity to converse with the minister of finances on the subject, to facilitate the matter, I obtained permission to address him directly by letter, instead of using the customary mode of employing the mediation of the minister of foreign affairs. But, after all, I fear you will think there has been unnecessary delay, as I have not received until now an answer to my letter, which was chiefly a transcript of yours to me. The truth is, as the minister of finances acknowledged to me a few days ago, this government has no systematic mode of gauging, each of the gaugers having his own process of arriving at the desired result; based, however, as you will perceive from the minister's letter, on mathematical principles.

The instruments received are two areometers and a still gauge, or scale, which I must forward by a sailing vessel from Rotterdam, as it would be difficult to pass them through the English custom-house. The letter I forward with this as received, preserving a copy. If I can do anything more to promote your views please inform me.

Very respectfully, your obedient servant,

GEO. FOLSOM.

A. D. BACHE, Esq.,
Superintendent of Weights and Measures.

Translation of letter to Hon. G. Folsom.

THE HAGUE, *June* 19, 1851.

SIR: I have had the honor, M. Chargé d'Affaires, to receive your letter of the 27th of March last, in which you request of me certain information relative to the gauging of casks, &c., in the Netherlands.

This sort of gauging has always been considered as an object sufficiently important to merit the attention of government, but at the same time it has been shown that it was very difficult, not to say impossible, to prescribe general instructions for its guidance. A provisional instruction was issued on March 15, 1806, compiled from the work of Professor Lulofs, but which cannot be applied to all kinds of casks appertaining to commerce; besides, by the introduction of the metrical system of weights and measures which is now in use in this kingdom, this provisional instruction has become altogether without object.

The difficulty of comprising in a general instruction the mode of gauging all the casks and barrels which present themselves in commerce, and the different sorts of gaugers which would be necessary, has resulted in this that, since 1812, all that relates to this part of the public business has been entrusted to special employees named gaugers, who, before obtaining their commission, undergo a scientific examination, in order to prove their knowledge of arithmetic including algebra and mathematics, and their skill in using all kinds of gauges; besides, they have to possess some slight acquaintance with physics. Thus having the necessary scientific knowledge, they seize the practice quite readily of obtaining by means of a gauge the capacity of casks both regular and irregular.

To prove the degree of density of liquids, two kinds of areometers are used, one of which is for liquids lighter than water, and the other for liquids heavier.

I do not consider it necessary here to enter into much detail in relation to the manner in which these areometers are constructed. Suffice it to say, that the one for liquids lighter than water is based upon the number 144, which is divided into degrees from $0°$ to $36°$. $0°$ is the specific weight of distilled water at the temperature of $55°$ Farenheit, and $36°$ that of pure alcohol. These degrees may be readily reduced to specific weights by calculation.

I should here add, that these areometers are constructed in such a manner that the thermometer is attached to them; and the administration has caused tables to be prepared indicating the influence which the difference of the degree of heat has upon the degree of immersion of the areometer. The scale of the areometer is divided into 200 degrees, the areometer marking 100 degrees at a temperature of $55°$ Fahrenheit, which indicates that in the liquid, distilled water and pure alcohol are found in equal parts.

The areometer for liquids heavier, as syrup, &c., is based upon the number 100, but the calculations are the same.

You will find herewith a gauge of the mode which the employés of the administration use generally, also a sample of each kind of areometer above referred to.

Please accept, M. Chargé d'affaires, the assurance of my very distinguished consideration.

VAN BORP.
The Minister of Finance.

APPENDIX No. 15. (3.)

Papers received from the government of Prussia, comprising a translation of the official instructions for gauging casks, by M. Van Düesberg, Minister of Finance, with table.

Translation of instructions for gauging casks.

§ 1. When the gauging officers are requested to gauge casks intended for wine, alcohol, beer, vinegar, or other liquids, their capacity is to be determined *in all cases* by the weight of the quantity of water that will fill them: for this purpose the following process is to be observed.

§ 2. Only such casks are admitted to be gauged, as are irreproachable in solidity of construction, well hooped, and clean of every foreign matter inside. The gauging officers have to examine into this carefully, and refuse all casks not fulfilling these requisitions.

§ 3. For filling, ordinary river, pond, or well water is to be used; the weight of the water is found by determining the weight of the empty cask, also when it is full, subtracting the first weight from the second. The filled cask must not be weighed until the water has been in it at least two hours. Immediately before proceeding to take the weight, the gauger must ascertain whether the cask is completely filled; should this not be the case, the necessary quantity of water must be added. Directly after taking the weight of the full cask, the temperature of the water by Reaumur's scale is to be determined and noted. It suffices to ascertain the weight of the filled vessel to the eighth of a pound, if it contain less than 100 quarts, and within a fourth of a pound if more. (Compare § 4.)

§ 4. From the weight of the water filling the vessel to be gauged, its contents in quarts is next computed by means of the subjoined table, in the arrangement and use of which the following has to be observed.

In order to avoid filling with distilled water, upon which are based the legal weight, and its reduction to cubic inches, the mean specific gravity of river and pond water, as well as of common well water, have been determined by careful experiments, in which the changes of temperature were taken into consideration. A table is subjoined, giving the data for both kinds of water, and at the various temperatures from 0° to 25°, Reaumur.

Column A gives the weight of a quart of water weighed in the open air.

Column B, the cubic contents of a pound of water expressed in fractions of a quart.

When the weight of water filling a cask to be gauged has been found, and the degree of temperature, Reaumur, the volume of the cask's contents in quarts is found by means of the number corresponding to the degree of temperature in the proper column of the table, according as river or well water has been used—dividing the number given in column A, by the weight of the water, or multiplying the number in column B by the same weight. The fractions of quarts are only considered for vessels of less than 100 quarts; for larger ones they may be neglected when they amount to only one half-quart or less; they are reckoned for the whole quart when more than half.

The following is an example of the computation. Suppose a vessel to have been weighed when filled with water at 10° Reaumur, and the weight of the water to have been found $= 496.75$ lbs; the table gives for well water opposite to 10° Reaumur, in column A, the number 2.4457, and in column B, 0.4089. The first makes the capacity of the caks $= \dfrac{49675}{24457} = 203.11$ quarts; the second, $4.9675 \times 4089 = 203.12$ quatrs. Neglecting the fraction after the decimal point, as it is smaller than 0.5, the capacity by both methods of calculation is to be set down as 203 quarts.

§ 5. The capacity in quarts found by the preceding method is to be branded in legible figures upon the head of the cask gauged, also the mark of the gauging officer, with the name of the place, and the year, and a voucher in the prescribed form is to be delivered to the officer who ordered the gauging.

VON DÜESBERG,
Minister of Finance.

BERLIN, *April* 3, 1847.

Table to determine the capacity of casks in quarts by means of the weight of water filling them at different temperatures.

[Refer to section 4 of Instructions of April 3, 1847.]

	River or pond water.				Well water.		
Fahr. Temp.	Reaumur Temp.	A. Weight of 1 qrt. water in air.	B. Cubic contents of 1 lb. water.	Fahr. Temp.	Reaumur Temp.	A. Weight of 1 qrt. water in air.	B. Cubic contents of 1 lb. water.
Degrees.	*Degrees.*	*Prussian lbs.*	*Prussian qts.*	*Degrees.*	*Degrees.*	*Prussian lbs.*	*Prussian qts.*
32.00	0	2.4448	0.4090	--------	0	2.4465	0.4087
34.25	1	449	090	--------	1	466	087
36.50	2	451	090	--------	2	468	087
38.75	3	452	090	--------	3	469	087
41.00	4	451	090	--------	4	468	087
43.25	5	450	090	--------	5	468	087
45.50	6	449	090	--------	6	466	087
47.75	7	448	090	--------	7	465	087
50.00	8	445	091	--------	8	462	088
52.25	9	443	091	--------	9	461	088
54.50	10	440	092	--------	10	457	089
56.75	11	436	092	--------	11	454	089
59.00	12	432	093	--------	12	449	090
61.25	13	428	094	--------	13	445	091
63.50	14	422	095	--------	14	440	092
65.75	15	417	096	--------	15	434	093
68.00	16	411	097	--------	16	428	094
70.25	17	406	097	--------	17	423	095
72.50	18	399	099	--------	18	416	096
74.75	19	392	100	--------	19	409	097
77.00	20	384	101	--------	20	401	098
79.25	21	376	102	--------	21	393	100
81.50	22	368	104	--------	22	385	101
83.75	23	359	105	--------	23	376	102
86.00	24	350	107	--------	24	367	104
88.25	25	342	108	--------	25	359	105

APPENDIX No. 16.

Letter of M. Moreau, Sub-director of International Exchanges, transmitting a complete collection of standard weights and measures as a present from France to the United States.

AGENCE CENTRALE DU SYSTEME D' EXCHANGE INTERNATIONAL,
56 RUE DE CLICHY, *Paris, April* 20, 1852.

SIR: I have the honor of informing your excellency, that I will forward to the President of the United States, by the steamer Humbolt, on the 9th of May next, a complete set of standard weights and measures of France.

This collection is presented by the minister of commerce of France, in the name of the government, to the government of the United States, in return for the splendid series of standard weights and measures so generously voted by Congress by the bill dated June 30, 1848, to be presented through me to the French Republic. I need not say, sir, that the collection was received with the warmest feelings of brotherhood and gratitude. The precious instruments that I forward to the President, are the best guarantee of the sympathy felt, in every moment, by France for the United States.

As illustrations of this collection, I have the honor of sending herewith to your excellency the report made to me on my request, by Mr. Sibermann, superintendent of the conservatory of arts and trades, to whom was entrusted the care and examination of the collection.

In this report, M. Silbermann relates the experiments made by himself, upon the weights and measures presented by the United States, gives the historical account of the adoption by France of the metrical system, and explains, in their smallest details, all the standards presented by France.

He concludes by saying, that his earnest hope is to see the American people adopt a system which will put an end to the troubles of commerce, and greatly co-operate to cement the bonds of fraternal feelings which have united for a long time our two respective countries.

Indeed, Mr. Secretary, I consider the reciprocal presentation of these two magnificent collections as the most glorious result of my system of international exchange.

Before concluding, sir, allow me to offer anew to your excellency the expression of my gratitude for your constant kindness towards me, and to assure you, that I will always do everything in my power to prove myself worthy of the confidence the American people have deigned to place in the humble advocate of a great cause.

Hoping, sir, that I have been agreeable to you, in fulfilling what I considered my duty, as agent of the United States, I have the honor to be, with great respect, sir, your excellency's most grateful and obedient servant, (for M. Vattemare, at present in Holland and Belgium,)

MOREAU, *Sub-director.*

His Excellency, THE SECRETARY OF THE TREASURY
of the United States.

APPENDIX No. 17.

Letter of M. Silbermann, superintendent of the Conservatory of Arts and Trades of France, to M. Alex. Vattemare, agent of International Exchanges, in relation to the standards of the United States and France.

PARIS, *March* 6, 1852.

DEAR MR. VATTEMARE: In answer to your request relative to my opinion concerning the weights and measures, and the instruments of weighing and measuring, you have entrusted to me for the Conservatory of Arts and Trades, one of the results of the system of international exchanges, of which you are the founder, and which has led to the execution of weights and measures, destined to be presented through you to the government of the United States, in the name of France, I feel impelled to subjoin some information relating to them, in view of the fact, that the greater part of them have for a long time been exhibited to the public in our gallery of weights and measures, side by side with the splendid collection which you have presented to us.

In the first place, I will communicate to you the opinion of connoisseurs, and I beg of you to believe that each instrument has been well examined and well appreciated. This opinion is, that all these articles are of an irreproachable execution; the two balances particularly are the object of universal admiration. Public opinion cannot go further. In testimony of the esteem in which I hold these balances, I cannot say more than that I used the small one to adjust the platinum kilogramme, which was exhibited at the World's Fair, in London; it is very delicate and especially most constant. I was able to make all my weighings with certainty to within half a milligramme. The form adopted for these balances is at once simple, well adapted to use, and distinguished by that taste which is only to be found in instruments made by master hands. These are justly to be termed instruments of precision.

What I have just said with regard to the small balance I may repeat with still more propriety respecting the large one; it is not inferior to the former in precision. In fact, I have tested it with 10 kilogrammes in each scale, and it promptly indicates a difference of one half a milligramme between the two weights, that is to say, one unit in twenty millions, in each scale. I have been obliged several times to repeat this experiment in the presence of incredulous persons, and it has always given the same result. What is most gratifying to me in the construction of these balances is the system adopted in the United States, which consists in preventing the oscillation of the balance and causing it to cant as soon as the equilibrium is destroyed; the weighings are effected very rapidly, and, as it has been seen, with as much precision as can be obtained with the most carefully made balances. For my part, I have ever regretted that all our balance makers have hitherto declined the adoption of this system. They assign, as the reason of this reluctance, that with an oscillating balance they can replace the small weights by arcs of oscillation, which enables them to estimate much smaller fractions of the milligramme. As for myself, I am inclined to believe that as much precision may be arrived at in one system as in the other, and in that case there will be a great gain of time in the system of canting. Moreover, I know from experience what confidence is to be placed in weights estimated by arcs; in spite of the utmost care, the above mentioned very small arcs are variable; and while they flatter us with the hope that we have obtained tenths of a milligramme, they cause us to commit, unwittingly, errors of more than one or two milligrammes.

I beg, however, to be permitted one observation, not upon the construction of these balances, but upon the manner of weighing in general. It is, that in the comparisons of standards the beam ought not to be lowered in reloading; the balance should remain fixed, the basin to be unloaded should be mechanically held in its position of equilibrium, and the weights should be taken off and replaced without any shock; then we are perfectly certain of an absolute regularity in the comparison. It is the method I employ in such cases. This regularity depends upon the knife-edges experiencing no displacement between the two weighings. Also, in order to use the method of the double weighings, or of Borda, in a simple manner, which allows me to control the reading of the weights, I proceed as follows: The basins are always loaded with the same weight, which is the largest unit that the balance will bear, say one kilogramme for balances of that capacity. I commence by verifying the copper counterpoise, which holds in equilibrium the standard kilogramme; then replacing that standard by the body to be weighed, and completing the equilibrium by marked weights taken from another kilogramme, very exact but subdivided, there will remain out of the scale precisely the weights replaced by the body to be weighed. I read them and have the weight of the body. On the other hand, if I subtract from one kilogramme the amount of the weights placed in the scale, I shall find the same weight again, if my readings have been faithful, if not, I am made aware of it in time, and I correct with accuracy. It is only from time to time that it is necessary to verify the exactness of the counterweight, and in successive weighings. In this way the double do not require much more time than the single weighings.

I have been highly pleased with the form given in the United States to the small weights. To represent polygons with wire of a convenient size, and having a number of sides equal to the figure expressed by those weights in units, is a very happy idea, which secures from false readings; we need no magnifying glass to distinguish a pentagon, which signifies five, from a quadrilateral, which represents four, from a triangle, or three, from an angle V, the two legs of which indicate two, and finally, from the single straight wire, making the unit. This form will certainly be appreciated in France; as for myself, I will do everything in my power to have it adopted by law, instead of the ancient form, which is subject to many errors, known only to those who use it often.

I have observed with pleasure even the hooks lined with buff to take up the weights without rubbing them; and the pincers also, lined with the same material, to take up the troy weights, have been used by me to take up the platinum kilogramme during its adjustment. I consider all these minute precautions, as the true stamp of the scrupulous experimenter.

As to the exactness of the weights and measures, what I have seen is to me a sure guaranty.

One point more—I allude to the alloyage adopted in the United States. I shall do my utmost to cause the brass employed in France in the fabrication of weights and measures to be of the same standard as that in the United States, and free from all hammering or rehardening whatever, simply cast, and as uniformly as possible, so as to have, like theirs, the least differences in the density and expansion of materials used. This necessity has long been felt, but it has not yet been sanctioned by law, as has been done in respect to the alloy of tin and lead, which forms the measures for capacity of liquids, for the verification of which a hydrostatical balance has even been made, as you will perceive in the list of the French articles which will be remitted to you.

Looking at the yard standard, I was at first quite amazed; it is divided in decimal parts. I thought I recognized decimeters and centimeters; but, unluckily, its total length is not quite that of the metre, it wants about eight centimeters and a half. Let Americans soon add them, and the two hemispheres, after having wisely adopted the decimal system, will soon be possessed of the uniform metrical system. The people of the United States, in such a good course should not stop. Allow me to justify my hope, with the example given by France to the whole world. They should listen to the history of the past, and of the enormous sacrifices made by France to obtain this laudable end.

The small degree of sympathy which existed formerly between the different States of the globe, the exclusiveness of each as regards all the rest, that unreflecting self-love which desires to command others, rather than accept their counsels, sacrificing even interest to vanity; all these causes tended to make each people, cloistering themselves, nay, fencing themselves in, insist upon having their own peculiar weights and measures. They cared but little for the annoyances of commerce in international transactions that were little known, and in fact of small extent. But this extravagant fondness for self regulation was not confined to the larger States; different provinces, even neighboring cities of the same nation were in perpetual rivalry with each other, and, whenever they could do so, assumed the power of nationalities, and decreed their own weights and measures. Why, then, in such a state of things, should not each individual take the same liberty, and construct his measures in accordance with his own interest? Imagine, if you can, the misreckonings experienced by commerce in such a relation of mutual interests, and such a profusion of measures of every kind. In the adjustment of imposts, the same difficulties were experienced, and the customhouse, that vidette on all frontiers, must have had many confused pages of records previous to the comparison of the various measures after they had been determined and legalized by the different States.

France, tired sooner than other nations of these divisions, which with her were even greater than elsewhere, formed at once a great resolution, the complete reformation of her weights and measures. This happened in 1790, at the very moment of her great political reformation. Accordingly, the constituent assembly, on the motion of Talleyrand, one of its members, ordered the Academy of Sciences to found a metrical system, based upon nature, and suitable for acceptance by all nations.

The academy fixed the unit at the millionth part of the quarter of the terrestrial meridian.

It adopted a provisional metre, deduced from the measures of the meridian, which, long before, the geometer Lacaille had measured in Peru; and, for greater certainty, ordered the measuring of the meridian passing through France, extending from Dunkirk to Barcelona, and which could be and was afterwards prolonged northward through England and Scotland, and from the Isle of Wight, southward, through Spain to the island of Formentara. This meridian was not selected because it passed through France, but because it was in Europe the longest meridian that could be chosen, not distant from France, and of which the two extremities might rest on the level of the sea. That gigantic work, accomplished in the midst of a revolutionary storm, was not to be the selfish work of France; such was not her desire. The provisional government invited foreign nations to co-operate in the definitive work by assembling a universal congress composed of the most illustrious learned men of each country.

This commission of weights and measures comprised the following gentlemen, viz:

Berthollet, Borda, Brisson, Coulomb, Darcet, Delambre, Haüy, Lagrange, Laplace, Lefevre-Gineau, Legendre, Mechain, Monge Prony, and Vandermonde, members of the Institute of France; Ænæ and Van Swinden, sent by the republic of the Netherlands; De Balbo, by Sardinia; Bugge, by Denmark; Ciscar and Pedrayès, by Spain; Fabbroni, by Tuscany; Franchini, by the Roman republic; Mascheroni, by the Cis-Alpine republic; Multedo, by the Ligurian republic; Trallès, by the Swiss confederation; Vassalli, by Piedmont; Lenoir, a French artist, who executed the metre and the apparatus relating to it, and Fortin, also a French artist, author of the kilogramme and its apparatus.

Lavoisier, Tillet, and General Meunier, also took an active part in these operations, though unfortunately for but a short time.

This illustrious commission received the work already accomplished, and, after minute verification and comment, deduced from it the new system, thanks to the untiring zeal of some of its members, such as Trallès, and Lefevre-Gineau, who performed the whole of the experiments of precision.

Trallès, as reporter of the commission, presented the platinum prototypes to the legislative body, after having presented them to the Institute of France. It is thus that under the shield of that most illustrious commission, and with the strongest sanction of the legislative body, the new system of weights and measures replaced the old uncertainties, and endowed the whole world with units suitable for the acceptance of all civilized nations.

That work, the fruit of the co-operation of all nations, will one day unite them all, as is well proved by the fact that this system is daily extending itself; for it has become law in Belgium, Spain, France, Greece, Holland, Lombardy, Poland, and Switzerland. The Zollverein has readjusted on it its common measures, making its pound five hundred grammes, its foot three decimeters, and its quart one litre and a half.

It has also been accepted on the other side of the Atlantic; for it is law in Chili and Colombia, and has been lately promulgated in Mexico.

How could it be otherwise? Did not America, by the measure of the meridian arc in Peru, furnish us with the length of the provisional metre, which, it is well known, does not differ, for the uses of civil life, from the definitive metre? For the provisional metre deposited in our collection in the conservatory is really only one-hundredth of a millimetre larger than those admitted as definitive. We

WEIGHTS AND MEASURES.

may justly say, therefore, that it is in America where we have sought this measure of union.

I am happy to be able thus to recall to mind the origin of the weights and measures, the list of which follows, that I may induce the people to whom they are presented to adopt them in practice. The weights and measures, as well as the instruments of weighing, measuring, and stamping, which the government of the French republic puts at your disposal to be presented in its name to the govern- of the United States, as a token of reciprocal sympathy, are the following, viz:

One complete collection of the whole apparatus, weights, and measures, composing in France the bureaus of verification of weights and measures, viz:

MEASURES OF LENGTH.

One brass metre, graduated in its whole length, used as a standard.
One wooden metre, bound with iron at its two ends.
One double decimetre.
One decimetre, (surveyor's chain,) with 10 stakes.
One chain metre for measuring the circumference of fagots and bundles of fire wood.

MEASURES OF CAPACITY.

Brass standards, with disks of ground glass.

One	double décalitre	= 20	litres.
"	décalitre	10	"
"	demi-décalitre	5	"
"	double litre	2	"
"	litre	1	"
"	demi-litre	0.5	"
"	double décilitre	0.2	"
"	décilitre	0.1	"
"	demi-décilitre	0.05	"
"	double centilitre	0.02	"
"	centilitre	0.01	"

SPECIMENS IN WOOD OF DRY MEASURES OF CAPACITY.

For grains.

One	hectolitre	100	litres.
"	demi-hectolitre	50	"
"	double décalitre	20	"
"	décalitre	10	"
"	demi-decalitre	5	"
"	double litre	2	"
"	litre	1	"
"	demi-litre	0.5	"
"	double décilitre	0.2	"
"	décilitre	0.1	"
'	demi-décilitre	0.05	"

For coal measures (with feet.)

One hectolitre	100	litres.
" demi-hectolitre	50	"

SPECIMENS IN LEGAL FORM OF THE BLOCK TIN MEASURES OF CAPACITY IN USE FOR LIQUIDS.

First Series, (cylindrical.)

One double litre	2	litres.
" litre	1	"
" demi-litre	0.5	"
" double décilitre	0.2	"
" décilitre	0.1	"
" demi-décilitre	0.05	"
" double centilitre	0.02	"
" centilitre	0.01	"

Second series, (with handles.)

One double litre	2	litres.
" litre	1	"
" demi-litre	0.5	"
" double décilitre	0.2	"
" décilitre	0.1	"
" demi-décilitre	0.05	"
" double centilitre	0.02	"
" centilitre	0.01	"

Third series, (with handle and cover.)

One double litre	2	litres.
" litre	1	"
" demi-litre	0.5	"
" double décilitre	0.2	"
" décilitre	0.1	"
" demi-décilitre	0.05	"
" double centilitre	0.02	"
" centilitre	0.01	"

SPECIMENS IN TIN PLATE OF MEASURES OF CAPACITY FOR MILK AND OIL.

Firt series, for milk and military rations.

One double litre	2	litres.
" litre	1	"
" demi-litre	0.5	"
" double décilitre	0.2	"
" décilitre	0.1	"
" demi-décilitre	0.05	"
" double centilitre	0.02	"
" centilitre	0.01	"

WEIGHTS AND MEASURES. 145

Second series, for lamp oil, marked B.

One	double litre	2	litres.
"	litre	1	"
"	demi-litre	0.5	"
"	double décilitre	0.2	"
"	décilitre	0.1	"
"	demi-décilitre	0.05	"
"	double centilitre	0.02	"
"	centilitre	0.01	"

Third series, for table oil, marked M.

One	double litre	2	litres.
"	litre	1	"
"	demi-litre	0.5	"
"	double décilitre	0.2	"
"	décilitre	0.1	"
"	demi-décilitre	0.05	"
"	double centilitre	0.02	"
"	centilitre	0.01	"

BRASS STANDARD WEIGHTS, (WITH KNOBS.)

One weight of 20 kilogrammes	= 20,000	grammes.
" " 10 "	10,000	"
" " 5 "	5,000	"
Two double kilogrammes	2,000	"
Two weights of 1 kilogramme	1,000	"
One demi-kilogramme	500	"
One double hectogramme	200	"
Two hectogrammes	100	"
One demi-hectogramme	50	"
One double décagramme	20	"
Two décagrammes	10	"
One demi-décagramme	5	"
Two double grammes	2	"
One gramme	1	"
" five décigrammes	0.5	"
" two décigrammes	0.2	"
" décigramme	0.1	"
" five centigrammes	0.05	"
" two centigrammes	0.02	"
" centigramme	0.01	"
" five milligrammes	0.005	"
Two two milligrammes	0.002	"
One milligramme	0.001	"

Nest of weights, forming altogether one kilogramme, and divided into—

500	grammes.
200	"
100	"
100	"
50	"
20	"
10	"
10	"
5	"
2	"
2	"
1	"

Cast-iron weights.

50 kilogrammes, in trapezoidal form

$\left.\begin{array}{r}20\\10\\5\\2\\1\end{array}\right\}$ in pyramidal form.

500	grammes.
200	"
100	"
50	"

The apparatus of verification consists of:

One balance capable of weighing 50 kilogrammes, sensitive to.. 0.02 gramme.
One balance capable of weighing 1 kilogramme, sensitive to...... .... 0.01 "
One assay balance capable, &c., 20 grammes, sensitive to.. 0.001 "
One hydrostatic balance, &c., 2 kilogrammes, sensitive to.. 0.01 "

The assay balance for the verification of small weights is accompanied by two series of weights, of grammes 20, 10, 10, 5, 2, and 1, also a series of the subdivisions of the gramme, and finally, two supernumerary dishes.

The hydrostatic balance is accompanied by a copper bucket for weighing in water. The balance serves, by its verification, to determine the standard of the alloy employed in the fabrication of pewter measures of capacity.

A *hopper* attached to an oaken bench is used to verify the wooden measures of capacity, and the strike to remove the surplus of the quantity of seed ascertained in advance, with which the measures are tested.

The seed used for this purpose is the rape seed, or any other, the form of which is round, small and regular.

On the bench is fastened a screw press intended to stamp the measure, for this purpose it is accompanied by a box containing a beak-iron and two small cushions, and also two keys to lighten the screw nuts.

The inspectors who, in their rounds of inspection, could not carry with them the above mentioned cumbrous apparatus, are provided simply with a small case, which will be found to contain the following articles, viz:

One wooden metre, in two parts.
One double décimetre, of boxwood.
One copper gauge, with projecting division marks for the verifica-

tion of the dimensions of the wooden measures of capacity from the double hectolitre to the semi-décilitre.

One double set balance, used as a steelyard of $\frac{1}{10}$, for weights from 20 to 2 kilogrammes, and a balance of equal arms for the kilogramme and its subdivisions.

One iron press, for stamping.
One heavy hammer.
Seven samples of stamps.
One kilogramme of nest weights, similar to the one above mentioned.
One kilogramme, with knob.

To this collection are added the official ordinances and instructions on the fabrication and verification of weights and measures, accompanied by an atlas representing all the weights and measures in their legal form, similar to those of the collection.

To this collection which does not aim at great precision, but only at a precision practicable for ordinary uses, has been added a collection of units, the perfect exactness of which is guaranteed by the name of their maker, *Gambey*.

These units are:
One brass graduated metre.
One brass litre.
One brass kilogramme, gilt.

Finally, to crown the collection, his excellency, the minister, has ordered to be added also a standard metre, in the construction of which I am at present occupied, and which will be compared with the greatest care with the platinum prototype metre deposited in the State archives.

That metre will be "à bout" and "a trait" (that is, it will have ends, projecting beyond the lines, between which the metre is measured,) and will constitute a *Borda thermometer*, by the addition of a second rule, upon which it will be fastened at one end. By this addition may be ascertained, at any instant, both the absolute length of the metre and its temperature.

These two rules will necessarily be made of two different metals; the metre of steel, gilded, to save it from rust, and the other, which supports it, of brass. The difference of expansion of these two metals is great enough to give appreciable divisions on the two corresponding scales, marked on the free ends of these two rules.

I will give you the details of the construction of this standard metre, when I send you the results of my experiments upon the expansion of the two metals, and upon the comparison of this metre with its prototype.

I am also about to verify the brass weights, as well as the measures of capacity. As soon as these labors are completed, the whole will be forwarded to you in good order. I venture to express the desire, if not the expectation, that these articles will serve as a foundation for the application of the metrical system in the United States. This is my earnest wish. I have exerted myself to the utmost to spare our old friends beyond the sea all additional labor, when they shall conclude to accept to our weights and measures. It is with this view that I have asked and obtained the funds necessary to the verification and fabrication of this last metre, the presentation of which was proposed by myself.

I believe, sir, I have fulfilled your wishes, while gratifying myself, by addressing you this long letter. At the first opportunity, I will communicate orally anything I may have omitted.

Meanwhile, believe me, sir, your most affectionate servant,
J. C. SILBERMANN,
Superintendent of the National Conservatory of Arts and Trades.

APPENDIX No. 18.

Letter of General A. Morin, Administrator of the Conservatory of Arts and Trades, transmitting the report of Mr. Silbermann, upon the French weights and measures presented to the United States.

Report upon the metrical weights and measures sent to the United States, by M. Silbermann, Superintendent of the Conservatory of Arts and Trades, of France.

The United States government, at the solicitation of Monsieur Vattemare, presented to France a beautiful collection of weights and measures, which Professor Bache, superintendent of weights and measures, was pleased to verify himself.

To this collection were added two balances, masterpieces of precision.

In return for this present, the French government wished to give to the United States a complete collection of measures of the metrical system, also accurately verified, in order to bring nearer that period, so desirable for commercial interests, when one system of measures shall be employed in both countries.

To the commerical and common measures have been added standards, the verification of which has been executed at the National Conservatory of Arts and Trades, by the director, by means of the standards of commerce, deposited there, which had been previously compared with those of the State archives.

The following report contains the results of these verifications.
A. MORIN.
General of artillery, member of the Institute, Administrator of the Conservatory of Arts and Trades.

Report of the operations executed by order of General A. Morin, member of the Institute, Superintendent of the Conservatory of Arts and Trades, for the verification of the measures presented to the United States by France, under the direction of M. Silbermann, director of the Conservatory of Arts and Trades.

The verification of the standards of weights and measures which the French government has presented to the government of the United

States, has been made at the Conservatory of Arts and Trades, in the gallery of weights and measures of that establishment, and with the prototypes of commerce which are deposited there.

These prototypes had been themselves compared with the official standards deposited in the archives of France.

The results of this comparison, as well as the manner in which they have been obtained, will be shown presently.

These two series of standards, (of commerce and of the archives,) consist each of a metre "á bout" (cut to length) of platinum, and a platinum kilogramme of a cylindrical form.

These measures were made at the same time by the celebrated artists Lenoir and Fortin, and verified by their colleagues of the international commission of weights and measures, in the 7th year of the republic, (1799.)

The comparison of the metre has been made by means of a special comparator, ("comparateur,") which shows a variation of one-ten-thousandth of a millimetre, that is to say $\frac{1}{10000000}$ of the whole length.

For the comparison of the kilogramme we used a balance which was sensitive to half a millegramme. The numbers obtained have been corrected for the loss which these weights have sustained in air—a loss which has been determined by means of a comparator, constructed with the object of ascertaining the linear dimensions of these cylindrical weights.

There is no standard of measures of capacity; in fact, it would be unnecessary, since the *litre*, the unit of this standard, is a cubic decimetre; and a cubic decimetre of distilled water, at its maximum density, weighs in a vacuum exactly one kilogramme.

The kilogramme, then, supplies the place of this unit.

The series of weights and measures presented to the United States, in exchange for those which have been transmitted to us by M. Vattemare, consists of three different series.

The first is composed of a standard metre of steel upon a bronze base, and a standard kilogramme of brass, gilt.

The second consists of a graduated brass metre, and of a litre, both made by *Gambey*.

The third consists of the series of weights and measures which compose the assortment of a bureau of verification of the first order. Finally, the apparatus for weighing, measuring, and sealing, necessary to these bureaus, complete this set.

150   WEIGHTS AND MEASURES.

CHAPTER I.

COMPARISON OF THE LENGTH MEASURES.

Comparison of the standard metre of commerce with that of the State archives.

This comparison was made by means of a lever-comparator, constructed, under my direction, by M. Brunner.

The accuracy of comparisons being dependent upon the precision of the apparatus for verification, I propose to give here a full description of this comparator, as well as the manner of using it.

1st. *The comparator.*

The base consists of two rules aa' bb', of the same breadth, and nearly of the same length; they are placed one above the other, and firmly pinned together at c', (to the right in fig 2.) The lower rule bb', is of bronze, the upper, aa', (upon which the metre under trial is placed,) of platinum. Each is 30 millimetres in breadth; their other dimensions are as follows:

	Length.	Thickness.
Platinum rule	1.12 millimetre.	3.50 millimetres.
Bronze rule	1.13 "	7.00 "

The length of the metre is obtained between the heel points dd', at the extremities of the short arms, df $d'f'$, of the two levers de $d'e'$, one lever at each extremity of the measure, the longer arms of which levers serve to multiply any minute differences of length in metres placed between the heelpoints. The axes ff', upon which the levers move, are firmly fixed to the lower rule. The shorter arms df $d'f'$, of these levers, are eight millimetres long, and are curved. The long arms fe $f'e'$ are 160 millimetres long. Their position is vertical above the rule to which they are united by the pieces supporting the axis of rotation.

This axis moves between the points of two screws secured in the support.

The lever $d'e'$ (situated on the side a', to the right in fig 2, where the two rules are united,) serves as a striker against one end of the metre under trial, the axis of rotation f of this lever being for this object firmly attached to the rule.

The other lever de (contact-lever) is brought into contact with the extremity of the introduced metre; and, to accomplish this, it is moved by the slide ghi by the action of a micrometric screw, $(s,)$ the nut k of which is fixed to the bronze rule by means of a projection which unites the two pieces.

In order not to injure the ends of the introduced metre, the two levers are held against the extremities only by means of a small spring $l\,l'$, the power of which does not exceed five grammes. The curved extremity $d\,d'$ of the short arms is cylindrical and horizontal, and presents, for contact with the introduced metre and edge, two millimetres in length.

At the summit $m\,m'$, of the piece constituting the support of each lever, there is a zero mark, and also another on the top of the lever ; the coincidence of these two gives the requisite length between the extremities of the short arms of the levers. To increase this precision, five marks are made instead of one, two either side of the zero mark, and the intervals on the top of the lever are slightly less than those on the support, in order that they may act as a vernier ; and to give still greater exactness to the observation, there is an eye-glass to each support. If the small arms of the levers $d\,d'$ are $\frac{1}{1000}$ of a millimetre out of the way, it is indicated at the extremity of the long arm by half a division on the vernier, a quantity quite appreciable by means of the lenses.

To make the delicate contact required, for which pushing with the hand alone would be unsatisfactory, there is a piece, p, (right end in fig. 2,) which presses against the side of the measure. This piece terminates in a horizontal tail piece q, which connects with a thumb-screw r, not very fine in its thread, that passes through the foot of the support. This screw is situated in the prolongation of the upper surface of the platinum rule, upon which surface the rule under trial rests.

The micrometric screw s, above alluded to, makes just a semi-millimetre each revolution. The head t is divided into 500 parts, and subdivided into 5,000 by a vernier (v) fixed to the support. The millimetre is thus graduated to 10,000 parts, which is equivalent to ten millionths of a metre, or the relation between a metre and a quarter of a terrestrial meridian. This screw turns between two points x, screwed into the slide which supports the contact lever, and is situated in the same line with the points of contact.

The delicacy of the points of contact being ascertained, there is still a condition to be provided for, viz : the invariability of the distance between the two heel points of the levers, an invariability constantly disturbed by variations of temperature. To insure an invariable length in the bronze rule, which serves as a support to the levers, M. Silbermann applies to this rule the rule $a\,a'$ of platinum, which, as the expansion of the two metals is very different, makes of the couple a Borda thermometer, (fig. 2 ;) and it indicates for each instant the temperature of the system. This is the object of uniting the two rules at one end e, by a pin which goes through both, while at the other end they are free. The difference of expansion is indicated by a scale c, divided into fourths of millimetres, traced upon the platinum rule. A vernier, made of a plate of platinum, is fixed against the bronze rule, which divides 24 of these fourths into 25 parts, and indicates thus hundredths of a millimetre. This plate serves also to guide the platinum rule, while the foot of the nut of the micrometric screw guides the rule on the other side.

For multiplying the movements of expansion of this Borda thermometer, the lever d'', f'', e'', (fig. 2,) is introduced. The arc e'', which terminates the arm of the lever f″ e″, carries a vernier which moves against a divided arc m″, whose foot carries the axis f″, of the lever fixed to the bronze rule b b′. The divisions of the vernier register $\frac{1}{50}$ of a degree of temperature. This apparatus for the comparisons ("comparateur") rests on several pieces, y, of equal thickness, and these on a brass support zz′, accurately planed.

The experiments which follow, and which have been made with the prototype of the archives, and that of commerce, as well as with the measures sent to the United States, will serve at the same time as examples for the use of the apparatus which has just been described

2d. Comparison of the standards of commerce with that of the archives.

These two metres, both of platinum, constructed at the same time, and deposited, one at the archives of State, the 4th Messidor, of the 8th year, (22d June, 1799,) and the other at the Department of the Interior, previously verified by the same operators, are found to be the same at the temperature of 10° (centigrade) after 24 hours continuance side by side.

I did not permit myself to put the standard in the ice; besides, the small co-efficient of expansion of platinum allows us to admit that there would not be a sensible difference between these two metres at the lawful temperature of 0° centigrade.

Either of these metres, then, can be replaced without hesitation by the other, as I have already done in the comparison of a standard intended for Spain.

Construction of the standard metre for the United States, and determination of its co-efficient of expansion.

This standard metre aa′ is of steel, annealed in a charcoal fire, which was extinguished as slowly as possible; was afterwards dressed by the planing machine without receiving a blow of the hammer or the touch of a file, then rubbed with emery to finish it on its four sides; finally, it was cut to the metric length at the temperature of melting ice, by means of a standard at the same temperature. These two ends were arranged, ground and polished by M. Brunner, by a method of his own devising.

This standard metre of the United States is at the same time "à bout" (cut to length) and "à trait," (the standard length being between the extreme division lines,) a small steel prism d d′ is screwed upon each end to make the joint visible; between the prism and the end a gold plate of the thickness of a hundredth of a millimetre is inserted.

Placed upon a thicker bronze bar, b b′, similar to that of the comparator, it forms with the co-operation of this a Borda thermometer, both are united at one of their extremities a′, by a conical pin c′, like the two bars of the comparator; the axis of this conical pin is 23 millimetres from the extremity of the metre. The two extremities a are free in their motions of expansion, each bears a divided scale; the scale on the bronze bar is engraved on a silver plate f′ screwed against this bar, its divisions are fourths of a millimetre. The vernier e is fixed on the steel bar ; it is composed of a silver plate set into the face of the bar, it gives 25ths of the division opposite, that is hundredths of millimetres.

The distance from the 0 of this vernier to the axis c' is 954 millimetres. Opposite to the divided plate of the bronze bar, on the other side at g, is a brass plate of the same dimensions ; these two plates serve as guides for the free end of the steel metre.

A vernier e', and a division on silver f', as well as a guide g of brass similar to the preceeding is shown at the fixed end a'. This second division will serve in case the axis should not be in exact contact, which would be immediately made known by the change of coincidence between the two divided scales placed on this extremity.

Difference of expansion between the two bars.

This system of bars was placed in melting ice, and there kept for two hours ; after which time, the coincidences being constant, the measures were proceeded with.

The vernier of the fixed end indicated........................... 4.88mm.
That of the free end... 4.42mm.

Two more hours immersion, in boiling water, gave the following numbers :

For the vernier of the fixed end................................... 4.88mm.
For that of the free end.. 3.80mm.

Difference between the free ends 4.42mm. - 3.80mm. = 0.62mm.

The difference of expansion from 0° to 100° between the two metals, steel and bronze, which constitute the two metres experimented on, is then 0.62mm. for 100° and for a length of 954mm. the distance from the axis of the fixed point to the 0 of the vernier placed at the free end.

Absolute expansion of the two bars.

To determine the absolute expansion of each of these two bars, I have been obliged to devise a special process which effectually admits the application of a constant length to each of the bars, for each degree of temperature from 0° to 100°.

The instrument, by means of which a constant length is inscribed on the bar, is a beam compass with very solid points, constantly kept in a trough of melting ice.

The compass consists of a bar of steel aa', 1.20m. long, 5 centimetres wide, and 8 millimetres thick ; it has two dry points, screwed on at the distance of a metre from each other. These points are of tempered steel and very solid their extremities are turned and sharpened with great care, and are of a conical form, the opposite sides of the cone making with each other an angle of about 60°. The distance between the two points is $\frac{1}{200}$ of a millimetre less than the metre in melting ice.

The trough in which this compass is placed is of a triangular form; one of the angles constitutes the bottom of it, in which are arranged two openings to allow passage for the points of the compass, so that these points may project about 15 millimetres. Whilst the compass is immersed in melting ice, the bar under trial is likewise placed in the same substance, the trough, which is intended to receive the bar, is furnished with a cast iron support, well straightened in its whole length, intended to receive lengthways the bar under trial. After remaining two hours in the trough, the bar has reached a temperature that may be considered uniform and invariable.

After this, to mark the bar with the compass, the extremities are lightly uncovered, then the trough containing the compass is carried there, so that the points may not be more than a millimetre from the surface of the bar ; then resting lightly one of the points on it, an arc of a circle of a millimetre or two in length is described with the other ; the point is stopped at the extremity of this arc, and another arc is then traced with the correspondent point at the other extremity of the bar.

After this first pointing, the compass is put aside, the bar with its support is taken away, and placed in a metal trough filled with distilled water, the temperature of which is raised to the boiling point by means of alcohol lamps. At the end of two hours of ebullition the second pointing is commenced ; this operation resembles the first, nevertheless precaution must be taken to place the first point within the trace made in the first pointing, and about half a millimetree from this trace ; then the other point will also fall within other mark and very near to it. The two last marks will then be found situated between the two first and they will consist equally of two arcs of circles; this precaution was omitted in the present case because the first point was carried outside ; it is for this reason that this portion must be subtracted from the other.

Four lines will thus be obtained belonging two and two to the temperature from 0° to 100° C.

When the pointing is finished, the distance between the arcs of the circles obtained at the two extreme temperatures is measured by the aid of the micrometer and the microscope 0 of the comparator.

The distance between the two lines of the free end of the bronze bar has thus been found to be 2.2459mm., which corresponds to the interval of the arcs of the fixed end 0.5429mm.; this last distance is negative.

The absolute expansion of the bronze bar is then 2.2459mm. — 0.5429mm. = 1.7030mm.

The distance measured by the micrometer between the two lines of the free end of the steel bar = 1.0680mm.; that of the fixed end = 0.5578mm., which is negative ; the absolute expansion of the steel metre is then from 0° to 100° = 1.6080mm. — 0.5578mm. = 1.0502mm.

3d. *Comparison between the differential expansion and the absolute expansion of the two bars.*

These two kinds of experiments took place simultaneously.

The expansion of the bronze having been.................. 1.7030mm.
That of the steel metre... 1.0502 "

We have for 1 metre, the difference = ... 0.6528mm.

Which for 0.954m., the distance of the vernier, gives 0.6228.
This quantity is confirmed by the reading 0.62 given in the first place, a reading made, as we know, to a hundredth of a millimetre.

From the preceding data it is easy to establish the co-efficient of correction for any temperature, by means of reading the two divisions which are traced on the extremity of the steel metre.

Let c represent the variation or actual difference with the metre at $0°$, l the difference the two verniers at $t°$ for the temperature c, l' the difference between the two verniers at $0°$ for the exact metre, then we shall have, $c = (l - l') \times \dfrac{1.7030}{0.6228}$.

For example, in the case of water boiling at $100°$:

At $0°$ $\begin{cases} \text{The fixed vernier} & 4.88 \text{ mm.} \\ \text{The free vernier} & 4.42 \\ \hline l' = & 0.46 \end{cases}$ At $100°$ $\begin{cases} \text{The fixed vernier} & 4.88 \text{ mm.} \\ \text{The free vernier} & 3.80 \\ \hline l = & 1.08 \end{cases}$

We then have $c = (1.08 - 0.46) \times \dfrac{1.70}{0.62} = \dfrac{0.62 \times 1.70}{0.62} =$ 1.70mm., and the metre is found 1.70mm. longer at $1°$ than at $0°$.

If the temperature of the apparatus is desired to be found, we shall have $t = \dfrac{l - l'}{0.0062}$.

If in any experiment the coincidence at the fixed end, under the number 4.88 for example, did not take place, the centre having become loosened, it will be sufficient to place the new indication in the first place in the two values l and l', or rather, to add its difference from 4.88 to $l' = 0.46$ — if the new number is smaller than 4.88, or to diminish in the contrary case.

Thus constructed, on the principal of the Borda thermometer, this metre offers the advantage of being easily reduced to $0°$, by the reading of the vernier, or to give the quantity to add to the absolute metre in order to have a standard measure at any temperature. By moving the verniers it is easily ascertained if the temperature is fixed. Finally, the standard is correct as a metre in its whole length, or between the extreme division lines.

4th. Comparison between the steel metre and the standard of the Conservatory of Arts and Trades.

The comparison was made in melting ice, whilst determining the preceeding expansion on the comparator, likewise in ice. When all the levers were invariable, the reading of the micrometric screw gave:

For the platinum standard.................................... 0.5219mm.
For the standard of steel...................................... 0.4993 "

The steel metre is then too short by........................ 0.0226 "

Its legal value, then, at the temperature of melting ice, is:
1m. — 0.0000226mm. = 0.9999774m.

§ *Comparison of the brass metre graduated by Gambey.*

This metre was compared at the same time as the former, its length at 0° is 1. 0002992m.

Its co-efficient of expansion, which has been determined by Gambey, is marked on it. I have not, therefore, verified it.

Brass graduated metre (for the bureaus of verification.)

This metre has been stamped in the bureau of verification; it possesses, therefore, the exactness required by law.

The wooden metre is likewise stamped and equally exact.

CHAPTER II.

COMPARISON OF WEIGHTS.

§ 1. *Comparison of the standard platinum kilogramme of the archives of State with the standard kilogramme of commerce, also of platinum deposited in the Conservatory of Arts and Trades.*

These two weights were compared in the open air on a balance sensitive to half a milligramme; they should consequently be corrected for the difference of weight of the volume of air which they displace at the moment of weighing.

The volume of these two kilogrammes has been determined by means of an instrument constructed expressly by Gambey, which is exact to a hundredth of a millimetre nearly, and serves to determine the height and diameter of these cylinders. The result of the operation has proved that their height is nearly equal to their diameter. The mean taken from a large number of measurements has given for the volume of the standard of the archives 48.6973 centimetre cubes, and of the standard of the conservatory 52.3220 cubic centimetres. Weight of 1 litre or 1,000 cubic centimetres of air.

The barometer marked 754.00$mm.$ at 14°.9; whence $H_0 =$ 752.17mm. The hygrometer for condensation gave the dew-point at 9°.7; whence $f = 9.305mm.$ for the elastic force of the vapor contained in the air.

The temperature of the air was 15°.7

Pressure of dry air $= 752.17 - 9.305 = 742.865,$ } At the temperature of 9°.7.
Pressure of the vapor in the air $= 9.305,$

One litre of dry air at 0°, under normal pressure of 760$mm.$, weighs 1.2991 *gms.*

One litre of vapor of water at 0°, under normal pressnre, will weigh 0.80559.*

One litre of dry air under 742.865$mm.$, and at 9°.7, weighs then $\frac{742.865 \times 1.2991}{760 \times (1 + 0.003666) \times 9.7} = 1.2248gms.$; and one litre of vapor under 9.305$mm.$, and at 9°.7, weighs $\frac{9.305 \times 0.80559}{760 \times (1 + 0.003666) \times 9.7} = 0.0095gm.$;

---

* This weight of the vapor of water at 0°, under the pressure of 760$mm.$, is deducted from its weight at 100°, under the same pressure, which is 0.58948gms.; corrected afterwards for its contraction from 100° to 0° by the coefficient of expansion of the air, which for $\frac{0}{1}$ is 0.00366.

then one litre of damp air under 752.170 mm., and at 9°.7, weighs 1.2343 gramme.

The weighing having been made at 15°.7 the preceding weight is too great by a quantity corresponding to the increase of volume which this weight of air experienced in passing from 9°.7 to 15°.7. We shall then have the weight of one litre of damp air, at a temperature of $15°.7 = \frac{1.2343}{1 + 0.003666 \times (15.7 - 9.7)} = 1.2077 gm.$; one litre, or 1,000 centimetres cubes, weighing $1.2077 gm$. One centimetre cube weighs 0.0012077.

Weight of the volume of displaced air.—P, the standard of the archives, displacing $48.6973 cms.$ of air, (cubic centimetres,) the correction becomes:

$$48.6973 cms. \times 0.0012077 gm. = 0.05881 gm.$$

P', the standard of the conservatory, displacing 52.3220 cms. of air, (cubic centimetres,) the correction becomes:

$$52.3220 cms. \times 0.0012077 gm. = 0.063891 gm.$$

The mean of the weighings gives for the equilibrium in the air:

$$P' + 0.001 gms. = P.$$

If the weights thus balanced in the air were balanced in a vacuum, the equilibrium would be destroyed; the body which has the most volume, experiencing the greatest loss in the air, would gain most in weight in passing from the air into a vacuum; it would then make the balance cant by a weight equal to the difference of the weight of the air previously displaced by each of them.

Subtracting, therefore, from each of these weights its loss in the air to restore the equilibrium in a vacuum, which is equivalent to taking away from the most voluminous the difference of the two losses, we shall have for equilibrium in a vacuum:

$$P' + 0.001 gm. - 0.06319 gm. = P - 0.05881, \text{ whence}$$
$$P' = P - 0.05881 gm. - 0.001 gm. + 0.06319 gm. = P + 0.00338 gm.,$$

or P = 1,000 gms.

$$P' = 1,000 gms. + 0.00338 gm. = 1,000.00338 gms.$$

§ 2. *Comparison of the standard platinum kilogramme of commerce, with the kilogramme of brass, gilt, for the United States.*

All the operations of weighing were performed with the two balances presented to France by the government of the United States.

Both these two balances are sensitive to the 0.0005 gramme; the smaller one being loaded with one kilogramme and the larger with ten kilogrammes.

To preserve this sensibility, and to avoid the alterations they might experience by a change of weight, it is necessary to leave the scales suspended with their loads, then to steady them underneath by means of the little spring which is found there for this purpose, and at the same time hold their basins and their weights firmly so as to avoid any variation while being suspended; not until then are the weights changed, the spring loosened and the balance left at perfect liberty.

These minute precautions are indispensable, else there is danger of committing errors of from 20 to 30 milligrammes in the larger and from 5 to 6 in the smaller balance.

The preceding platinum weights P′ was used in the comparison of the gilt, brass, kilogramme made by Gambey, for international exchanges, amongst which is comprised No. 6, intended for the United States.

The volume of this No. 6 is deducted from the volume of water which it displaces at the temperature of 12°.

(NOTE.—It is quite certain that the knob, which is tightly screwed on, did not allow the water to penetrate into the interior, not even into the joint.)

The weight of water displaced at $12° = 123.945 gms.$; the volume of this brass kilogramme is then, according to the table of Despretz, $\frac{123.945}{0.999634} = 123.9903 ce.$

These corrections, rendered indispensable by the loss of weight in the air, were applied with the assistance of the following observations made during the weighing.

The barometer was at $760.60 mm.$ at $13°.1$, whence $H_o = 758.99 mm.$; the hygrometer at the dew point at $4°.5$ C: then $f = 6.74$; the pressure of the dry air $= 758.99 mm. - 6.74 mm. = 752.25 mm.$, the temperature of the air $13°.1$ C, whence one litre of dry air, under $752.25 mm.$ and at $4°.5$, weighs $\frac{752.25 \times 1.2991}{760 \times (1 + 0.003666) \times 4.5} = 1.2691$, and one litre of vapor, under $6.74 mm.$ and at $4°.5$, weighs $\frac{6.74 \times 0.80559}{760 \times (1 + 0.003666) \times 4.5} = 0.0070.$ One litre of vapor, under $758.99 mm.$, at $4°.5$, weighs $1.2761.$

The weighing having been made at $13°.1$, the preceding weight is too great by a quantity corresponding to the surplus of expansion which the volume of air experiences in passing from $4°.5$ to $13°.1$, or for $8°.6$.

We have then for the weight of one litre at $13°.1$, $\frac{1.2761}{(1 + 0.00366) \times 8.6}$ $= 1.2492 gm.$, and, consequently, 1ce. of air weighs $0.0012492 gm.$ The standard P′ loses, therefore, of its weight, $52.3220 \times 0.0012492 = 0.06536 gm.$, and the brass kilogramme No. 6, $123.9903 \times 0.0012492 = 0.15489 gm.$ The comparison of these two kilogrammes having been made in air, it is necessary, in order to bring it back to what it would be in a vacuum, to subtract from each the loss experienced by it in the air. The double weighings of No. 6 have given the following results:

No. $6 + 0.1320 gm. = $ P′ $+ 0.0420$; introducing the correction in returning to the vacuum we have:

No. $6 + 0.1320 gm. - 0.15489 gm. = $ P′ $+ 0.0420 gm. - 0.06536 gm.$; from whence:

No. $6 = $ P′ $+ 0.0420 - 0.06536 gm. - 0.1320 gm. + 0.15489 gm. = $ P′ $0.00047.$

Replacing P′ by its value, which is 1000.00338, we have No. $6 = 1000.00338 gm. - 0.00047 gm. = 1000.00291 gm.$

All the kilogrammes which have been used for the comparison were thus verified, and they gave in a vacuum the following results, which have, besides, been the object of a direct verification:

	Grammes.
No. 1	1000.00291
No. 2	1000.00690
No. 3	1000.00890
No. 4	1000.00590
No. 5	1000.00990
No. 6	1000.00291

§ 3. *Direct comparison, in the vacuum of the air-pump, between the standard kilogramme of commerce and the gilt brass kilogramme, No. 1, of the preceding series.*

This comparison has been heretofore considered impracticable; at all events it has not been undertaken. The method which I have adopted perfectly accomplishes the object; it had not been fully determined upon at the time I compared the kilogramme intended for the United States, but that kilogramme is the same as No. 1, which here serves as a standard. This method is very simple in practice, and free from the effects of the temperature, or of pressure, or dampness, as well as from the variations produced by the differences of volume or of density.

Two small glass, receivers, fig. 1, a. a', having exactly the capacity necessary to contain a brass kilogramme, k, equal in volume (0.2 litre) and in weight, are provided at their top with a small cock; each receiver is placed on a disk of ground glass, which serves as a moveable plate. The cementing between the receiver and the disk is effected by a process of Monsieur Poinsot, chemist to the Conservatory of Arts and Trades; it consists in covering the edge of the receivers with a band of vulcanized India rubber, from which the excess of sulphur has been removed by immersing it in a solution of potash; this band is stretched round the edge of the receiver, and so applied to the glass plate. The vacuum is perfectly preserved if the band is sufficiently thin.

The standard kilogramme p. being placed under one of the receivers, and a kilogramme serving for counterpoise having been placed under the other, a vacuum is made in both receivers at the same time, and dry hydrogen is introduced before completing the vacuum. After the hydrogen has been expelled by the air-pump, the remaining pressure is stopped at two millimetres; the weight of hydrogen left in each receiver under this pressure is inappreciable in the balance; moreover, the weight to be considered is but the difference of the weights of the volumes displaced, a weight inferior to the preceding, which is itself only $\dfrac{0.2 \text{ lit.} \times 0.0898 \text{ gm.} \times 3 \text{ mm.}}{760 \text{ mm.}} = 0.00047$, or nearly five-hundredths of a milligramme. After the air was exhausted from the two receivers, each was placed upon a dish of the balance.

After restoring the equilibrium very exactly with some small weights, I withdrew the bell containing the platinum standard, and replaced the latter by the kilogramme No. 1. I then produced the vacuum as before, and above all I reduced it to the same degree of interior pressure.

Again, replacing the receiver in this condition on the dish, I obtained an equilibrium by increasing by half a milligramme the weight in the other dish.

This last result agrees extremely well with what was obtained by the ordinary corrections for reducing the weighings in the open air to those in a vacuum.

	Kil. Gr.
In this way the weight of the standard was found... =	1000.00338
The weight of the kilogramme No. 1..................... =	1000.00291
Difference between these weights in air.............. =	0.00047
And, finally, difference between these weights in a vacuum... =	0.0005

This identity of the two differences confirms the first operations as well as the process of verification above described.

§. 4 *Comparison of the standard weights of the collection intended for the United States, with the preceding kilogrammes taken as standards.*

I have supposed that all the brass weights were of the same density as the preceding, and as in this case they will balance equally in a vacuum and in the open air, their volume of air displaced being the same, there has not been applied to these weights the loss they experience in the air; their value is therefore what they have in a vacuum.

The series of the standard weights is composed of the following pieces:

```
A  weight of 20 kilogrammes ............ or 20,000   grammes.
   "       "  10      "         ............    10,000      "
   "       "   5      "         ............     5,000      "
2d "       "   2      "         ............     2,000      "
1st "      "   2      "         ............     2,000      "
2d "       "   1      "         ............     1,000      "
1st "      "   1      "         ............     1,000      "
A  weight of  5 hectogrammes............       500  ⎫
   "       "  2      "         ............      200  |
   "       "  1      "         ............      100  |
   "       "  1      "         ............      100  |
   "       "  5 decagrammes............          50  |
   "       "  2      "         ............      20  ⎬ 1,000 gms.
   "       "  1      "         ............      10  |
   "       "  1      "         ............      10  |
   "       "  5 grammes...................        5  |
   "       "  2      "         ............       2  |
   "       "  2      "         ............       2  |
   "       "  1      "         ............       1  ⎭
```

Fractions of the gramme.

A weight of	5 decigrammes	0.5	
" "	2 "	0.2	
" "	1 "	0.1	
" "	1 "	0.1	
" "	5 centigrammes	0.05	
" "	2 "	0.02	
" "	1 "	0.01	} 1 gr.
" "	1 "	0.01	
" "	5 milligrammes	0.005	
" "	2 "	0.002	
" "	1 "	0.001	
" "	1 "	0.001	
" "	1 "	0.001	

We commenced by verifying each of the weights of 1 kilogramme, then the weight of the 2 kilogrammes, then that of 5 kilogrammes, 10 kilogrammes, and of 20 kilogrammes; the multiples of the gramme from 1 gramme to 5 hectogrammes, making together 1,000 grammes, have been compared with the 1 kilogramme only. The subdivisions of the grammes, forming together 1 gramme, have been compared with the 1 gramme.

The double weighings have given the following gross results:

No. 1 of the 1 kilogramme = No. 6 + 0.0040 g. = 1,000.0029 g. + 0.0040 g. = 1000.0069 grammes.
No. 2 of the 1 kilogramme = No. 6 + 0.0020 g. = 1000.0029 g. + 0.0020 g. = 1000.0049 grammes.
No. 1 of the 2 kilogrammes = No. 6 + No. 1 — 0.076 g. = 2000.0058 g. — 0.076 g. = 1999.9298 grammes.
No 2 of the 2 kilogrammes = No. 6 + No. 1 — 0.064 g. = 2000.0058 g. — 0.064 g. = 1999;9418 grammes.
5 kilogrammes = No. 2 + No. 3 + No. 4 + No. 5 + No. 6 — 0.020 g. = 5000.0145 grammes.
10 kilogrammes = No. 2 + No. 3 + No. 4 + No. 5 + No. 6 + 5000.0145 g. — 0.088 = 9999.9610 grammes.
20 kilogrammes = 2d. 1 k. + 2 k. + 2 k. + 5 k. + 10 k. preceding + 0.040 g. = 19999.848 g. + 0.040 g. = 19999.888 grammes.
The weight of 5 h., 2 h., 1 h., 1 h., 5 d., 2 d., 1 d., 1 d., 5 g., 2 g., 1 g., 1 g,, = No 6 + 0.002 g. = 1000.0049 grammes.
The nest kilogramme of 1 k. = No. 6 + 0.002 = 1000.0049 gr.

After being verified separately, the fractions of the gramme of the large series were again verified by a gramme adjusted by Fortin; these small weights added together ought to make exactly a gramme; their value was found equal to 1.00020 grammes on a gramme balance, by Devrine, made at the commencement of this century, and in which a division of 1 millimetre in size marks $\frac{1}{25}$ of a milligramme. In such a good condition for weighing, I was enabled to read with the naked eye the fourths of millimetres, or the division which corresponds to hundredths of a milligramme; this balance is provided with a spring similar to those of the United States.

Ex. Doc. 27——11

§ . *Iron weights.*

The weights of cast iron having been subjected by the inspectors to the ordinary verification of weights, and their correctness being within the limits prescribed by law, have not undergone a second verification.

CHAPTER III.

COMPARISON OF THE MEASURES OF CAPACITY.

§ 1. *Definition and correction.*

The unit of the measures of capacity is the litre; it is in relation to the metre a cubic decimetre; for the weight of a cubic decimetre of distilled water, taken at its maximum density, is, at the temperature of 4° cent., and in a vacuum, exactly a kilogramme, or 1,000 grammes.

Under these conditions of legal connexion between the weight of water and its volume, the capacity of a vessel is determined by using the weight of distilled water which this vessel contains. But as the material of which the measures of capacity are made expands under the influence of heat, the legal condition is that their standard capacity shall be exact at the temperature of melting ice, or at 0° centigrade.

As the verifications are not practicable with these conditions of 0° for the vessel, and 4° for the water it contains, and for the whole in a vacuum, we are obliged, as regards the weight, to use calculation to assimilate the practical to the legal conditions.

For the corrections relative to the temperature of water, the loss of weight in the air, the humid state of the latter, and the expansion of the vessels, we consult, in the practice of verification, a table of corrections arranged, by an order of government, by Monsieur Coriolis, member of the institute.

This table supposes the barometrical pressure to be constant, and at the normal height of 760 millimetres at 0° of temperature; the hygrometrical state of the air at 72° of Saussure, which corresponds to the 0.5 of the maximum tension of the vapor contained in the air for the temperature of the observation, the cubic expansion of the brass of which the measures, weights, and counterpois are constructed, are supposed $= 3 \times 0.00002108 = 0.00006324$ for 1° centigrade; finally, for the expansion of water, we have admitted that given by Hälström, for each degree of temperature between 0° and 30° centigrade.

In the first column of this table is found the temperature of water; in the second, the weight of one litre of water at 10°; and in the third, the corresponding loss of weight which should be placed on the dish, if we have previously counterbalanced 1 kilogramme, in order to replace it by water.

WEIGHTS AND MEASURES.

Table of corrections for one litre.

Degrees centigrade.	Weight of one litre of water.	Loss of one kilogramme of water.	Degrees centigrade.	Weight of one litre of water.	Loss of one kilogramme of water.
		Grammes.			*Grammes.*
0	998.754	1.246	16	999.067	0.933
1	998.870	1.130	17	998.984	1.016
2	998.971	1.029	18	998.889	1.111
3	999.057	0.943	19	998.782	1.218
4	999.132	0.868	20	998.664	1.336
5	999.195	0.805	21	998.535	1.465
6	999.245	0.755	22	998.394	1.606
7	999.283	0.717	23	998.243	1.757
8	999.307	0.693	24	998.080	1.920
9	999.320	0.680	25	997.905	2.095
10	999.320	0.680	26	997.720	2.280
11	999.308	0.692	27	997.524	2.476
12	999.285	0.715	28	997.318	2.682
13	999.249	0.751	29	997.101	2.899
14	999.200	0.800	30	996.880	3.120
15	999.139	0.861			

This table secures an exactness of less than 5 milligrammes for the capacity of the litre, an exactness which is much greater than is necessary in practice, and which is even sufficient for theoretical uses. It has been employed in all the following verifications of capacity:

M. Parent, balance maker to the administration, employs a very sure method for adjusting the measures of capacity. He takes care during their construction to have them a few fractions of a cubic centimetre smaller than the legal capacity which is shown by the overflowing of the water contained in a stamped measure. The final adjustment is made by the weight of the water the vessel contains, and the capacity being too small, the weight of water will be less than that given in the preceding table. Multiplying the difference between these two weights by 8°.5, the approximate density of brass, we shall have the weight of the brass to be taken off the interior of the vessel, which occupies the place of the lacking quantity of water. As this brass is taken away by the scraper, it is sufficient to weigh in scrapings about seven times the weight of the difference, because emery paper, or any other polishing, will gradually make up 8°.5, and will allow a second correction.

This trial, which is but a determination of capacity, is similar to the one that will be used for the litre.

§ 2. *Verification of the capacity of the standard litre.*

The standard brass litre made by Gambey, covered with a disk of ground glass, surmounted by the standard kilogramme No. 6 and the additional weight 0.792 gms. placed in one of the dishes, exactly balance the other dish loaded with a similar litre, covered by its disk and with one kilogramme.

Unloading then the first dish, and replacing the kilogramme No. 6 by distilled water poured into the litre, taking care to remove by means of a feather the bubbles of air adhering to the inner sides of this measure, the temperature of this water showing $12°.2$ being taken, slide the glass disk to the edge of the vessel, cautiously removing by means of a small pipe, the surplus water, so as not to spill it on the outside, avoiding always the heating by the hands; after which, place on its dish the measure thus prepared. In accordance with the preceding table, the cubic decimetre or litre of water in brass weighs, at $12°.2$, only 999.2778 gms., or rather its loss is 0.7222 gms.; after having added this loss to complete one kilogramme (weight of the litre of water at $4°$) it was found necessary to add 0.863 gms. to complete the equilibrium, which indicates that the capacity of this measure is too small.

To determine this capacity, we have the following quantities, which have counterbalanced each other:

1000.00291 *gms.* $+$ 0.792 $=$ water $+$ 0.7222 $+$ 0.863, whence we obtain for the weight of the water at $4°$ contained in this measure, water $+$ 0.7222 $=$ 1000.00291 $+$ 0.792 $-$ 0.863 $=$ 999.93191 *gms.*

1,000 grammes of water at $4°$ are equal to one litre, and 999.93191 *gr.* are equal to 0.99993191 litre.

This capacity could again be determined by means of the following experimental data, in which the co-efficient of expansion of the vessel is wanting:

The volume of the kilogramme No. 6 $=$ 123.993 cc. the litre of water, at $12°.2$, weighs according to Hälström, 999.6989 *gms.*, and according to Despretz 999.594 *gms.*

The barometer at $12°.2 = 762.35$ *mm.* and at $0°$, 760.840 *mm.*

The hygrometer for condensation gives the dew-point at $5°.50$, whence f, the elastic force of vapor $= 7.171$ *mm*; finally the temperature of the air $= 12°.2$.

I yet prefer the preceding capacity to that which could be found by calculation by means of the above given quantities; first it will differ from it very little; besides, for comparisons, it is more regular to employ this method, which is used by the government to preserve uniformity.

§ 3. *Verification of the series of brass standards.*

This series is composed of eleven measures of capacity. They have undergone the same process as the litre. To weigh the water contained, I made use of the first six weights of the series of the preceding paragraphs for the multiples of the litre.

WEIGHTS AND MEASURES. 165

The double décalitre (water at 13°.5 ; correction at 15.510 *gms.*:)
Water + 15.510 $g.$ = 19999.888 — 0 = 19999.888.
20 $l.$ real value = 19.999888 $l.$

The décalitre (water at 15° ; correction 8.610 $g.$:)
Water + 8.610 $g.$ = 9999.961 $g.$ — 2.497 = 9997.464 $g.$
10 $l.$ real value 9.997464 $l.$

The half décalitre (water at 14°.5 ; correction 4.152 $g.$:)
Water + 4.152 $g.$ = 5000.145 — 0.025 = 4,999.9895
5 $l.$ real value = 4.9999895 $l.$

The double litre (water at 14°.3 ; correction 1.637 $g.$:)
Water + 1.637 = 1999.9298 — 0.412 = 1999.5178.
2 $l.$ real value = 1.9995178 $l.$

The litre (water at 14°.0 ; correction 0.800 $g.$:)
Water + 0.800 = 1000.009 — 0.299 = 999.7019 $g.$
1 $l.$ real value 0.9997019 $l.$

The half litre (water at 13°.5 ; correction 0.387 $g.$:)
Water + 0.387 = 500.000 $g.$ — 0.123 = 499.878 $l.$,
0.5 $l.$ value 0.499878 $l.$

The double décilitre (water at 13°.5 ; correction 0.155 $g.$:)
Water + 0.155 = 200.000 $g.$ — 0.135 = 199.865
0.2 $l.$ real value = 0.199865 $l.$

The décilitre (water at 13°.5 ; correction 0.078 $g.$:)
Water + 0.078 $g.$ = 100.000 — 0.042 = 99.958
01. $l.$ real value = 0.099958 $l.$

The demi-décilitre (water 13°.5 ; correction 0.039 $g.$:)
Water + 0.039 = 50.000 $g.$ — 0.001 = 49.999.
0.05 $l.$ real value = 0.49999 $l.$

The double centilitre (water at 13°.5 ; correction 0.016 $g.$:)
Water + 0.016 = 20.000 $g.$ — 0.006 = 19.994.
0.02 $l.$ real value 0.019994 $l.$

The centilitre (water at 13°.5 ; correction 0.008 $g.$:)
Water + 0.008 = 10.000 $g.$ — 0 = 10.000 $g.$
0.01 $l.$ real value = 0.010000 $l.$

If we wish to calculate these capacities directly, the following elements may be used : At the commencement of this verification we had for barometric pressure, 764.40 *mm.* at 13°.0 or H_0 = 762.79 ; hygrometer at the dew-point, 4°.5 f = 6.7 mm. ; the temperature of the air 13°.0. At the end of this verification we had : for barometric pressure 763.95 mm. at 13°.5 or H_0 = 762.34 ; hygrometer at the dew-point, 4°.5 f = 6.7 mm. ; the temperature of the air 13°.0.

It will be necessary to find the expansion of each of the measures, as well as the volume of each of the weights which have been used, knowing that the six gilt standard brass kilogrammes have all the same volume.

§ 4. *Pewter measures of capacity.*—The three series, each one of eight measures, being only the usual legal forms for liquids, have not been verified anew, because they had been stamped by the verifiers of weights and measures ; each of these series commences with the double litre and ends with the centilitre.

§ 5. *Tin measures.*—The two series of which these measures are composed are used, one with a straight handle for the sale of milk ; the other, with a curved handle, for the sale of oil ; the measures intended for the sale of table oil bear the mark M., (manger,) and those which are intended for lamp oil are marked B., (bruler.) All these measures bear the legal stamp of the verifier of weights and measures.

These two series are each composed of seven measures, beginning with the double litre, and ending with the double centilitre.

§ 6. *Wooden measures for corn, grain, &c.*—The wooden measures used for dry materials are of large dimensions and capacity. The series is composed of eleven measures, which are the hectolitre, the half hectolitre, the double décalitre, the décalitre, the half décalitre, the double litre, the litre and the half litre, the double décilitre, the décilitre, and the half décilitre. These measures have been verified and stamped by the inspector of weights and measures. Their verification is made with fine round grain, such as rape seed, or any others of regular shape. For this operation a hopper of linen cloth, bordered with iron, is used ; it is fixed against the table of the press for stamping the measures of capacity ; the valve attached below the hopper permits the regular flowing out and uniform settling up of the grain employed, either for filling the standard or for receiving that which has been thus measured by the standards, after having taken away the surplus by the aid of the striker, (a bar which serves to strike the measure.) The two wooden measures with feet, the hectolitre and the demi-hectolitre, are used to measure charcoal. The verifiers in their circuit, not being able to have with them such heavy apparatus for verification, have in their travelling case a brass rule, which, at one end, has straight notches, serving as limits to the height and to the diameter which each of these wooden measures ought to have to be of the legal admissible capacity ; for a difference of $\frac{1}{100}$ on the dimensions is tolerated considering the shrinking of the wood by drying ; but this difference should be in excess for new measures.

CHAPTER IV.

OF MONEY.

The monetary system, joined to the preceding, completes the metrical system ; it is united to it through the weight of its unit, the franc, which is five grammes. The series is as follows :

Name and value of the pieces.	Composition.		Weight.		Diameter.
	Exact.	Tolerated.	Exact.	Tolerated.	
20 francs	Gold 0.9 ⎫	⎫	6.45161	± 0.002	21 mm.
10 francs	Copper 0.1 ⎭	0.002 ⎭	3.22580	± 0.002	20
5 francs	⎫	⎫	25.	± 0.003	37
2 francs	Silver 0.9 ⎬	⎬	10.	± 0.005	27
1 franc	Copper 0.1 ⎭	0.003 ⎭	5.	± 0.005	23
5 decimes			2.5	± 0.007	18
2 decimes			1.	± 0 010	15
1 decime			10.	± 0.01	30
5 c	Pure copper 95 ⎫		5.	+ 0.01	25
	Tin 4 ⎬				
2 c	Zinc 1 ⎭		2.	+ 0.015	20
1 centime			1.	+ 0.015	15

Observations.—According to the diameter of the piece the length of the metre is found by putting edge to edge. 19 pieces of 5 f. + 11 pieces of 2 fr.; 20 pieces of 2 f. + 20 pieces of 1 fr.; 20 pieces of 5 c. + 20 pieces of 1 fr.; 29 pieces of 5 c. + 7 pieces of 10 fr., &c. The pieces of 10 f. and 2 deci. are new; the piece of 2 c. is not yet issued.

The legal value of coinable metals is as follows:

Kind.	Produce.	VALUE OF THE KILOGRAMME.			
		Of alloy at 0.9.		Of pure metal.	
		Coined.	Ingot.	At par.	By exchange.
		Francs.	*Francs.*	*Francs.*	*Francs.*
Gold	620	3,100	3,094	3,444.44	3,437.77
Silver	40	200	198	222.22	220.
Copper	1.	5.			

NOTE.—The notes of 100f., 200f., 500f., and 1,000f., issued by the bank continue this series. The piece or bank note of 50f. (intermediate element) has not yet been created.

Done at Paris, May 5, 1852.

J. C. SILBERMANN,
Conservator of the Conservatory of Arts and Trades.

Approved.

A. MORIN,
General of Artillery, Member of the Institute,
Administrator of the Conservatory of Arts and Trades.

Nomenclature of the metrical system.

The metrical system has one unit for its basis, is universal and decimal.

From the unit of length all the other units are derived.

In order that this unit might belong equally to all nations, it was taken on the actual dimensions of our globe. It is the ten millionth part of the quarter of the terrestrial meridian.*

This unit of length is called *metre;* to adapt it to the decimal calculation, the metre was subdivided into parts of ten, and those into others ten times smaller; and its multiples are by ten, and those by ten again.

The metre serves as a basis to the other units in the following manner:

The are, or the unit of superficial measure, is a square the size of which is ten metres long.

The stère, or the unit of cubature for wood, is a cubic metre.

The *litre*, or the unit for gauging vessels for dry or liquid materials, is a cube, the side of which is one-tenth of a metre.

The *gramme*, or the unit of weight, is the weight of a cube of $\frac{1}{100}$ of a metre, or one cubic centimetre of distilled water, at its maximum density, (4° c.,) weighed in a vacuum.

The *franc*, or the monetary unit, is 5 grammes of an alloy composed of 9 parts of fine silver and 1 part of pure copper, and made under guaranty.

All these units are multiplied and divided like the metre. To systematize the denomination, we have taken the names of the multiples from the Greek language, and those of the divisors from the Latin, thus: *deca* for 10, *hecto* for 100, *kilo* for 1,000, *myria* for 10,000, *deci* for 0.1, *centi* for 0.01, *milli* for 0.001. These names are written before that of the kind of unit in question; thus, we say 1 decametre for 10 metres, kilometre for thousand metres, kilogramme for thousand grammes, centimetre, centilitre, centigramme for 0.01 of metre, of litre, and of gramme.

Each of these multiples or divisors may in the calculation be taken for principal units. It is thus that the kilometre serves as unit of topographical length for railroads; the millimetre for micrometrical measures; the kilogramme for the weights of commerce, &c. Custom has adopted all these Greek and Latin names only for the

---

* The length taken, it is said, is not precise; it is further added, that it can never be so, since the meridians are not equal. Let us see, then, what is the value of this incorrectness. The unit taken equals 443.296 lines; the error, according to Delambre, would be +0.032 lines, or only 0.026 lines. M. Puissant found it a little greater. This point is not settled. As to the inequality of the two meridians, that of Peru appears, thus far, to give the largest result: it is 443.44 lines, which is the length of the provisional metre. The difference is + 0.144 lines.

These differences are of no account in commerce, for much greater are tolerated in the verification. Regarding the wants of science, they only demand the perfect preservation of the platinum standard deposited in the archives, and the possibility of comparison without alteration. This preservation is also assured by the length of the sexagesimal seconds pendulum at Paris, which is 440.5595 lines = 0.9938267 of a metre, according to Borda, at the temperature of 0°, and in a vacuum, or ˙9.993846, according to other more recent determinations.

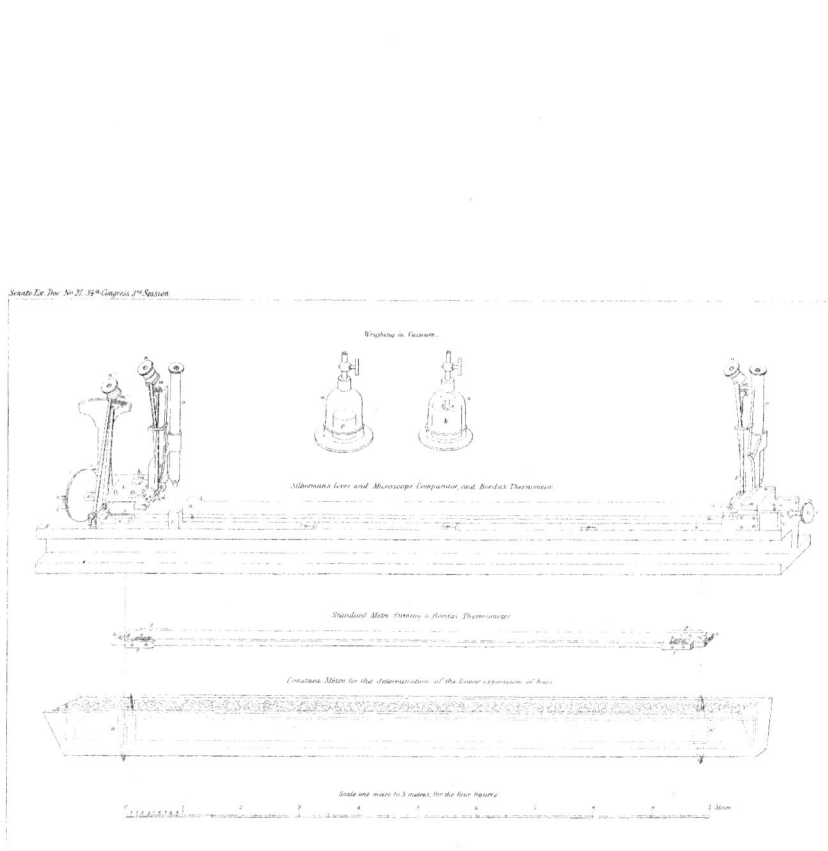

metre, the litre, and the gramme. Those which belong to the *are* are only the hectare and the centiare.
Those which relate to the stère are the decistère and the centistère. For the franc, the names of decime and centime, taken for 0.1 f., 0.01 f., are the only ones that are made use of.

APPENDIX No. 19.

Letter of W. H. Vesey, esq., United States consul at Havre, transmitting books and instruments illustrative of the French system of gauging.

AMERICAN CONSULATE,
Havre, September 22, 1853.

DEAR SIR: I have the honor to acknowledge receipt of your letter of the 16th of August, and, agreeably to your desire, have obtained a graduated gauge, in iron, the same as used by the officers of the *contributions indirectes*, of this country, for establishing the capacity or measures of casks, which I forward by this opportunity. I also forward a ribbon measure, used for the same purpose, but it is seldom or never had recourse to, except for the ascertaining the measures of casks of immense size. They are accompanied by two works, printed under the authority of this government, which, I believe, supply the fullest information on the system practiced by the official gaugers of this country, and which serve as their guide in all cases of difficulty or dispute.

The gauge is calculated to measure casks of the capacity of a tun, or four hogsheads, and the mode of using this instrument (which you will perceive is in three pieces) is, first, after placing the cask bung up, and inserting the instrument in an oblique direction to the lower part of the right hand end, then by taking the number on the gauge, at the centre of the *bunghole* in a line with the inner part of the stave, you will ascertain the number of *litres* the cask is capable of containing. If in adopting the same method on the other end of the cask a different number should be found, the two must be added together and the *mean* taken as the measurement.

There are two sides of the gauge graduated: that having the greater number of scores or lines, shows the quantity in *litres*, indicating by the number 1, (which can only apply to very small casks,) that its contents are 10 *litres;* the second line indicates 20, and every succeeding line the additional quantity of 10 litres, up to 100, which indicates 1,000 litres. The *fractional parts between the two lines* are computed as accurately as possible by the eye.

The other marked side of the gauge is used for the purpose of ascertaining the extent of leakage, but as it would be impossible to exemplify the manner of arriving at this, unless a *cask* could accompany this note, I beg to refer you to page 124 of the accompanying "Manual" for fuller information.

For the cost of the instrument and books now transmitted, as well as a trifling gratuity to the person who procured them for me, I shall take the liberty to draw upon you in a few days.

I have the honor to be, &c.,

W. H. VESEY.

A. D. Bache, Esq.,
   Superintendent Weights and Measures.

APPENDIX No. 20.

Letter of D. K. McRae, esq., consul at Paris, transmitting books, papers, and instruments in relation to the French system of gauging.

United States Consulate,
Paris, September 26, 1853.

Dear Sir: I had the honor, some time since, to receive your favor of the 16th August last, and immediately set about to supply myself with the means of fulfilling your requests.

I have this day forwarded by the Humboldt, which sails on the 30th, three volumes of the "Annales des Contributions indirectes et des Octrois," one "Manuel Alphabetique," one "Municipale Revue et Gazette réunis," two volumes "Manuel de l'Employé de l'Octroi," a "Table of Directions," a "Note Instructive, Directions Generales des Douanes," with three reports.

These are all packed in a box to your address, with two different instruments which are used here. You will find in the small tin boxes an instrument which is very delicate, and I have been requested to ask you to open them with great care; this I have made a memorandum of on the box.

I am very much indebted to Mons. Vattemare for efficient aid in procuring these things, and through his instrumentality the cost of all the articles does not exceed forty francs, which you can remit me through the State Department, on which I will draw at the end of six months, in settlement of accounts.

I am but little versed in mechanics of any kind, and therefore do not know if I have been able to render you a service, but I shall be gratified if I have done so. I shall be further pleased if, when your report is made, you will place it in my power to reciprocate a kindness of Mons. Vattemare, who is engaged in his system of international exchange, and is always happy to contribute and receive acts of courtesy between the United States and France.

I enclose, with this—

Letter of the Prefect of the Seine.
Letter of Mons. Vattemare.
Statement of instruments used in France.

The bill for the instruments Mons. Vattemare has not handed me, but he informs me it is 25 francs.

I have the honor to be, sir, very respectfully, yours,

D. K. McRAE,
United States Consul.

APPENDIX No. 20. (1.)

Letter from M. Alex. Vattemare, agent of international exchanges, to D. K. McRae, esq., consul at Paris, in relation to the French system of gauging.

PARIS, *September* 7, 1853.

MY DEAR SIR: In reply to your honored letter of the 2d instant, I have the pleasure to communicate to you the result of my inquiries relative to the method used and instruments required by the official gaugers in France, viz:

The custom-house.
Indirect contributions.
The city tolls.

The best works, and in fact the only ones, used by the officers of the above bureaus (although not officially acknowledged) for gauging and weighing, are:

1. D'Agar's Manuel des droits réunies, 1 vol. 8vo., Paris, 1813.
2. Alonard —— —— Contributions indirectes, 1 vol.
3. Girard Manuel des Contributions et de l'octroi, 1 vol.
4. Bonnet, Manuel de l'employé de l'octroi, 2 vols. 8vo., 1852.
5. Doursther's Dictionaire universel des poids et mesures, 1 vol. 8vo., Bruxelles, 1840.
6. Dareste Annales des Contributions indirectes, 3 vols. 8vo., Paris, 1836, 1840, 1844.
7. Note instructive sur la gauge á ruban fabriqué d'aprés le noveau systéme metrique, Paris, 1807.
8. Circulaire *du* 29 *Aout*, 1853, instructions sur l'emploi de l'alambre partatif adopté pour la verification des vins.

Instruments.

1. Gauge, in parts.
2. Gauge hooks.
3. Gauge ribbon.
4. Areometer.
5. A portable alembic for the verification of wines, (just adopted.)

Of the books, I have already procured D'Agar's Manuel, Dareste's Annales, Note Instructive, the Circulaire de 29 Aout, 1853, and Bonnet's Manuel de l'employé de l'octroi. I have added to these a copy of No. 80 of the *Gazette Municipale*, of August 16, 1851, containing a very interesting article on (dépotoir) gauging of vessels, by Mr. Lair, conservator of the entrepôt (magazine) of liquids.

I found every officer of the above mentioned bureaus most readily disposed to give me every possible information; it is from them I learned the titles of the books and names of the instruments used by them. But as neither of the books, &c., are official except the note and circular, I could not, without the authorization of the chief clerk, just now out of town, obtain these books, and was obliged to buy Bonnet's Manuel, althongh it is against my rule to procure anything except by way of exchange; but considering the nature of the object, the proposed aim, and my desire of being agreeable to you and Professor Bache, I have done this with pleasure. Yet you will remark that the system of international exchange has been taken into consideration, for the booksellers as well as the instrument makers have, without my asking it, reduced their prices more than 25 per cent. of their regular prices. The following is, as much as I have been able to ascertain, the price of the wooden gauges:

Small gauge and parts... 18 francs.
Large gauge and parts... 28 francs.
Portable alembic, for the verification of wines............... 20 francs.

As for the Girard, Alonard, and Doursther, (the two former out of print long ago, and the last published in Belgium,) I will do my best to procure them. They are said to be very valuable for the intended purpose. The four accompanying volumes are presented (the Annales des Contributions) by the Hon. M. Dupont, member of the legislative chamber and publisher of this work; the other proceeds from the Department of the Treasury.

The enclosed is the price of the iron instruments used by the officers of the custom-house, and "*contributions indirectes*" for gauging and measuring, manufactured by Mr. Meyer, Faubourg St. Antoine, No. 69, for the government. This bill is made in accordance with the deduction granted in behalf of our system.

Placing myself, my humble means and influence, at your disposal, and that (of our) of your great and noble country, whose kindness and hospitality is forever engraved on my grateful memory, I have the honor to be, my dear sir, your very humble and devoted friend and servant,

ALEXANDER VATTEMARE.

Monsieur McREA,
   United States Consul, Paris.

APPENDIX No. 20. (2)

Letter from Mons. M. F. Hausemann, Prefect of the Seine, to Mons. Alex. Vattemare, in relation to the instruments used in gauging tuns at the gates of Paris.

1*st. Division* 2, 267.—2*d. Bureau.*—*Nos. of registry of the secretaryship of the bureau* 2,267.—*Objects of the letters or resolutions.*—*Tolls.*—*Gauges in use for this service.*

PREFECTURE OF THE DEPARTMENT OF THE SEINE,
Paris, September 16, 1853.

SIR: You have requested to have placed at your disposal some models of instruments which are made use of at the barriers of Paris, by the employés of the tolls, for gauging tuns.

I recognize all the advantages which exchanges of different types can offer when the instruments are determined by the laws of the country, or, still further, when they regulate commercial conventions; but I must observe to you that the gauge of the *octroi* of Paris offers nothing of this kind. It is entirely special, and is only in use at the barriers. Commerce neither knows it nor its use; it is not to be found with any merchant of gauging or weighing instruments; and is made upon a model given by the administration.

Matters are thus, because the *octroi* does not determine the taxable quantity; the tax gatherer is obliged to declare it, and the employés verify the exactness of the declaration, but they are not qualified to give to this verification an authentic character. If the law had given to them the constitution of the quantities to submit to the customs, it would have made expert juries, and would have obliged them to employ only the measures established in virtue of the law.

The gauge in use at the barriers is only definitive as a means furnished by the administration to its employés, to approach, as nearly as possible by the inspection of casks, a knowledge of their contents. It is yet left for estimation, and cannot be considered as an instrument of precision which could be sent abroad.

Under these circumstances, sir, I find myself obliged to decline your request.

Accept, sir, the assurance of my very distinguished consideration.

M. F. HAUSEMANN,
Prefect of the Seine.

Monsieur VATTEMARE,
Rue de Clichy 56.

APPENDIX No. 20. (3.)

Price current of the instruments employed for the use of the indirect contributions of the custom-house.

Gauges in three parts, divided to the decalitre and centimetres, one	4.70
Gauges flat, with rings, 1 division	3.50
Gauges flat, with rings, 2 divisions	4.00
Gauges, square for gauging boats, double meters	35.00
Gauges or plummets to verify casks of oil	50.00
Plummets for sugar, with relative chambers	25.00
Plummets, enclosed in cane	12.00
Plummets, enclosed in bamboo	10.00
Plummets, enclosed in form of bamboo	9.00
Plumb-lines, folding with eight branches, one	.50
Plumb-lines, centesimally divided	.40
Metres divided with spare pieces, for wood	6.50

Metres in copper for gauges, for boats	2.50
Pincers to lead cooked articles, No. 1	35.00
Pincers to lead cooked articles, No. 2	50.00
Lead to strike 10 ± the thousand	10.00
Bores (assorted)	1.40

Utensils for the use of the Octroi.

Plumb-lines with grades, No. 1	1.40
Plumb-lines with grades, No. 4	
Plumb-lines, No. 6, for forage, large	4.00
Plumb-lines, for forage, small	3.75
Plumb-lines, for cotton	2.00
Plumb-lines, for glass	2.50
Plumb-lines, for small tubs	4.50
Plumb-lines bent for boats	8.00
Plumb-lines, in cross, for stone, small	5.00
Plumb-lines, in cross, for stone, large	6.00
Plumb-lines (plottes)	3.50
Quarries, large	3.50
Quarries, small	3.00
Gauges with divisions	9.00
Instruments for taking the thickness of (doms)	.75
Scissors for unpacking	1.50
Hammers, strong, with pincers	2.75
Gimlets with iron handles, large	1.25
Gimlets with iron handles, medium	1.30
Hammer with screw	2.50
Bores for casks	5.00
Bores for boats	7.00
Pincers to solder	50.00
Leads at 10 the thousand	10.00
Leads strong, 80 the 100 kilos	
Axes for splitting wood	3.00
Compass of large thickness	14.00
Compass of small thickness, tinned	9.00
Axes for (margerer) wood	14.00
Gauges for grain	2.00
Meters simple, square	3.50
Meters double, not jointed	3.50
Meters double, jointed	6.50

LOUIS MAYER,

Faubourg St. Antoine, 69.

APPENDIX No. 21.

Table showing the result of the comparisons of the following yard measures with the United States standard, at 62° Fahrenheit.

Date.	Number of yard.	Temperature.	Distance between junct'n of matrix and yard.		Comparison of scales on matrix.		Destination, or remarks.
			No. of comparisons.	Result. — Too long. + Too short	No. of comparisons.	Result. — Too long. + Too short.	
				Inch.		*Inch.*	
1849. Dec. —			3	+0.0009	3	1st foot, —0.00 2d foot, +0.0002 3d foot, +0.0007	Bureau of Ordnance and Hydrography, Navy Department.
1850.	62		5	+0.0003	5	+0.0004	
1853.	97		3	+0.0001	5	+0.0001	
Feb. —	99		3	+0.0009	3	0.00*	*Coinciding exactly with the standard.
	100		3	+0.0009	3	0.00*	For Mexico.
1856. Nov. 4	101		4	+0.0010	4	—0.0003	Iowa, November 6, 1856.
1853. Feb. —	102		3	+0.0015	3	0.000	Alexandria, Va.
	103		3	+0.0020	3	+0.0002	
May —	104		3	+0.0014	3	0.000	
1854. Dec. 18	105		3	+0.0012	3	0.000	California, December 18, 1854.
July 10	106		3	+0.0007	3	+0.0002	Tennessee, July 10, 1854.
Nov. 11	107		3	+0.0011	3	+0.0002	Wisconsin, November 11, 1854.
	108		3	+0.0019	3	0.000	For China.
1850.	113		4	+0.0004	4	+0.0003	California.
	114		3	+0.0002	3	+0.0002	
	118		4	+0.0001	3	+0.0002	France.
1853. May —	132		3	+0.0021	3	0.000	
1850.	133		6	+0.0013	6	+0.0002	
	134		3	+0.0009	3	+0.0002	California.
	135		4	+0.0011	3	+0.0002	Do.
April 2	138		3	+0.0010	3	+0.0002	Custom-house, Astoria, Oregon.
1852.	139		3	+0.0013	3	+0.0005	Kingdom of Siam.
Apr. 24	145		3	+0.0020	3	+0.0002	State of Alabama.
1852. Feb. —	146		3	+0.0023	3	+0.0004	Japan.
1851. Mar. —	150		3	+0.0010	3	+0.0002	Scottsville custom-house, Wash'n Ter'y.
Jan. —	151		4	+0.0007	4	+0.0002	Olympia, Oregon.
Mar. 24	Standard yard divided into— Feet, inches, tenths, and eighths of inch. Feet, tenths, hundredths of feet. Links, tenths and hundredths of links.						General land office in California.
"	Same as above..						General land office, Oregon.
Apr. 10	......do..						General land office of Iowa, Wisconsin, and Minnesota.
1854. Nov. 8	......do..						General land office, Washington Ter'y.
	......do..						General land office, Ter. of New Mexico.
	......do..						General land office, Territories of Kansas and Nebraska.
1855. Feb. 22	......do..						General land office, Utah Territory.

APPENDIX No. 22.

TABLE I.

Comparisons of new British standard yard, (bronze No. 11,) and of the mean yard, 27 to 63 inches on Troughton scale, with the yard on the dividing machine.

Date.	No.	Yard.	Temperature.	Microm. div.	Inches.
1856.					
May 1	1	British bronze standard	60.5	+27	0.00090
	2	......do......	60.5	+26	.00087
	3	......do......	60.5	+31	.00103
	4	......do......	60.5	+34	.00113
	5	......do......	60.5	+33	.00110
	6	......do......	60.5	+32	.00107
	Mean		60.5		.00102
	1	Troughton scale	60.5	+12	0.00040
	2	......do......	60.5	+11	.00037
	3	......do......	60.6	+10	.00033
	4	......do......	60.6	+11	.00037
	5	......do......	60.6	+12	.00040
	6	......do......	60.7	+10	.00033
	Mean		60.6		.00037
May 2	7	Troughton scale	59.5	+ 6	0.00020
	8	......do......	60.4	+ 7	.00023
	9	......do......	60.6	+ 9	.00030
	10	......do......	60.7	+ 7	.00023
	11	......do......	60.9	+ 9	.00030
	12	......do......	61.0	+ 8	.00027
	Mean		60.5		.00025
	7	British bronze standard	61.3	+29	0.00097
	8	......do......	61.4	+28	.00093
	9	......do......	61.5	+27	.00090
	10	......do......	61.5	+29	.00097
	11	......do......	61.5	+28	.00093
	12	......do......	61.5	+29	.00097
	Mean		61.4		.00094
Oct. 14	1	Troughton scale	61.5	+ 1	0.0001
	2	......do......	61.5	+ 1	.0001
	3	......do......	61.5	+ 1	.0001
	4	......do......	61.5	+ 1	.0001
	5	......do......	61.5	+ 1	.0001
	Mean		61.5		.00010
	1	British bronze standard	61.8	+ 9.5	0.00095
	2	......do......	61.8	+10.0	.00100
	3	......do......	61.8	+10.0	.00100
11 a. m.	4	......do......	61.8	+10.0	.00100
	5	......do......	61.8	+ 9.5	.00095
	6	......do......	61.8	+10.0	.00100
	7	......do......	61.8	+ 9.5	.00095
p. m.	8	......do......	60.0	+10.0	.00100
	9	......do......	60.0	+10.0	.00100
	10	......do......	60.0	+10.0	.00100
	11	......do......	60.0	+ 9.5	.00095
	Mean		61.2		0.00098

APPENDIX No. 22—Continued.

Date.	No.	Yard.	Temperature.	Microm. div.	Inches.
1856. Oct. 15	1	British bronze standard	60.8	+10.0	0.00100
	2	do.	60.8	+10.0	.00100
	3	do.	60.8	+10.0	.00100
	4	do.	60.8	+ 9.5	.00095
	5	do.	60.8	+10.0	.00100
	6	do.	60.6	+10.0	.00100
	7	do.	60.6	+10.0	.00100
	8	do.	60.7	+ 9.0	.00090
	9	do.	61.0	+10.0	.00100
	1	Troughton scale	61.0	+ 1.0	0.00010
	2	do.	61.2	+ 0.0	.00000
	3	do.	61.2	+ 1.0	.00010
	Mean		61.1		0.00007
	10	British bronze standard	61.5	+ 9.5	0.00095
	11	do.	61.5	+ 9.5	.00095
	12	do.	61.5	+ 9.5	.00095
	Mean		61.0		0.00098

NOTE.—One division of the micrometer used in the observations made in May was equal to one thirty-thousandth part of an inch; in October, one division of the micrometer was equal to one ten-thousandth part of an inch. Previous to the comparisons in October, the stops for the yard on the dividing machine had been frequently verified, and their distance found to be one ten-thousandth of an inch greater than the standard yard on the Troughton scale, as confirmed by the above comparisons. Equal weight is therefore attached to the comparisons in May and October, notwithstanding the less number of observations on the Troughton scale recorded with the latter.

TABLE II.

Comparison of United States standard commercial pound with the new British standard pound No. 5.

No.	Date.	Comparison.		No.	Date.	Comparison.	
	1856.		Gr.				Gr.
1	Nov. 14	British pound heavier	0.005	21	Nov. 15	British pound heavier	.005
2		do	.005	22	Nov. 16	do	.000
3		do	.020	23		do	.005
4		do	.020	24		do	.015
5		do	.015	25		do	.018
6		do	.010	26		do	.000
7		do	.000	27		do	.010
8		do	.010	28		do	.000
9		do	.005	29		do	.005
10		do	.015	30		do	.010
11	Nov. 15	do	.010	31		do	.010
12		do	.003	32		do	.000
13		do	.020	33		do	.010
14		do	.015	34		do	.005
15		do	.020	35		do	.000
16		do	.005	36		do	.010
17		do	.015	37		do	.000
18		do	.005	38		do	.010
19		do	.010	39		do	.010
20		do	.004	40		do	.015
						Mean	0.009

Ex. Doc. 27——12

TABLE III.

Comparison of Silbermann's kilogramme with the committee kilogramme, belonging to the American Philosophical Society.

No.	Date.	Comparison.	Gr.
	1856.		
1		Silbermann's kilogramme heavier	0.15
2		......do............do	0.14
3		......do............do	0.16
4		......do............do	0.16
5		......do............do	0.14
6		......do............do	0.16
7		......do............do	0.16
8		......do............do	0.18
9		......do............do	0.17
10		......do............do	0.17
11	November 27	......do............do	0.18
12		......do............do	0.19
13		......do............do	0.19
14		......do............do	0.16
15		......do............do	0.15
16	November 29	......do............do	0.18
17		......do............do	0.18
18		......do............do	0.18
19		......do............do	0.17
20		......do............do	0.19
21		......do............do	0.19
22		......do............do	0.18
23	December 1	......do............do	0.18
24		......do............do	0.17
25		......do............do	0.17
26		......do............do	0.17
		Mean	0.170

Probable error of one comparison $= \pm$ 0.01 gr., of mean $= \pm$ 0.002 gr.

The Silbermann kilogramme is equal to 1000.0029 grammes, or 0.045 grains heavier than the standard kilogramme.

TABLE IV.

Comparisons of platinum kilogramme, by Fortin, with committee kilogramme, belonging to the American Philosophical Society.

No.	Date.	Barometer.	Comparison.		Corrected to bar. 30 inches.
	1856.			Gr.	Gr.
1	December 1		Platinum kilogramme heavier.	1.58	1.56
2			....do............do.........	1.62	1.60
3			....do............do.........	1.62	1.60
4			....do............do.........	1.62	1.60
5			....do............do.........	1.62	1.60
6			....do............do.........	1.62	1.60
7		30.48	....do............do.........	1.62	1.60
8	December 2	30.20	....do............do.........	1.64	1.63
9			....do............do.........	1.65	1.64
10			....do............do.........	1.64	1.63
11	December 3	29.20	....do............do.........	1.59	1.62
12			....do............do.........	1.60	1.63
13			....do............do.........	1.59	1.62
14		29.40	....do............do.........	1.63	1.65
15	December 5	30.34	....do............do.........	1.64	1.63
16			....do............do.........	1.64	1.63
17			....do............do.........	1.66	1.65
18			....do............do.........	1.65	1.64
19	December 6	30.37	....do............do.........	1.67	1.65
20			....do............do.........	1.67	1.65
21			....do............do.........	1.67	1.65
22	December 7	30.55	....do............do.........	1.68	1.65
23			....do............do.........	1.69	1.66
24			....do............do.........	1.69	1.66
25	December 8	30.66	....do............do.........	1.65	1.62
26			....do............do.........	1.68	1.65
27	December 9	29.93	....do............do.........	1.63	1.63
28		29.81	....do............do.........	1.62	1.63
29	December 13	30.50	....do............do.........	1.62	1.60
30			....do............do.........	1.63	1.61
31			....do............do.........	1.62	1.61
32		30.33	....do............do.........	1.63	1.62
			Mean.....................		1.626 ± 0.004

Probable error of one comparison ± 0.02 gr., of mean ± 0.004 gr.

TABLE V.

Comparison of the length of the Mexican vara with the United States standard yard.

Number of observation.	Temperature.	Length of vara.	Reduced to 62° by difference of expansion of iron and brass.
	Fahr.	*Inches.*	*Inches.*
1	57.5	32.9703	32.9698
2	57.5	663	658
3	58.5	662	658
4	58.5	664	660
5	55.3	695	687
6	55.5	700	692
7	57.3	693	687
8	61.8	682	682
9	58.7	705	701
10	61.1	685	684
11	61.3	676	675
12	61.8	674	674
Means	58.7	32.9684	32.9680

The probable error of any single observation is ± .00106, and of the mean of all the observations ± .0003.

The comparison was made on the duodecimal side of the vara. The division lines were, however, so coarse that the edges of the divisions were taken as the points for the comparison. Assuming the length of the decimal and duodecimal sides to be the same, the length of the vara at the mean temperature of the observations 58°.7 Fahrenheit is 32.9682 inches.

APPENDIX No. 23.

Comparison of the half-bushel measures.

No. of standard.	Date.	Barometer.	Temp. of water.	Difference from standard.	Corrections for temp.	Result: — too large, + too small. Single.	Mean.	Corrected mean.	Destination.
		Inches.	*Fah.*	*Grains.*	*Grains.*	*Grains.*	*Grains.*	*Grains.*	
1	....	29.30	53.4	+ 4.7	....	—0.411	....	....	State of Maryland.
2	....	29.90	53.0	+ 2.0	....	—0.378	....	....	
3	....	30.14	51.5	— 7.4	....	+1.335	....	....	
4	....	29.62	51.9	— 6.2	....	+0.128	....	....	
5	....	29.50	51.1	—12.0	....	—6.931	....	....	
6	....	30.14	50.6	—14.4	....	—0.419	....	....	
7	....	29.50	50.0	—17.8	....	—0.771	....	....	
8	....	29.50	50.1	—15.7	....	+0.848	....	....	
9	....	30.20	52.0	— 6.2	....	—0.541	....	....	
10	....	30.20	50.6	—13.5	....	+0.381	....	....	
11	....	29.95	50.1	—16.4	....	+0.148	....	....	
12	....	29.95	49.5	—19.4	....	—0.407	....	....	
13	....	29.95	51.6	— 8.8	....	—0.644	....	....	
14	....	30.36	48.2	—24.0	....	—0.502	....	....	
15	....	30.30	49.2	—20.4	....	—0.177	....	....	
16	....	30.36	50.0	—16.7	....	+0.329	....	....	
17	....	30.07	49.0	—21.8	....	—0.739	....	....	
18	....	30.25	48.1	—23.9	....	—0.197	....	....	
19	....	30.12	47.8	—23.5	....	+0.819	....	....	
20	....	30.00	48.7	—21.8	....	+0.242	....	....	
21	....	30.15	48.0	—24.5	....	—0.592	....	....	
22	....	30.12	47.3	—26.0	....	—0.406	....	....	
23	....	30.12	47.3	—25.7	....	—0.106	....	....	
24	....	29.54	48.9	—20.8	....	+0.588	....	....	
25	....	29.60	48.4	—22.5	....	+0.434	....	....	
26	....	29.60	48.4	—22.0	....	....	+0.934	....	
27	....	29.60	48.4	—22.6	....	....	+0.334	....	
28	....	29.59	48.9	—21.5	....	....	—0.112	....	
29	....	29.95	47.0	—26.5	....	....	—0.087	....	
30	....	29.84	49.5	—18.5	....	....	+0.493	....	
		29.84	49.2	—20.8	....	—0.557			
		29.68	47.7	—25.0	....	—0.431	} —0.377	....	Great Britain.
		29.90	47.5	—25.0	....	+0.070			
	....	30.14	47.7	—25.2	....	—0.591			
	1844.								
31	Mar. 19	30.24	50.2	—16.5	—16.06	—0.44	....	....	
	April 1	30.60	48.0	—23.3	—23.90	+0.60	+0.08	*—0.40	
32	Mar. 19	30.24	50.1	—16.3	—16.54	+0.24	....	....	
	April 1	30.60	50.6	—14.2	—13.98	—0.22	+0.01	—0.47	California.
33	Mar. 22	29.80	47.8	—24.8	—24.32	—0.48	....	....	
	April 1	30.65	50.3	—13.8	—15.58	+1.78	+0.65	+0.17	
34	Mar. 21	29.90	50.9	—12.6	—12.26	—6.34	....	....	
	Mar. 22	29.80	50.5	—17.2	—14.54	—2.66	....	....	
	April 1	30.65	49.9	—17.2	—17.42	+0.22	—0.93	—1.41	
36	Mar. 20	29.82	49.7	—18.4	—18.20	—0.20	....	....	
	April 1	30.65	49.7	—19.3	—18.20	—1.10	—0.65	—1.13	Astoria, April, 1850.
37	Mar. 21	29.90	50.4	—15.8	—15.10	—0.70	....	....	
	Mar. 22	29.80	50.4	—14.3	—15.10	+0.80	....	....	
	April 1	30.65	49.4	—18.6	—19.38	+0.78	+0.29	—0.19	
38	Mar. 18	29.55	50.2	—15.7	—16.00	+0.30	....	....	
	April 1	30.65	49.2	—21.5	—20.22	—1.28	—0.46	—0.94	
39	Mar. 20	29.80	49.4	—19.1	—19.38	+0.28	....	....	
	April 1	30.63	49.0	—21.4	—21.06	—0.34	—0.03	—0.51	
40	Mar. 21	29.90	50.3	—15.3	—15.58	+0.28	....	....	
	Mar. 22	29.80	50.2	—16.4	—16.06	—0.34	....	....	
	April 1	30.63	48.9	—21.9	—21.38	—0.52	—0.19	—0.67	
41	Mar. 22	29.80	50.6	—14.3	—13.98	—0.32	....	....	
	April 2	30.72	49.6	—18.9	—18.60	—0.30	—0.31	—0.79	California.
43	Mar. 25	30.11	49.2	—19.8	—20.22	+0.42	....	....	
	April 2	30.72	49.5	—19.0	—18.99	—0.01	+0.20	—0.28	
44	April 2	30.72	49.4	—20.2	—19.38	—0.82	—0.82	—1.30	
45	April 4	30.15	53.4	+ 4.7	+ 5.11	—0.41	....	....	
	1845.								
	Jan. 15	30.26	49.0	—18.5	—21.06	+2.56	....	....	
	Feb. 10	30.17	48.6	—20.8	—22.37	+1.57	....	....	
	Mar. 1	29.92	49.8	—19.1	—17.81	—1.29	....	....	

* The correction was by inadvertance applied with the wrong sign in my report for 1846.

WEIGHTS AND MEASURES.

Comparison of the half bushel measures—Continued.

No. of standard.	Date.	Barometer.	Temp. of water.	Difference from standard.	Corrections for temp.	Result: — too large, + too small.			Destination.
						Single.	Mean.	Corrected mean.	
		Inches.	Fah.	Grains.	Grains.	Grains.	Grains.	Grains.	
	1846. Jan. 5	30.23	49.3	—17.2	—19.81	+2.61	+1.00	+0.52	
46	1845. Jan. 15	30.26	48.7	—20.9	—22.04	+1.14			
	Mar. 1	29.92	50.0	—18.4	—17.02	—1.38	—0.12	—0.60	
47	1844. April 4	30.15	53.4	+ 5.7	+ 5.11	+0.59			
	1845. Jan. 15	30.26	48.4	—23.8	—22.93	—0.87			
	Mar. 5	29.50	50.4	—16.1	—15.10	—1.00	—0.43	—0.91	
48	Jan. 15	30.26	48.3	—23.8	—23.21	—0.59			
	Mar. 5	29.50	50.3	—17.6	—15.58	—2.02			
	Mar. 6	30.30	51.5	—10.5	— 8.73	—1.77	—1.46	—1.94	
49	1844. Mar. 27	30.05	55.3	+22.4	+22.53	—0.13			
	April 2	30.72	49.4	—18.6	—19.38	+0.78	+0.32	—0.16	Bureau of Ordnance.
50	April 4	30.15	53.3	+ 5.2	+ 4.42	+0.78			
	1845. Jan. 15	30.26	48.2	—24.7	—23.49	—1.21			
	Mar. 5	29.50	50.3	—16.6	—15.58	—1.12	—0.52	—1.00	
51	1844. April 3	30.45	49.4	—19.8	—19.38	—0.22			
	April 4	30.15	53.2	+ 6.0	+ 3.75	+2.25	+1.02	+0.54	
52	1845. Jan. 21	29.89	49.9	—18.1	—17.42	—0.68			
	Mar. 5	29.50	50.3	—18.2	—15.58	—2.62	—1.65	—2.13	China.
53	Jan. 21	29.89	49.8	—17.1	—17.80	+0.71			
	Mar. 6	30.27	51.9	— 8.1	— 6.32	—1.78	—0.53	—1.01	Olympia, W. T., March 26, 1851.
54	Jan. 20	30.20	49.6	—19.3	—18.60	—0.70			
	Feb. 4	29.33	49.0	—19.7	—21.06	+1.36			
	Mar. 6	30.27	51.8	— 7.5	— 6.99	—0.51	+0.05	—0.43	
55	Jan. 21	29.90	49.7	—18.9	—18.20	—0.70			
	Mar. 6	30.27	51.7	— 8.0	— 7.57	—0.43	—0.56	—1.04	
56	Jan. 22	30.24	50 0	—16.8	—17.02	+0.22			
	Feb. 4	29.37	48.7	—21.3	—22.04	+0.74			
	Mar. 6	30.27	51.6	—10.0	— 8.15	—1.85	—0.30	—0.78	
57	Jan. 21	29.90	49.4	—20.0	—19.38	—0.62			
	Mar. 6	30.30	51.5	—10.3	— 8.73	—1.57	—1.09	—1.57	
58	Jan. 22	30.24	49.9	—16.6	—17.42	+0.82			
	Mar. 7	30.22	54.0	+ 9.0	+ 9.95	—0.95	—0.06	—0.54	
59	Jan. 21	29.90	49.3	—20.1	—19.81	—0.29			
	Mar. 7	30.22	53.7	+ 7.5	+ 7.37	+0.13	—0.08	—0.56	
60	Jan. 25	29.47	52.6	— 1.4	— 1.47	+0.07			
	Mar. 7	30.22	53.7	+ 5.1	+ 7.37	—2.27	—1.10	—1.58	
61	Jan. 23	30.50	50.5	—14.6	—14.51	—0.10			
	Mar. 7	30.22	53.5	+ 7.0	+ 5.79	+1.29	+0.59	+0.11	
62	Jan. 25	29.47	52.3	— 4.1	— 3.60	—0.50			
	Mar. 7	30.22	53.5	+ 6.5	+ 5.79	+0.71	+0.10	—0.38	France, November 1850.
63	Jan. 25	29.47	52.2	— 4.7	— 4.32	—0.38			
	Mar. 7	30.22	53.4	+ 4.2	+ 5.11	—0.91	—0.64	—1.12	
64	Jan. 25	29.50	51.9	— 6.8	— 6.32	—0.48			
	Mar. 10	29.99	53.5	+ 3.0	+ 5.79	—2.79	—1.63	—2.11	
66	Jan. 27	30.20	50.2	—15.5	—16.06	+0.56			
	Feb. 4	29.37	48.5	—24.6	—22.65	—1.95			
	Mar. 10	29 99	53.4	+ 5.2	+ 5.11	+0.09	—0.43	—0.91	
67	Jan. 27	30.20	51 2	— 9.5	—10.47	+0.97			
	Mar. 10	29.99	53.3	+ 3.3	+ 4.42	—1.12	—0.07	—0.55	
68	Jan. 27	30.20	50.9	—12.3	—12.26	—0.04			
	Mar. 10	29.99	53.4	+ 7.5	+ 5.11	+2.29	+1.13	+0.65	
69	Jan. 29	30.12	52.4	— 2.3	— 2.89	+0.59			
	Mar. 10	29.99	53.3	+ 2.8	+ 4.42	—1.62	—0.51	—0.99	
70	Feb. 8	30.24	49.0	—20.6	—21.06	+0.46			
	Mar. 10	29.99	53.3	+ 6.0	+ 4.42	+1.58	+1.02	+0.54	
71	Jan. 31	30.04	52.0	— 6.2	— 5.65	—0.55			
	Mar. 10	29.99	53.2	+ 2.4	+ 3.75	—1.35	—0.95	—1.43	California.
72	Jan. 30	30.20	51.2	—11.0	—10.47	—0.53			
	Feb. 4	29.37	48.3	—26.1	—23.21	—2.89			
	Mar. 10	29.99	53.2	+ 4.0	+ 3.75	+0.25	—1.06	—1.54	
73	Jan. 31	30.06	51.6	— 7.3	— 8.17	+0.87			
	Mar. 11	29.83	51.3	—11.6	— 9.89	—1.71	—0.42	—0.90	
74	Feb. 3	30.45	47.7	—25.1	—24.56	—0.54			
	Mar. 11	29.83	51.3	— 8.9	— 9.89	+0.99	+0.22	—0.26	
75	Feb. 1	30.40	50.5	—13.8	—14.54	—0.74			
	Mar. 11	29.87	51.2	— 9.6	—10.47	+0.87	+0.06	—0.42	

Comparison of the half bushel measures—Continued.

No. of standard.	Date.	Barometer.	Temp. of water.	Difference from standard.	Corrections for temp.	Result: — too large, + too small. Single.	Mean.	Corrected mean.	Destination.
		Inches.	Fah.	Grains.	Grains.	Grains.	Grains.	Grains.	
76	1845. Jan. 30	30.23	50.3	—16.2	—15.58	—0.72	....	....	
	Mar. 11	29.91	51.1	—11.0	—11.06	+0.06	—0.33	—0.81	Scottsville, Puget's Sound W. T., March 26, 1851.
77	Feb. 6	29.79	50.3	—16.0	—15.58	—0.42	....	....	
	Mar. 11	29.91	51.0	—12.4	—11.66	—0.74	—0.58	—1.06	Mexico.
78	Feb. 4	29.44	47.6	—25.2	—24.82	—0.37	....	....	
	Mar. 11	29.96	51.1	—11.0	—11.06	+0.06	—0.16	—0.64	
79	Feb. 11	29.75	48.4	—23.1	—22.93	—0.17	....	....	
	Mar. 12	30.35	50.7	—11.4	—13.41	+2.01	....	....	
	1846. Jan. 5	30.22	50.2	—14.0	—16.06	+2.06	+1.30	+0.82	
80	1845. Feb. 4	29.44	47.4	—26.0	—25.32	—0.68	....	....	
	Mar. 12	30.35	51.3	—12.2	— 9.89	—2.11	—1.40	—1.88	
81	Feb. 10	30.22	50.6	—14.4	—13.98	—0.42	....	....	
	Mar. 12	30.35	51.2	— 9.7	—10.47	+0.77	+0.17	—0.31	
82	Feb. 7	30.20	50.4	—15.3	—15.10	—0.20	....	....	
	Mar. 12	30.35	51.0	—10.3	—11.66	+1.36	+0.58	+0.10	
83	Feb. 8	30.30	49.0	—21.5	—21.06	—0.44	....	....	
	Mar. 12	30.35	50.8	— 9.8	—12.85	+3.05	....	....	
	Mar. 13	30.24	50.6	—13.4	—13.98	+0.58	....	....	
	1846. Jan. 5	30.22	49.8	—20.4	—17.81	—2.59	....	....	
	Jan. 6	30.36	50.6	— 9.3	—13.98	+4.68	+1.06	+0.58	
84	1845. Feb. 13	30.28	52.8	— 0.4	+ 0.45	—0.85	....	....	
	Feb. 14	30.42	49.1	—21.1	—20.64	—0.46	....	....	
	Mar. 12	30.35	50.7	—12.2	—13.41	+1.21	—0.03	—0.51	
85	Feb. 7	30.20	49.0	—20.2	—21.06	+0.86	....	....	
	Mar. 12	30.35	50.5	—14.1	—14.54	+0.44	+0.65	+0.17	
86	Feb. 7	30.20	48.4	—22.3	—22.93	+0.63	....	....	
	Mar. 12	30.35	50.4	—14.8	—15.10	+0.30	+0.46	—0.02	
87	Feb. 10	30.22	49.7	—18.8	—18.20	—0.60	....	....	
	Mar. 13	30.24	51.5	—10.1	— 8.73	—1.37	—0.98	—1.46	
88	Feb. 12	29.60	50.2	—16.5	—16.06	—0.44	....	....	
	Mar. 13	30.24	51.5	— 8.9	— 8.73	—0.23	—0.33	—0.81	
89	Feb. 14	30.42	48.6	—23.1	—22.37	—0.73	....	....	
	Mar. 13	30.24	51.3	— 9.9	— 9.89	—0.01	—0.37	—0.85	
91	Feb. 14	30.42	48.4	—23.2	—22.93	—0.27	....	....	
	Mar. 13	30.24	51.1	—10.5	—11.06	+0.56	+0.14	—0.34	
92	Feb. 13	30.35	52.1	— 4.5	— 4.99	+0.49	....	....	
	Feb. 14	30.42	48.9	—23.0	—21.38	—1.62	....	....	
	Mar. 13	30.24	51.0	— 9.7	—11.66	+1.96	....	....	
	1846. Jan. 5	30.22	49.8	—16.0	—17.81	—1.81	—0.24	—0.72	State of Alabama.
93	1845. Feb. 12	29.60	49.7	—18.1	—18.20	+0.10	....	....	
	Mar. 13	30.24	50.9	—12.8	—12.26	—0.54	—0.22	—0.70	
94	Feb. 13	30.35	51.9	— 6.3	— 6.32	+0.02	....	....	
	Feb. 14	30.42	48.8	—22.5	—21.71	—0.79	....	....	
	Mar. 13	30.24	50.7	—12.8	—13.41	+0.61	—0.05	—0.53	
95	Feb. 15	30.14	49.7	—18.5	—18.20	—0.30	....	....	
	Mar. 13	30.24	50.6	—15.0	—13.98	—1.02	—0.66	—1.14	Wisconsin, Nov. 11 1854.
96	Feb. 15	30.14	49.6	—18.8	—18.60	—0.20	....	....	
	Feb. 14	29.84	51.6	— 9.0	— 8.15	—0.85	—0.52	—1.00	
97	Feb. 19	30.20	51.6	— 7.3	— 8.15	+0.85	....	....	
	Feb. 14	29.84	51.4	—10.3	— 9.31	—0.99	—0.07	—0.55	
98	Feb. 25	30.00	53.5	+ 5.5	+ 5.79	—0.29	....	....	
	Mar. 14	29.84	51.3	— 8.5	— 9.89	+1.39	+0.55	+0.07	
99	Feb. 25	30.00	53.6	+ 7.2	+ 6.47	+0.73	....	....	
	Mar. 14	29.84	51.1	—10.3	—11.06	+0.76	+0.74	+0.26	
100	Feb. 26	29.82	53.8	+ 8.5	+ 8.26	+0.24	....	....	
	Mar. 14	29.70	51.0	— 8.7	—11.66	+2.96	+1.60	+1.12	
101	Feb. 25	30.00	53.5	+ 6.0	+ 5.79	+0.21	....	....	
	Mar. 14	29.70	50.9	—11.1	—12.26	+1.16	+0.68	+0.20	
102	Feb. 25	30.00	53.5	+ 6.5	+ 5.79	+0.71	....	....	
	Mar. 14	29.70	50.8	—10.5	—12.85	+2.35	+1.53	+1.05	
103	Feb. 27	29.90	51.7	— 6.9	— 7.57	+0.67	....	....	
	Mar. 14	29.70	50.7	—13.5	—13.41	—0.09	+0.29	—0.19	
105	Feb. 27	29.90	51.4	—10.0	— 9.31	—0.69	....	....	

Comparison of the half bushel measures—Continued.

No. of standard.	Date	Barometer.	Temp. of water.	Difference from standard.	Corrections for temp.	Result: — too large, + too small.			Destination.
						Single.	Mean.	Corrected mean.	
	1845.	Inches.	Fah.	Grains.	Grains.	Grains.	Grains.	Grains.	
105	Mar. 15	29.94	51.0	—11.3	—11.66	+0.36	—0.16	—0.64	
106	Feb. 28	29.99	50.6	—13.7	—13.98	+0.28			
	Mar. 15	29.94	50.9	—11.7	—12.26	+0.56	+0.42	—0.06	
107	Mar. 1	29.90	50.1	—15.7	—16.54	+0.84			
	Mar. 15	29.94	50.8	—11.9	—12.85	+0.95	+0.89	+0.41	
108	Feb. 27	29.90	51.3	— 9.2	— 9.89	+0.69			
	Mar. 15	29.94	50.7	—12.9	—13.41	+0.51	+0.60	+0.12	
109	Mar. 1	29.90	49.9	—17.6	—17.42	—0.18			Sent August 29, 1853, to custom-house at Alexandria, Va.
	Mar. 15	29.94	50.5	—15.8	—14.54	—1.26	—0.72	—1.20	
110	Feb. 28	29.99	50.4	—14.2	—15.10	+0.90			
	Mar. 15	29.94	50.4	—16.0	—15.10	—0.90	0.00	—0.48	
112	Mar. 1	29.92	49.8	—18.0	—17.81	—0.19			Dist. of Columbia, 1849.
	Mar. 15	29.94	50.4	—13.0	—15.10	+2.10	+0.95	+0.47	
113	Mar. 5	29.50	50.4	—14.2	—15.10	+0.90			
	Mar. 15	29.94	50.3	—13.8	—15.58	+1.78	+1.34	+0.86	
114	Mar. 5	29.50	50.6	—13.6	—13.98	+0.38			
	Mar. 17	29.30	49.3	—16.6	—19.81	+3.21			
	Mar. 20	30.10	47.9	—23.4	—24.11	+0.71			
	Mar. 21	30.17	50.7	—13.6	—13.41	—0.19			
	1846.								
	Jan. 6	30.36	49.9	—13.8	—17.42	+3.62	+1.55	+1.07	
	1845.								
115	Mar. 1	29.92	49.8	—18.0	—17.81	—0.19			
	Mar. 17	29.30	49.1	—19.4	—20.64	+1.24	+0.52	+0.04	
116	Mar. 7	30.22	53.5	+ 5.9	+ 5.79	+0.11			
	Mar. 17	29.25	48.9	—20.8	—21.38	+0.58	+0.34	—0.14	
117	Mar. 11	29.96	51.0	—10.9	—11.66	+0.66			
	Mar. 17	29.25	48.6	—23.1	—22.37	—0.73	—0.03	—0.51	
118	Mar. 10	29.90	53.1	+ 3.9	+ 3.07	+0.83			
	Mar. 17	29.25	48.5	—22.0	—22.65	+0.65	+0.74	+0.26	
119	Mar. 11	29.83	51.5	— 9.2	— 8.73	—0.47			
	Mar. 17	29.28	48.4	—23.0	—22.93	—0.07	—0.27	—0.75	
120	Mar. 13	30.24	50.6	—14.6	—13.98	—0.62			
	Mar. 17	29.28	48.4	—24.2	—22.93	—1.27	—0.94	—1.42	
121	Mar. 12	30.30	50.0	—17.4	—17.02	—0.38			
	Mar. 17	29.32	48.4	—24.0	—22.93	—1.07	—0.72	—1.20	
122	Mar. 20	30.10	49.6	—18.8	—18.60	—0.20			
	Mar. 22	30.27	50.0	—16.6	—17.02	+0.42	+0.11	—0.37	
124	Mar. 22	30.30	51.6	— 7.2	— 8.15	+0.95			
	Mar. 24	30.03	49.7	—17.9	—18.20	+0.30	+0.62	+0.14	
125	Mar. 20	30.10	48.8	—20.9	—21.71	+0.81			
	Mar. 22	30.27	50.1	—16.7	—16.54	—0.16	+0.32	—0.16	
126	Mar. 20	30.10	48.6	—21.7	—22.37	+0.67			
	Mar. 24	30.03	49.6	—16.7	—18.60	+1.90			
	Mar. 25	30.30	50.8	—13.3	—12.85	—0.45	+0.71	+0.23	
127	Mar. 19	29.94	49.9	—17.1	—17.42	+0.32			
	Mar. 25	30.30	50.7	—12.1	—13.41	+1.31	+0.81	+0.33	
128	Mar. 20	30.10	48.4	—22.4	—22.93	+0.53			
	Mar. 25	30.30	50.9	—11.7	—12.26	+0.56	+0.54	+0.06	
129	Mar. 18	29.64	50.2	—16.0	—16.06	+0.06			
	Mar. 25	30.30	51.0	—10.9	—11.66	+0.76	+0.41	—0.07	
130	Mar. 19	29.94	49.5	—18.2	—18.99	+0.79			
	Mar. 26	30.50	51.3	—11.0	— 9.89	—1.11			
	1846.								
	Jan. 5	30.23	49.4	—21.5	—19 38	—2.12	—0.81	—1.29	
131	Jan. 7	29.75	50.0	—16.2	—17.02	+0.82			
	Jan. 22	30.20	50.2	—13.7	—16.06	+2.36			
	Mar. 28	29.90	52.50	+ 2.2	— 2.18	+4.38			
	Mar. 30	30.25	51.25	— 7.3	—10.18	+2.88	+2.61	+2.13	
	1845.								
132	Mar. 22	30.30	50.7	—13.6	—13.41	—0.19			
	Mar. 26	30.50	51.3	— 8.6	— 9.89	+1.29	+0.55	+0.07	
133	Mar. 21	30.17	50.0	—16.2	—17.02	+0.82			San Francisco custom-house, Dec. 20, 1849.
	Mar. 26	30.50	51.2	— 9.9	—10.47	+0.57	+0.69	+0.21	
134	Mar. 25	30.28	51.3	—10.5	— 9.89	—0.71			
	Mar. 26	30.50	51.1	—13.7	—11.06	—2.64			
	1846.								
	Jan. 8	30.00	50.3	—14.4	—15.58	+1.18			
	Jan. 22	30.20	49.9	—18.0	—17.42	—0.58	—0.66	—1.14	
	1845.								
136	Mar. 24	30.03	49.9	—18.1	—17.42	—0.68			

Comparison of the half bushel measures—Continued.

No. of standard.	Date.	Barometer.	Temp. of water.	Difference from standard.	Corrections for temp.	Result: — too large, + too small.			Destination.
						Single.	Mean.	Corrected mean.	
	1845.	Inches.	Fah.	Grains.	Grains.	Grains.	Grains.	Grains.	
136	Mar. 26	30.50	50.9	—12.7	—12.26	—0.44	—0.56	—1.04	
	1846.								
137	Jan. 9	29.98	50.9	—11.3	—12.26	+0.96	....	....	
	Jan. 22	30.20	49.6	—21.1	—18.60	—2.50	—0.77	—1.25	
138	Jan. 8	30.00	49.8	—18.0	—17.81	—0.19	....	....	
	Jan. 22	30.20	49.5	—20.0	—18.99	—1.01	—0.60	—1.08	
139	Jan. 9	29.98	50.6	—13.0	—13.98	+0.98	....	....	
	Jan. 23	30.55	51.6	— 9.8	— 8.15	—1.65	—0.33	—0.81	
140	Jan. 10	30.00	49.1	—20.4	—20.64	+0.24	....	....	
	Jan. 23	30.55	51.5	— 5.2	— 8.73	+3.53	....	....	
	Mar. 28	29.90	52.2	— 3.6	— 4.32	—0.72	....	....	
	Mar. 30	30.25	51.1	—10.1	—11.06	+0.96	+0.99	+0.51	
141	Jan. 10	30.00	49.0	—21.0	—21.06	+0.06	....	....	
	Jan. 23	30.55	51.1	—11.0	—11.06	+0.06	+0.06	—0.42	
143	Jan. 10	30.00	48.9	—20.7	—21.38	+0.68	....	....	
	Jan. 23	30.55	50.7	—18.2	—13.41	—4.79	....	....	
	Jan. 24	30.40	51.1	—10 4	—11.06	+0.66	—1.15	—1.63	
144	Jan. 14	30.20	48.5	—23.1	—22.65	—0.45	....	....	
	Jan. 23	30.55	50.4	—16.0	—15.10	—0.90	—0.67	—1.15	
145	Jan. 20	30.50	49.8	—19.3	—17.81	—1.49	....	....	
	Jan. 23	30.55	50.0	—18.9	—17.02	—1.88	—1.68	—2.16	Government of Japan.
146	Jan. 13	30.23	49.6	—19.3	—18.60	—0.70	....	....	
	Jan. 24	30.40	50.5	—16.0	—14.54	—1.46	—1.08	—1.56	Iowa, Nov. 6, 1856.
147	Jan. 14	30.90	47.8	—25.2	—24.31	—0.89	....	....	
	Jan. 24	30.40	50.0	—18.3	—17.02	—1.28	....	....	
	Mar. 28	29.90	51.95	— 6.2	— 5.98	—0.22	....	....	
	Mar. 30	30.25	50.95	—11.3	—11.96	+0.66	—0.43	—0.91	
148	Jan. 13	30.23	48.9	—21.7	—21.38	—0.32	....	....	
	Jan. 24	30.40	49.8	—19.0	—17.81	—1.11	....	....	
	Jan. 26	29.92	50.7	—13.2	—13.41	+0.21	—0.41	—0.89	
149	Jan. 14	30.20	47.5	—25.8	—25.07	—0.73	....	....	
	Jan. 24	30.40	49.4	—20.7	—19.38	—1.32	—1.02	—1.50	
150	Jan. 17	29.70	50.7	—14.3	—13.41	—0.89	....	....	
	Jan. 24	30.40	49.1	—22.3	—20.64	—1.66	—1.27	—1.75	California, Dec. 18, 1854.
151	Jan. 21	29.78	51.5	— 9.5	— 8.73	—0.77	....	....	
	Jan. 24	30.40	48.8	—22.0	—21.71	—0.29	—0.53	—1.01	
152	Jan. 20	30.50	50.4	—13.4	—15.10	+1.70	....	....	
	Jan. 26	29.92	50.4	—17.0	—15.10	—1.90	—0.10	—0.58	
154	Jan. 19	30.49	48.0	—23.0	—23.90	+0.90	....	....	
	Jan. 26	29.92	50.3	—18.0	—15.58	—2.42	—0.76	—1.24	
155	Jan. 20	30.50	49.5	—19.7	—18.99	—0.71	....	....	
	Jan. 26	29.87	50.2	—19.2	—16.06	—2.14	....	....	
	Jan. 27	29.75	51.3	—10.4	— 9 89	—0.51	—1.12	—1.60	
156	Jan. 21	29.78	50.6	—15.0	—13.98	—1.02	....	....	
	Jan. 26	29.87	51.8	— 8.0	— 6.99	—1.01	—1.01	—1.49	
157	Jan. 22	30.20	51.6	— 7.7	— 8.15	+0.45	....	....	
	Jan. 26	29.80	51.5	— 8.6	— 8.73	+0.13	....	....	
	Jan. 27	29.75	51.1	—12.2	—11.06	—1.14	—0.19	—0.67	
159	Jan. 21	29.72	52.0	— 4.7	— 5.65	+0.95	....	....	
	Jan. 27	29.75	51.0	—13.2	—11.66	—1.54	....	....	
	Jan. 28	30.03	52.5	— 0.7	— 2.18	+1.48	....	....	
	Jan. 28	30.03	51.9	— 6.0	— 6.32	+0.32	....	....	
	Jan. 28	30.03	51.4	—10.3	— 9.31	—0.99	....	....	
	Jan. 28	30.03	51.2	— 9.1	—10.47	+1.37	....	....	
	Jan. 28	30.03	51.0	—12.6	—11.66	—0.94	+0.09	—0.39	
160	Jan. 23	30.55	48.1	—24.1	—23.70	—0.40	....	....	
	Jan. 27	29.75	50.9	—10.7	—12.26	+1.56	....	....	
	Jan. 28	30.03	52.0	— 5.3	— 5.65	+0.35	....	....	
	Jan. 28	30.03	51.7	— 5.6	— 7.57	+1.97	....	....	
	Jan. 28	30.03	51.3	— 8.3	— 9.89	+1.59	....	....	
	Jan. 28	30.03	51.0	—12.0	—11.66	—0.34	....	....	
	Jan. 28	30.03	50.9	—13.5	—12.26	—1.44	+0.47	+0.01	
161	Jan. 22	30.20	50.6	—15.0	—13.98	—1.02	....	....	
	Jan. 27	29.75	50.7	—15.2	—13.41	—1.79	—1.40	—1.88	
162	Jan. 27	29.75	51.3	—10.6	— 9.89	—0.71	....	....	
	Jan. 27	29.75	50.6	—14.4	—13.98	—0.42	....	....	
	Mar. 28	29.90	51.8	— 8.1	— 6.99	—1.11	....	....	
	Mar. 30	30.25	51.0	— 9.6	—11.66	+2.06	—0.04	—0.52	Government of Siam.

APPENDIX No. 24.

Comparison of the gallon measures.

No. of standard.	Date.	Barometer.	Temp. of water.	Difference from standard.	Corrections for temp.	Result: — too large, + too small.			Destination.
						Single.	Mean.	Corrected mean.	
	1842.	Inch.	Fah.	Grains.	Grains.	Grains.	Grains.	Grains.	
1	Previous to April 5.	30.00	51.0	—2.5	....	....	+0.0214	....	
2	....do....	30.00	45.7	—5.7	....	....	+0.0848	....	
3	....do....	30.00	46.2	—5.8	....	....	+0.0236	....	
4	....do....	30.00	46.8	—5.65	....	....	+0.0887	....	
5	....do....	30.00	47.2	—5.5	....	....	+0.0592	....	
6	....do....	30.00	53.8	+1.6	....	....	—0.1659	....	
7	....do....	30.00	53.1	+0.55	....	....	—0.1867	....	State of Maine.
8	....do....	30.00	53.0	+0.5	....	....	—0.0117	....	State of New Hampshire.
9	....do....	30.00	54.7	+3.5	....	....	—0.1415	....	State of Vermont.
10	....do....	30.00	53.8	+1.6	....	....	—0.1659	....	State of Rhode Island.
11	....do....	30.00	52.6	—0.4	....	....	—0.0826	....	State of Massachusetts.
12	....do....	30.00	53.3	+0.6	....	....	—0.4470	....	State of Connecticut.
13	....do....	30.00	53.3	+0.7	....	....	—0.3470	....	State of New York.
14	....do....	30.00	50.2	—3.4	....	....	+0.0520	....	State of New Jersey.
15	....do....	30.00	51.5	—1.8	....	....	+0.0769	....	State of Pennsylvania.
16	....do....	30.00	51.5	—1.8	....	....	+0.0769	....	State of Delaware.
17	....do....	30.00	51.8	—1.5	....	....	+0.0037	....	State of Maryland.
18	....do....	30.00	52.8	+0.05	....	....	—0.0471	....	State of Virginia.
19	....do....	30.00	53.0	+0.55	....	....	+0.0383	....	State of North Carolina.
20	....do....	30.00	52.1	—1.2	....	....	—0.1249	....	State of South Carolina.
21	....do....	30.00	52.2	—1.0	....	....	—0.0677	....	State of Georgia.
22	....do....	30.00	52.4	—0.6	....	....	+0.0248	....	State of Louisiana.
23	....do....	30.00	51.6	—1.6	....	....	+0.1525	....	State of Alabama.
24	....do....	30.00	52.5	—0.4	....	....	+0.0711	....	State of Ohio.
25	....do....	30.00	52.0	—1.2	....	....	+0.0180	....	State of Missouri.
26	....do....	30.00	52.4	—0.6	....	....	+0.0248	....	State of Mississippi.
27	....do....	30.00	52.4	—0.65	....	....	—0.0252	....	State of Kentucky.
28	....do....	30.00	52.4	—0.6	....	....	+0.0248	....	State of Indiana.
29	....do....	30.00	52.7	—0.1	....	....	+0.0101	....	State of Illinois.
30	....do....	30.00	52.8	+0.05	....	....	—0.0471	....	State of Tennessee.
31	....do....	30.00	53.0	+0.5	....	....	—0.0117	....	State of Arkansas.
32	....do....	30.00	53.2	+0.87	....	....	—0.0917	....	State of Michigan.
33	....do....	30.00	53.0	+0.5	....	....	—0.0117	....	Portland and Falmouth, Maine.
34	....do....	30.00	53.2	+1.0	....	....	+0.0383	....	Salem, Mass.
35	....do....	30.00	53.2	+1.0	....	....	+0.0383	....	Boston and Charlestown, Mass.
36	....do....	30.00	50.8	—2.6	....	....	+0.1928	....	Newburyport, Mass.
37	....do....	30.00	49.5	—3.93	....	....	+0.1472	....	New Bedford, Mass.
38	....do....	30.00	50.8	—2.7	....	....	+0.0928	....	Providence, R. I.
39	....do....	30.00	50.5	—3.1	....	....	+0.0324	....	Newark, N. J.
40	....do....	30.00	50.5	—3.2	....	....	—0.0676	....	New Haven, Conn.
41	....do....	30.00	49.5	—3.9	....	....	+0.1772	....	New York, N. Y.
42	....do....	30.00	50.8	—2.7	....	....	+0.0928	....	Philadelphia, Pa.
43	....do....	30.00	50.6	—2.97	....	....	+0.0492	....	Wilmington, Del.
44	....do....	30.00	49.9	—3.8	....	....	—0.0621	....	Baltimore, Md.
45	....do....	36.00	54.1	+2.3	....	....	—0.0344	....	Norfolk, Va.
46	....do....	30.00	53.7	+1.7	....	....	—0.1206	....	Alexandria, Va.
47	....do....	30.00	53.8	+1.9	....	....	+0.1341	....	Richmond, Va.
48	....do....	30.00	53.8	+1.93	....	....	+0.1641	....	Wilmington, N. C.
49	....do....	30.00	53.8	+1.65	....	....	—0.1159	....	Charleston, S. C.
50	....do....	30.00	50.9	—2.6	....	....	+0.0571	....	Savannah, Geo.
51	....do....	30.00	50.3	—3.25	....	....	+0.0988	....	Mobile, Ala.
52	....do....	30.00	50.2	—3.3	....	....	+0.1520	....	Key West, Fla.
53	....do....	30.00	50.3	—3.25	....	....	+0.0988	....	Apalachicola, Fla.
54	....do....	30.00	51.4	—2.0	....	....	+0.0012	....	New Orleans, La.
55	....do....	30.00	51.4	—2.0	....	....	+0.0012	....	Passamaquoddy, (Eastport,) Me.
56	....do....	30.00	51.5	—1.8	....	....	+0.0769	....	Machias, Maine.
57	....do....	30.00	52.2	—0.93	....	....	+0.0023	....	Frenchman's Bay, Maine.
58	....do....	30.00	51.1	—2.35	....	....	+0.0357	....	Penobscot, Maine.
59	....do....	30.00	51.6	—1.8	....	....	—0.0475	....	Waldoboro', Maine.
60	....do....	30.00	50.6	—3.0	....	....	+0.0192	....	Wiscasset, Maine.
61	....do....	30.00	51.0	—2.53	....	....	—0.0086	....	Bath, Maine.
62	....do....	30.00	51.4	—2.1	....	....	—0.0988	....	Saco, Maine.
63	....do....	30.00	51.1	—2.37	....	....	+0.0157	....	Kennebunk, Maine.
64	....do....	30.00	52.9	+0.3	....	....	—0.0044	....	York, Maine.
65	....do....	30.00	52.4	—0.65	....	....	—0.0252	....	Belfast, Maine.
66	....do....	30.00	50.6	—3.0	....	....	+0.0192	....	Portsmouth, N. H.
67	....do....	30.00	50.5	—3.0	....	....	+0.1324	....	Burlington, Vt.
68	....do....	30.00	50.6	—3.0	....	....	+0.0192	....	Gloucester, Mass.
69	....do....	30.00	54.8	+3.9	....	....	—0.0182	....	Marblehead, Mass.

Comparison of the gallon measures—Continued.

No. of standard.	Date.	Barometer.	Temp. of water.	Difference from standard.	Corrections for temp.	Result: — too large, + too small.			Destination.
						Single.	Mean.	Corrected mean.	
	1842.	Inch.	Fah.	Grains.	Grains.	Grains.	Grains.	Grains.	
	Previous								
70	to April 5.	30.00	50.5	−3.1			+0.0324		Ipswich, Mass.
71	...do....	30.00	51.4	−2.07			−0.0688		Plymouth, Mass.
72	...do....	30.00	50.5	−3.0			−0.1324		Fall River, Mass.
73	...do....	30.00	50.4	−3.25			−0.0044		Barnstable, Mass.
74	...do....	30.00	51.4	−2.0			+0.0012		Edgartown, Mass.
75	...do....	30.00	51.4	−1.93			+0.0612		Nantucket, Mass.
76	...do....	30.00	51.5	−1.9			−0.0231		Bristol, (Bristol & Warren,) R. I.
77	...do....	30.00	51.5	−1.9			−0.0231		Newport, R. I.
78	...do....	30.00	51.6	−1.8			−0.0475		Middletown, Conn.
79	...do....	30.00	54.8	+3.8			−0.0818		New London, Conn.
80	...do....	30.00	52.4	−0.6			+0.0248		Fairfield, Conn.
81	...do....	30.00	51.8	−1.4			+0.1037		Sackett's Harbor, N. Y.
82	...do....	30.00	51.7	−1.7			−0.0713		Rochester, N. Y.
83	...do....	30.00	51.6	−1.6			+0.1525		Oswego, N. Y.
84	...do....	30.00	55.1	+4.2			−0.2479		Lewistown, N. Y.
85	...do....	30.00	51.6	−1.7			+0.0525		Buffalo, N. Y.
86	...do....	30.00	55.3	+4.6			−0.2253		Ogdensburgh, N. Y.
87	...do....	30.00	51.6	−1.8			−0.0475		Sag Harbor, N. Y.
88	...do....	30.00	50.9	−2.8			−0.1429		Jersey City, N. Y.
89	...do....	30.00	51.6	−1.7			+0.0525		Plattsburg, N. Y.
90	...do....	30.00	51.5	−1.9			−0.0231		Cape Vincent, N. Y.
91	...do....	30.00	51.5	−2.0			−0.1231		Perth Amboy, N. J.
92	...do....	30.00	52.0	−1.2			+0.0180		Bridgeton, N. J.
93	...do....	30.00	51.8	−1.6			−0.0963		Lumberton, N. J.
94	...do....	30.00	52.5	−0.4			+0.0711		Bargaintown, N. J.
95	...do....	30.00	51.6	−1.7			+0.0525		Tuckerton, N. J.
96	...do....	30.00	51.6	−1.7			+0.0525		Erie, Pa.
97	...do....	30.00	54.0	+2.1			−0.0390		Annapolis, Md.
98	...do....	30.00	52.0	−1.2			+0.0180		Snow Hill, Md.
99	...do....	30.00	52.0	−1.2			+0.0180		Oxford, Md.
100	...do....	30.00	51.7	−1.7			−0.0713		Vienna, Md.
101	...do....	30.00	53.9	+2.0			+0.0476		Port Tobacco, Md.
102	...do....	30.00	52.2	−1.0			−0.0677		Georgetown, D. C., Oct. 27, 1853.
103	...do....	30.00	53.9	+1.9			−0.0524		Tappahannock, Va.*
104	...do....	30.00	52.0	−1.3			−0.1819		Wheeling, Va.
105	...do....	30.00	53.1	+0.7			−0.0367		
106	...do....	30.00	53.2	+0.9			−0.0617		Yorktown, Va., Oct. 27, 1853.
107	...do....	30.00	52.2	−1.0			−0.0677		Petersburg, Va., Oct. 27, 1853.
108	...do....	30.00	50.8	−2.7			+0.0928		Memphis, Tenn.
109	...do....	30.00	52.3	−0.9			−0.1214		Elizabeth City, N. C.
110	...do....	30.00	54.7	+3.6			−0.0415		Edenton, N. C., Oct. 27, 1853.
111	...do....	30.00	52.0	−1.2			−0.0180		Plymouth, N. C.*
112	...do....	30.00	52.9	+0.25			−0.0544		Washington, N. C.*
113	...do....	30.00	52.4	−0.6			+0.0248		Newbern, N. C., Oct. 27, 1853.
114	...do....	30.00	52.0	−1.1			+0.1180		Ocracoke, N. C.
115	...do....	30.00	52.6	−0.3			+0.0174		Beaufort, N. C., Oct. 27, 1853.
116	...do....	30.00	53.0	+0.5			−0.0117		Georgetown, S. C.*
117	...do....	30.00	54.6	+3.4			−0.0013		Beaufort, S. C., Oct. 27, 1853.
118	...do....	30.00	52.0	−1.2			+0.0180		St. Louis, Mo.
119	...do....	30.00	52.4	−0.6			+0.0248		Darien, Ga.*
120	...do....	30.00	52.4	−0.6			+0.0248		St. Mary's, Ga.*
121	...do....	30.00	52.9	+3.1			−0.0610		Chicago, Ill.
122	...do....	30.00	52.7	−0.2			−0.0899		Miami, Ohio.*
123	...do....	30.00	53.5	+6.1			−0.1521		Cincinnati, Ohio.
124	...do....	30.00	56.1	+6.8			+0.0864		Iowa, Nov. 6, 1856.
125	...do....	30.00	52.4	−0.6			+0.0248		Michilimackinac, Mich.*
	1844.								
126	Jan. 29	30.34	48.6	−4.75	−4.807	+0.06			
	Feb. 16	29.90	48.8	−5.10	−4.666	−0.43			
	Feb. 29	30.31	48.8	−4.05	−4.666	+0.62			
	Feb. 29	30.34	48.6	−4.75	−4.8072	+0.0572			
	Mar. 1	30.12	50.7	−2.95	−2.906	−0.04	+0.053		Detroit, Mich.*
127	Jan. 30	29.90	48.7	−4.80	−4.737	−0.06			
	Feb. 6	29.90	47.8	−5.60	−5.225	−0.37			
	Feb. 29	30.31	48.8	−4.90	−4.666	−0.23			
	Mar. 1	30.12	50.6	−2.60	−3.019	+0.42			
	Mar. 5	30.46	49.3	−4.20	−4.255	+0.05	−0.04		Wisconsin, Nov. 11, 1854
128	Jan. 31	30.24	47.1	−5.60	−5.637	+0.02			
	Feb. 2	30.05	47.4	−6.00	−5.445	−0.55			
	Feb. 17	29.94	47.5	−5.40	−5.390	−0.01			
	Feb. 29	30.31	48.8	−4.43	−4.666	+0.24			
	Mar. 1	30.12	50.6	−3.40	−3.019	−0.38			
	Mar. 5	30.46	49.3	−4.00	−4.255	+0.20	−0.08		Pensacola, Fla.*

* Have not been sent, but are directed, and will be sent as soon as practicable.

WEIGHTS AND MEASURES.

Comparison of the gallon measures—Continued.

No. of standard.	Date.	Barometer.	Temp. of water.	Difference from standard.	Corrections for temp.	Result: — too large, + too small. Single.	Mean.	Corrected mean.	Destination.
	1844.	Inch.	Fah.	Grains.	Grains.	Grains.	Grains.	Grains.	
129	Jan. 29	30.34	47.8	—5.20	—5.225	+0.02			
	Feb. 2	30.05	47.4	—5.80	—5.445	—0.35			
	Feb. 29	30.31	48.8	—5.19	—4.666	—0.52			
	Mar. 1	30.10	50.5	—4.75	—3.132	—1.618			
	Mar. 5	30.46	49.2	—4.55	—4.345	—0.20	—0.533		St. Augustine, Fla.*
130	Jan. 29	30.34	47.7	—5.30	—5.280	—0.02			
	Feb. 16	29.90	48.8	—4.40	—4.666	+0.27			
	Feb. 29	30.31	48.8	—4.35	—4.666	+0.32			
	Mar. 1	30.10	50.5	—3.40	—3.132	—0.27	+0.07		St. Mark's, Fla.
131	Feb. 5	29.96	46.2	—5.70	—5.824	+0.12			
	Feb. 6	29.90	47.8	—5.30	—5.225	—0.07			
	Feb. 20	30.06	47.2	—6.15	—5.599	—0.55			
	Feb. 21	29.92	48.8	—4.60	—4.666	+0.07			
	Feb. 22	29.95	50.6	—3.35	—3.019	—0.33			
	Feb. 27	29.98	47.9	—5.1	—5.1809	+0.084			
	Feb. 28	30.23	49.3	—5.70	—4.255	—1.44	—0.302		Jacksonville, Fla.*
132	Feb. 3	30.26	47.1	—5.70	—5.637	—0.06			
	Feb. 17	29.94	47.6	—5.30	—5.335	+0.03			
	Feb. 29	30.29	48.8	—4.65	—4.666	+0.02			
	Mar. 1	30.10	50.5	—3.50	—3.132	—0.37	—0.09		Pearl River, Miss.
133	Feb. 1	30.37	47.6	—5.40	—5.335	—0.06			
	Feb. 29	30.29	48.8	—5.00	—4.666	—0.33			
	Feb. 29	30.29	48.85	—5.00	—4.666	—0.334			
	Mar. 1	30.07	50.5	—3.65	—3.132	—0.52	—0.311		Natchez, Miss.*
134	Jan. 31	30.27	46.7	—5.70	—5.723	+0.01			
	Feb. 16	29.90	48.8	—4.50	—4.666	+0.17			
	Feb. 20	30.18	47.0	—5.80	—5.676	—0.12			
	Feb. 21	29.98	49.2	—4.00	—4.345	+0.34			
	Feb. 22	30.00	50.7	—2.85	—2.906	+0.06			
	Feb. 27	29.98	48.1	—5.2	—5.0927	—0.107			
	Feb. 28	30.23	49.1	—5.46	—4.436	—1.02			
	Feb. 28	30.23	49.15	—5.46	—4.436	—1.024			
	Feb. 28	30.23	46.8	—5.53	—5.738	+0.208			
	Feb. 29	30.28	46.2	—5.8	—5.823	+0.023			
	Mar. 4	30.08	53.2	+0.9	+0.962	—0.062			
	Mar. 5	30.45	48.6	—5.1	—4.807	—0.293			
	Mar. 7	30.40	48.1	—4.8	—5.092	—0.292	—0.162		China.
135	Feb. 1	30.40	47.8	—5.10	—5.225	+0.12			
	Feb. 29	30 28	48.9	—4.20	—4.596	+0.40			
	Mar. 4	29.96	54.8	+4.05	+3.882	—0.17			
	Mar. 8	30.30	50.0	—3.47	—3.658	+0.19	+0.22		Government of Japan.
136	Jan. 31	30.27	46.5	—5.60	—5.739	+0.14			
	Feb. 29	30.28	48.9	—4.23	—4.596	+0.39			
	Mar. 4	29.96	54.6	+3.33	+3.351	—0.02			
	Mar. 8	30.30	50.0	—3.40	—3.658	+0.26	+0.19		
137	Feb. 3	30.26	47.3	—5.50	—5.552	+0.02			
	Feb. 5	29.96	46.2	—5.60	—5.824	+0.22			
	Feb. 29	30.28	48.9	—3.53	—4.596	+1.07			
	Mar. 4	29.96	54.5	+3.20	+3.136	—0.06			
	Mar. 8	30.28	49.9	—3.60	—3.738	+0.13			
	Mar. 8	30 28	49.9	—3.60	—3.738	+0.138	+0.253		Cherrystone, (Eastville,) Va., sent Oct. 27, 1853.
138	Feb. 6	29.89	48.6	—4.70	—4.807	+0.11			
	Feb. 16	29.90	48.8	—4.60	—4.666	+0.07			
	Feb. 20	30.06	47.2	—5.70	—5.599	—0.10			
	Feb. 21	29 92	48.7	—4.60	—4.737	+0.74			
	Feb. 22	29.95	50.4	—3.00	—3.246	+0.25			
	Feb. 27	30.00	47.9	—5.19	—5.1809	—0.009			
	Feb. 28	30.23	49.3	—5.50	—4.255	—1.24	—0.035		Government of Siam; sent by Com. Perry in June, 1852.
139	Feb. 3	30.26	47.2	—5.60	—5.599	0.00			
	Mar. 4	29.99	54.3	+3.40	—2.725	+0.67			
	Mar. 5	30.46	50.0	—3.30	—3.658	+0.36	+0.34		Astoria, Oregon.
140	Feb. 6	29.89	48.4	—4.80	—4.928	+0.13			
	Feb. 7	29.90	47.2	—5.60	—5.599	0.00			
	Feb. 8	29.62	48.5	—5.00	—4.867	—0.13			
	Feb. 20	30.14	47.2	—5.10	—5.599	+0.45			
	Feb. 21	29.98	49.0	—4.25	—4.526	+0.28			
	Feb. 22	30.00	50.6	—4.05	—3.019	—1.03			
	Feb. 27	29.98	48.0	—4.9	—5.1368	+0.237			
	Feb. 28	30.23	49.2	—5.02	—4.345	—0.67			
	1849.								
	Jan. 9	30.00	48.7	—4.5	—4.87	+0.37			
	Mar. 23	30.00	52.7	+0.4	—0.11	+0.51	—0.015		

* Have not been sent, but are directed, and will be sent as soon as practicable.

Comparison of the gallon measures—Continued.

No. of standard.	Date.	Barometer.	Temp. of water.	Difference from standard.	Corrections for temp.	Result: — too large, + too small. Single.	Mean.	Corrected mean.	Destination.
	1844.	Inch.	Fah.	Grains.	Grains.	Grains.	Grains.	Grains.	
141	Feb. 7	29.91	47.0	−5.50	−5.676	+0.18	......	......	
	Mar. 4	29.99	54.1	+2.10	+2.334	−0.23	......	......	
	Mar. 5	30.46	50.0	−4.00	−3.658	−0.34	−0.13	......	Scottville, Puget's Sound, W. T.
142	Feb. 6	29.90	48.2	−4.90	−5.049	+0.15	......	......	
	Feb. 7	29.90	47.4	−5.20	−5.445	+0.24	......	......	
	Feb. 17	29.90	47.4	−5.50	−5.445	−0.05	......	......	
	Feb. 20	30.06	47.3	−4.00	−5.522	+1.52	......	......	
	Feb. 21	29.92	48.7	−3.60	−4.737	+1.14	......	......	
	Feb. 22	29.95	50.4	−2.75	−3.246	+0.50	......	......	
	Feb. 27	30.00	47.9	−3.9	−5.1899	+1.281	......	......	
	Feb. 28	30.23	49.3	−4.85	−4.255	−0.59	+0.524	......	California.
143	Feb. 9	29.94	46.4	−5.60	−5.770	+0.17	......	......	
	Mar. 4	30.03	53.9	+1.60	+1.952	−0.35	......	......	
	Mar. 5	30.46	49.9	−4.20	−3.738	−0.46	−0.21	......	Olympia, W. T.
144	Feb. 10	30.18	46.8	−5.70	−5.739	+0.04	......	......	
	Mar. 4	30.08	53.6	+1.00	+1.393	−0.39	......	......	
	Mar. 5	30.46	49.8	−4.40	−3.817	−0.58	−0.31	......	Mexico.
145	Feb. 9	29.94	46.6	−5.80	−5.707	−0.09	......	......	
	Feb. 10	30.18	46.2	−5.80	−5.824	+0.02	......	......	
	Mar. 4	30.08	53.4	+0.90	+1.132	−0.23	......	......	
	Mar. 5	30.46	49.6	−4.20	−3.991	−0.01	−0.08	......	California.
146	Feb. 12	30.22	48.6	−5.00	−4.807	−0.19	......	......	
	Feb. 13	30.20	47.0	−6.00	−5.676	−0.32	......	......	
	Feb. 17	29.90	47.3	−5.60	−5.522	−0.08	......	......	
	Feb. 20	30.12	47.2	−5.85	−5.559	−0.25	......	......	
	Feb. 21	29.98	48.9	−4.04	−4.596	+0.56	......	......	
	Feb. 22	30.00	50.6	−4.00	−3.019	−0.98	......	......	
	Feb. 27	29.98	47.95	−5.3	−5.1809	−0.141	......	......	
	Feb. 28	30.23	49 25	−5.13	−4.345	−0.785	......	......	
	Feb. 28	30.23	49.2	−5.13	−4.345	−0.78	−0.329	......	
147	Feb. 10	30.18	46.6	−5.70	−5 707	+0.01	......	......	Alexandria, Va. Delivered in September, 1853, in lieu of the old set, become injured.
	Mar. 4	30.08	53.4	+0.90	+1.132	−0.23	......	......	
	Mar. 5	30.46	49.5	−4.45	−4.077	−0.37	−0.20	......	
148	Feb. 9	29.94	46.3	−5.80	−5.797	0.00	......	......	
	Mar. 4	30.08	53.2	+0.73	+0.962	−0.23	......	......	
	Mar. 5	30.00	49.6	−5.00	−3.991	−1.009	......	......	
	Mar. 6	30.48	49.2	−4.27	−4.345	−0.07	−0.436	......	Shipped in December, 1850, to California.
149	Feb. 13	30.30	47.2	−5.80	−5.599	−0.20	......	......	
	Mar. 6	30.55	49.9	−3.35	−3.738	+0.39	......	......	
	Mar. 7	30.50	49.2	−4.53	−4.345	−0.18	0.00	......	
150	Feb. 13	30.30	46.8	−5.80	−5.739	−0.06	......	......	
	Feb. 17	29.94	47.3	−6.10	−5.522	−0.58	......	......	
	Mar. 6	30.55	49.9	−3.05	−3.738	+0.69	......	......	
	Mar. 7	30.50	49.2	−3.90	−4.345	+0.44	+0.12	......	Shipped in December, 1850, to California.
151	Feb. 16	29.90	48.8	−4.50	−4.666	+0.17	......	......	
	Mar. 6	30.55	49.8	−3.83	−3.817	−0.01	......	......	
	Mar. 7	30.50	49.2	−4.60	−4.345	−9.25	−0.03	......	Sent, October 27, 1853, to Yeocomico, Va.
152	Feb. 12	30.28	47.8	−5.30	−5.225	−0,07	......	......	
	Mar. 6	30.55	49.7	−3.80	−3.904	+0.10	......	......	
	Mar. 7	30.50	49.1	−4.83	−4.436	−0.39	−0.12	......	Shipped in December, 1850, to California.
153	Feb. 16	29.90	48.8	−4.50	−4.666	+0.17	......	......	
	Mar. 6	30.55	49.6	−3.60	−3.991	+0.39	......	......	
	Mar. 7	30.49	49.1	−4.00	−4.436	+0.43	+0.33	......	Pittsburg, Pa.; sent Oct. 27, 1853.
154	Feb. 14	30.21	48.4	−5.00	−4.928	−0.07	......	......	
	Feb. 17	29.94	47.5	−5.20	−5.390	+0.19	......	......	
	Mar. 6	30.55	49.6	−3.50	−3.991	+0.49	......	......	
	Mar. 7	30.49	49.1	−4.30	−4.435	−0.13	+0.12	......	
155	Feb. 17	29.90	47.4	−5.30	−5.445	+0.14	......	......	
	Mar. 6	30.55	49.5	−3.95	−4.077	+0.12	......	......	
	Mar. 7	30.49	49.0	−4.90	−4.525	−0.37	−0.12	......	Wheeling, Va.; sent October 27 1853.
156	Feb. 16	29.90	48.8	−4.70	−4.666	−0.03	......	......	
	Mar. 6	30.50	49.4	−3.70	−4.165	+0.46	......	......	
	Mar. 7	30.44	48.9	−4.45	−4 596	+0.15	+0.19	......	Camden, N. J.; sent October 27, 1853.
104	Feb. 15	30.15	49.1	−4.50	−4.436	−0.06	......	......	
	Mar. 6	30.50	49.3	−4.10	−4.255	+0.15	......	......	
	Mar. 7	30.44	48.9	−4.70	−4.596	−0.11	−0.01	......	
106	Feb. 16	29.90	48.8	−4.50	−4.666	+0.17	......	......	
	Mar. 6	30.50	49.3	−3.70	−4.255	+0.55	......	......	
	Mar. 7	30.44	48.9	−4.40	−4.596	+0.20	+0.31	......	Yorktown, Va.; sent October 27 1853.
107	Feb. 17	29.90	47.4	−5.50	−5.445	−0.05	......	......	
	Mar. 6	30.50	49.2	−3.85	−4.315	+0.49	......	......	
	Mar. 7	30.40	48.9	−4.35	−4.696	+0.25	+0.23	......	Petersburg, Va.; sent Oct. 27, '53

APPENDIX No. 25.

Comparison of the parts of gallon measures.

No. of standard.	Denomination.	Date.	Barometer.	Temp. of water.	Difference from standard.	Corrections for temp.	Result: — too large, + too small. Single.	Mean.	Corrected mean.	Destination.
		Previous to	Inches.	Fah.	Grains.	Grains.	Grains.	Grains.	Gr'ns.	
1	Half gall.	Apr. 5, 1842.		48.6	—2.4			+0.0036		
1	Quart	....do		47.4	—1.3			+0.0611		
1	Pint	....do		53.6	+0.15			—0.0241		
1	Half pint.	....do		52.8	—0.03			—0.0361		
2	Half gall.	....do		47.4	—2.65			+0.0723		
2	Quart	....do		56.8	+1.98			—0.1097		
2	Pint	....do		52.4	—0.12			—0.0319		
2	Half pint.	....do		49.5	—0.3			—0.0452		
3	Half gall.	....do		53.8	+0.8			—0.0899		
3	Quart	....do		56.4	+1.78			—0.1026		
3	Pint	....do		52.2	—0.15			—0.0335		
3	Half pint.	....do		49.5	—0.25			+0.0048		
4	Half gall.	....do		50.0	—1.85			—0.0208		
4	Quart	....do		48.6	—1.17			+0.0318		
4	Pint	....do		53.0	+0.05			—0.0139		
4	Half pint.	....do		49.5	—0.27			—0.0252		
5	Half gall.	....do		54.3	+1.3			—0.0626		
5	Quart	....do		53.7	+0.37			—0.0248		
5	Pint	....do		52.0	—0.15			+0.0022		
5	Half pint.	....do		49.8	—0.27			—0.0322		
6	Half gall.	....do		52.6	—0.2			—0.0413		State of Alabama.
6	Quart	....do		54.5	+0.73			—0.0602		
6	Pint	....do		51.6	—0.2			+0.0115		
6	Half pint.	....do		50.0	—0.22			+0.0086		
7	Half gall.	....do		54.0	+1.1			+0.0305		State of Maine.
7	Quart	....do		52.3	—0.1			+0.0946		
7	Pint	....do		51.8	—0.17			—0.0179		
7	Half pint.	....do		50.4	—0.15			+0.0520		
8	Half gall.	....do		53.0	+0.15			—0.1058		State of N. Hampshire.
8	Quart	....do		52.0	—0.25			+0.0545		
8	Pint	....do		51.5	—0.25			—0.0154		
8	Half pint.	....do		50.6	—0.17			+0.0187		
9	Half gall.	....do		53.6	+0.07			+0.0036		State of Vermont.
9	Quart	....do		51.7	—0.4			+0.0072		
9	Pint	....do		52.1	—0.1			+0.0343		
9	Half pint.	....do		50.8	—0.15			+0.0245		
10	Half gall.	....do		53.9	+0.08			—0.1762		State of Rhode Island.
10	Quart	....do		52.0	—0.3			+0.0045		
10	Pint	....do		51.7	—0.17			+0.0336		
10	Half pint.	....do		51.0	—0.17			—0.0125		
11	Half gall.	....do		53.3	+0.03			—0.2235		State of Massachusetts.
11	Quart	....do		52.2	—0.15			+0.0830		
11	Pint	....do		51.2	—0.25			+0.0312		
11	Half pint.	....do		51.8	—0.10			—0.0061		
12	Half gall.	....do		50.8	—1.5			—0.1036		State of Connecticut.
12	Quart	....do		52.2	—0.2			+0.0330		
12	Pint	....do		52.8	—0.07			—0.0891		
12	Half pint.	....do		52.3	—0.10			—0.0514		
13	Half gall.	....do		53.9	+0.9			—0.0762		State of New York.
13	Quart	....do		56.6	+1.93			—0.0561		
13	Pint	....do		53.3	+0.07			—0.0608		
13	Half pint.	....do		53.0	+0.03			—0.0019		
14	Half gall.	....do		51.2	—1.15			—0.0250		State of New Jersey.
14	Quart	....do		53.5	+0.2			—0.1156		
14	Pint	....do		54.0	+0.23			—0.0373		
14	Half pint.	....do		56.8	+0.55			+0.0276		
15	Half gall.	....do		54.0	+1.03			—0.0369		State of Pennsylvania.
15	Quart	....do		51.7	—0.35			+0.0572		
15	Pint	....do		53.5	+0.2			+0.0422		
15	Half pint.	....do		56.8	+0.57			+0.0476		
16	Half gall.	....do		50.0	—1.85			—0.0208		State of Delaware.
16	Quart	....do		51.8	—0.33			+0.0459		
16	Pint	....do		53.2	+0.12			0.0000		
16	Half pint.	....do		56.7	+0.55			+0.0406		
17	Half gall.	....do		50.1	—1.8			—0.0224		State of Maryland
17	Quart	....do		51.8	—0.32			+0.0559		
17	Pint	....do		53.3	+0.1			—0.0208		
7	Half pint.	....do		56.7	+0.5			—0.0094		

WEIGHTS AND MEASURES.

Comparison of the parts of gallon measures—Continued.

No. of standard.	Denomination.	Date.	Barometer.	Temp. of water.	Difference from standard.	Corrections for temp.	Result: — too large, + too small. Single.	Mean.	Corrected mean.	Destination.
		Previous to	Inches.	Fah.	Grains.	Grains.	Grains.	Grains.	Gr'ns.	
18	Half gall.	April 5,1842		54.0	+1.1			+0.0305		State of Virginia.
18	Quart	....do.		51.8	—0.33			+0.0459		
18	Pint	...do.		53.0	+0.07			+0.0061		
18	Half pint.	....do.		56.6	+0.45			—0.0465		
19	Half gall.	....do.		50.6	—1.4			—0.1096		State of North Carolina.
19	Quart	....do.		51.7	—0.33			+0.0772		
19	Pint	....do.		53.1	+0.07			—0.0220		
19	Half pint.	....do.		56.6	+0.43			—0.0665		
20	Half gall.	....do.		51.1	—1.15			+0.0028		State of South Carolina.
20	Quart	....do.		52.0	—0.32			+0.0155		
20	Pint.	...do.		53.5	+0.13			—0.0278		
20	Half pint.	....do.		56.7	+0.4			—0.1094		
21	Half gall.	....do.		51.9	—0.07			—0.0196		State of Georgia.
21	Quart	....do.		52.1	—0.3			—0.0311		
21	Pint	....do.		53.1	+0.07			—0.0220		
21	Half pint.	....do.		56.5	+0.4			—0.0836		
22	Half gall.	....do.		52.2	—0.43			+0.0361		State of Louisiana.
22	Quart	....do.		51.7	—0.35			+0.0572		
22	Pint	....do.		52.8	—0.05			—0.0628		
22	Half pint.	....do.		56.4	+0.4			—0.0706		
23	Half gall.	....do.		51.1	—1.2			—0.0072		State of Alabama.
23	Quart	....do.		52.2	—0.2			+0.0330		
23	Pint	....do.		52.9	+0.03			—0.0080		
23	Half pint.	...do.		56.4	+0.45			—0.0206		
24	Half gall.	....do.		50.4	—1.53			+0.0928		State of Ohio.
24	Quart	....do.		51.7	—0.38			+0.0272		
24	Pint	....do.		52.5	0.1			—0.0412		
24	Half pint.	....do		52.2	0.00			+0.0852		
25	Half gall.	....do.		48.2	—2.55			—0.0257		State of Missouri.
25	Quart	....do.		51.9	—0.3			+0.0402		
25	Pint	....do.		53.2	+0.1			—0.0200		
25	Half pint.	....do.		52.4	—0.05			—0.0110		
26	Half gall.	....do.		49.0	—2.2			+0.0629		State of Mississippi.
26	Quart	....do.		51.9	—0.37			—0.0298		
26	Pint	....do.		53.4	+0.15			+0.0085		
26	Half pint.	....do.		51.0	—0.13			+0.0275		
27	Half gall.	....do.		49.1	—2.27			—0.0522		State of Kentucky.
27	Quart	....do.		53.4	+0.25			—0.0330		
27	Pint	....do.		53.5	+0.17			+0.0122		
27	Half pint.	....do.		51.0	—0.2			—0.0425		
28	Half gall.	....do.		49.1	—2.25			—0.0322		State of Indiana.
28	Quart	....do.		53.1	+0.1			—0.0841		
28	Pint	....do.		53.5	+0.17			+0.0122		
28	Half pint.	...do.		50.5	—0.2			—0.0043		
29	Half gall.	....do.		49.1	—2.2			+0.0178		State of Illinois.
29	Quart	....do.		53.0	+0.12			+0.0079		
29	Pint	....do.		53.8	+0.2			—0.0207		
29	Half pint.	....do.		51.2	—0.15			—0.0099		
30	Half gall.	....do.		49.5	—1.87			+0.1686		State of Tennessee.
30	Quart	....do.		53.0	+0.13			+0.0021		
30	Pint	....do.		53.6	+0.2			+0.0259		
30	Half pint.	....do.		51.2	—0.17			+0.0045		
31	Half gall.	....do.		49.7	—2.05			—0.1078		State of Arkansas.
31	Quart	....do.		53.0	+0.1			—0.0279		
31	Pint	....do.		53.0	+0.05			—0.0139		
31	Half pint.	....do.		51.7	—0.07			+0.0318		
32	Half gall.	....do.		50.5	—1.6			—0.0338		State of Michigan.
32	Quart	....do.		53.2	+0.17			—0.0701		
32	Pint	....do.		53.7	+0.2			+0.0026		
32	Half pint.	....do.		51.5	—0.15			—0.0327		
33	Half gall.	....do.		52.8	—0.05			—0.0987		Portland, Me.
33	Quart	....do.		52.6	—0.1			—0.0207		
33	Pint	....do.		56.7	+1.02			+0.0011		
33	Half pint.	....do.		51.5	—0.15			—0.0327		
34	Half gall.	....do.		46.6	—2.8			+0.0536		Salem, Mass.
34	Quart	....do.		52.5	—0.1			—0.0177		
34	Pint	....do.		56.8	+1.07			+0.0251		
34	Half pint.	....do.		51.6	—0.1			+0.0057		
35	Half gall.	....do.		46.8	—2.8			+0.0693		Boston, Mass.
35	Quart	....do.		52.4	—0.17			—0.0138		
35	Pint	....do.		56.8	+1.07			+0.0251		
35	Half pint.	....do.		51.7	—0.05			+0.0518		
36	Half gall.	....do.		52.8	—0.05			—0.0987		Newburyport, Mass.
36	Quart	....do.		52.4	—0.17			—0.0108		

Comparison of the parts of gallon measures—Continued.

No. of standard.	Denomination.	Date.	Barometer.	Temp. of water.	Difference from standard.	Corrections for temp.	Result: — too large, + too small. Single.	Mean.	Corrected mean.	Destination.
		Previous to	Inches.	Fah.	Grains.	Grains.	Grains.	Grains.	Gr'ns.	
36	Pint......	April 5, 1842	....	56.6	+0.93	....	....	—0.0630	......	Newburyport,
36	Half pint.	....do.....	....	52.2	0.00	....	....	+0.0582	......	Mass.
37	Half gall.	....do.....	....	52.8	0.00	....	....	—0.0485	......	New Bedford,
37	Quart ..	....do.....	....	52.5	—0.13	....	....	—0.0123	......	Mass.
37	Pint......	....do.....	....	55.0	+0.57	....	....	+0.0376	......	
37	Half pint.	....do.....	....	53.0	+0.07	....	....	+0.0381	......	
38	Half gall.	....do.....	....	52.8	0.00	....	....	—0.0485	......	Providence, R. I.
38	Quart ..	....do.....	....	52.6	—0.1	....	....	—0.0207	......	
38	Pint......	....do.....	....	54.8	+0.52	....	....	+0.0348	......	
38	Half pint.	....do.....	....	52.7	—0.05	....	....	—0.0431	......	
39	Half gall.	....do.....	....	52.4	—0.3	....	....	+0.0124	......	Newark, N. J.
39	Quart ..	....do.....	....	52.2	—0.2	....	....	+0.0330	......	
39	Pint......	....do.....	....	54.8	+0.47	....	....	—0.0152	......	
39	Half pint.	....do.....	....	52.3	—0.07	....	....	—0.0214	......	
40	Half gall.	....do.....	....	47.6	—2.7	....	....	—0.0326	......	New Haven, Ct.
40	Quart ..	....do.....	....	52.4	—0.15	....	....	+0.0062	......	
40	Pint......	....do.....	....	55.0	+0.57	....	....	+0.0376	......	
40	Half pint.	....do.....	....	52.1	—0.03	....	....	+0.0371	......	
41	Half gall.	....do.....	....	48.2	—2.5	....	....	+0.0243	......	NewYork, N. Y.
41	Quart ..	....do.....	....	52.6	—0.07	....	....	+0.0093	......	
41	Pint......	....do.....	....	55.0	+0.06	....	....	—0.0676	......	
41	Half pint.	....do.....	....	52.5	—0.03	....	....	—0.0006	......	
42	Half gall.	....do.....	....	52.5	—0.17	....	....	+0.0655	......	Philadelphia.
42	Quart ..	....do.....	....	46.8	—1.4	....	....	+0.0346	......	
42	Pint......	....do.....	....	54.9	+0.5	....	....	—0.0088	......	
42	Half pint.	....do.....	....	52.5	—0.05	....	....	—0.0206	......	
43	Half gall.	....do.....	....	52.9	+0.05	....	....	—0.1022	......	Wilmington, Del.
43	Quart ..	....do.....	....	46.8	—1.17	....	....	—0.0034	......	
43	Pint......	....do.....	....	53.2	+0.05	....	....	—0.0700	......	
43	Half pint.	....do.....	....	52.6	0.00	....	....	+0.0198	......	
44	Half gall.	....do.....	....	50.8	—1.4	....	....	—0.0036	......	Baltimore, Md.
44	Quart....	....do.....	....	52.9	+0.03	....	....	—0.0461	......	
44	Pint......	....do.....	....	52.9	+0.03	....	....	—0.0080	......	
44	Half pint.	....do.....	....	52.6	0.00	....	....	+0.0198	......	
45	Half gall.	....do.....	....	53.8	+0.77	....	....	—0.1129	......	Norfolk, Va.
45	Quart ...	....do.....	....	53.8	+0.4	....	....	—0.0414	......	
45	Pint......	....do.....	....	52.9	0.00	....	....	—0.0380	......	
45	Half pint.	....do.....	....	52.7	—0 03	....	....	—0.0231	......	
46	Half gall.	....do.....	....	52.6	—0.2	....	....	—0.0413	......	Alexandria, Va.
46	Quart ...	....do.....	....	53.7	+0.37	....	....	—0.0248	......	
46	Pint......	....do.....	....	52.6	—0.07	....	....	—0.0394	......	
46	Half pint.	....do.....	....	52.7	—0.05	....	....	—0.0431	......	
47	Half gall.	....do.....	....	52.6	—0.17	....	....	—0.0113	......	Richmond, Va.
47	Quart....	....do.....	....	52.8	0.00	....	....	0.0000	......	
47	Pint......	....do.....	....	52.6	—0.07	....	....	—0.0394	......	
47	Half pint.	....do.....	....	52.8	0.00	....	....	—0.0060	......	
48	Half gall.	....do.....	....	52.5	—0.2	....	....	+0.0355	......	Wilmington, N.C.
48	Quart ...	....do.....	....	51.7	+0.4	....	....	+0.0072	......	
48	Pint......	....do.....	....	52.6	—0.05	....	....	—0.0104	......	
48	Half pint.	....do.....	....	53.2	+0 05	....	....	—0.0100	......	
49	Half gall.	....do.....	....	52.4	—0.3	....	....	+0.0124	......	Charleston, S. C.
49	Quart ...	....do.....	....	52.3	—0.15	....	....	+0.0446	......	
49	Pint......	....do.....	....	53.6	+0.17	....	....	—0.0041	......	
49	Half pint.	....do.....	....	53.0	0.00	....	....	—0.0319	......	
50	Half gall.	....do.....	....	46.6	—2.9	....	....	—0.0464	......	Savannah, Ga.
50	Quart ...	....do.....	....	50.2	—0.87	....	....	—0.0070	......	
50	Pint......	....do.....	....	49.7	—0.47	....	....	+0.0181	......	
50	Half pint.	....do.....	....	49.8	—0.2	....	....	+0.0378	......	
51	Half gall.	....do.....	....	52.5	—0.2	....	....	+0.0355	......	Mobile, Ala.
51	Quart....	....do.....	....	49.4	—0.97	....	....	+0.0713	......	
51	Pint......	....do.....	....	52.7	+0.05	....	....	+0.0637	......	
51	Half pint.	....do.....	....	53.3	+0.1	....	....	+0.0346	......	
52	Half gall.	....do.....	....	52.6	—0.2	....	....	—0.0413	......	Key West, Fla.
52	Quart....	....do.....	....	50.0	—0.85	....	....	+0.0646	......	
52	Pint......	....do.....	....	52.9	+0.07	....	....	+0.0320	......	
52	Half pint.	....do.....	....	53.2	+0.07	....	....	+0.0100	......	
53	Half gall.	....do.....	....	47.0	—2.8	....	....	+0.0379	......	Apalachicola, Fla.
53	Quart...	....do.....	....	50.0	—0.9	....	....	+0.0146	......	
53	Pint......	....do.....	....	53.1	+0.07	....	....	—0.0230	......	
53	Half pint.	....do.....	....	53.0	+0.03	....	....	—0.0019	......	
54	Half gall.	....do.....	....	45.0	—2.8	....	....	—0.0155	......	New Orleans, La.
54	Quart ...	....do.....	....	50.2	—0.85	....	....	+0.0130	......	
54	Pint......	....do.....	....	52.9	+0.07	....	....	+0.0320	......	
54	Half pint.	....do.....	....	53.6	+0.1	....	....	—9.0130	......	

WEIGHTS AND MEASURES. 193

Comparison of parts of gallon measures—Continued.

No. of standard.	Denomination.	Date. 1851.	Barometer. Inches.	Temp. of water. Fahr.	Difference from standard. Grains.	Corrections for temp. Grains.	Result: — too large + too small. Single. Grains.	Mean. Grains.	Corrected mean. Gr'ns.	Destination.
55	Half gall.	March 8	30.00	50.2	—1.75	—1.776	+0.026			
		March 12	30.25	52.4	—0.75	—0.3124	—0.4376			
		March 13	30.17	52.6	—0.5	—0.1587	—0.3413	—0.251		
55	Quart...	March 4	30.30	50.0	—0.97	—0.914	—0.056			
		March 14	30.20	53.6	+0.43	+0.348	+0.082			
		March 15	30.13	54.6	+0.95	+0.784	+0.166	+0.064		
55	Pint......	March 13	30.18	52.9	+0.03	+0.0380	—0.008			
		March 17	29.72	54.0	+0.45	+0.267	+0.183	+0.087		
55	Half pint.	March 8	30.00	50.6	—0.2	—0.188	—0.012			
		March 18	29.55	51.4	—0.14	—0.125	—0.015	—0.013		
56	Half gall.	March 11	30.19	51.0	—1.25	—1.26	+0.01			
		March 12	30.25	52.4	—0.72	—0.3124	—0.4076			
		March 13	30.17	52.6	—0.45	—0.1587	—0.2913	—0.230		
56	Quart...	March 5	30.10	52.6	+0.02	—0.079	+0.099			
		March 14	30.20	53.6	+0.37	+0.348	+0.022			
		April 16	29.61	51.3	—0.37	—0.5314	+0.1614	+0.094		
56	Pint......	March 13	30.18	52.8	+0.1	+0.012	+0.088			
		March 17	29.72	54.0	+0.33	+0.267	+0.063	+0.075		
56	Half pint.	March 8	30.00	50.6	—0.17	—0.188	+0.018			
		March 18	29.55	51.2	—0.15	—0.143	—0.007	+0.005		
57	Half gall.	March 8	30.00	50.2	—1.77	—1.776	+0.006			
		March 13	30.15	52.6	—0.4	—0.1587	—0.2413			
		March 15	30.10	54.6	+1.75	+1.568	+0.183	—0.017		
57	Quart...	March 4	30.30	49.8	—1.04	—0.954	—0.086			
		March 14	30.20	53.6	+0.45	+0.348	+0.102			
		March 15	30.13	54.6	+0.84	+0.784	+0.056	+0.024		California, Dec. 18, 1854.
57	Pint.....	March 14	30.20	53.6	+0.13	+0.174	+0.044			
		March 17	29.70	53.9	+0.35	+0.2437	+0.107	+0.076		
57	Half pint.	March 11	30.16	50.6	—0.15	—0.188	+0.038			
		March 18	29.55	51.1	—0.1	—0.1491	+0.0491	+0.043		
58	Half gall.	March 10	30.20	48.2	—2.6	—2.524	—0.076			
		March 13	30.13	52.6	—0.25	—0.1587	—0.0913			
		March 15	30.10	54.4	+1.3	+1.460	—0.160	—0.109		
58	Quart...	March 4	30.30	49.8	—2.05	—0.954	—0.096			
		March 14	30.20	53.6	+0.22	+0.348	—0.128	—0.112		France.
58	Pint.....	....do.....	30.20	53.6	+0.35	+0.174	+0.076			
		March 17	29.70	53.8	+0.38	+0.220	+0.16	+0.118		
58	Half pint.	March 10	30.15	48.6	—0.3	—0.30045	+0.00045			
		March 18	29.55	51.1	—0.2	—0.1491	—0.0509	—0.025		
59	Half gall.	March 12	30.25	52.4	—0.63	—0.3124	—0.3176			
		March 13	30.13	52.6	—0.19	—0.1587	—0.0313	—0.174		
59	Quart...	March 8	30.00	50.4	—0.75	—0.811	+0.061			
		March 14	30.20	53.6	+0.4	+0.348	+0.052	+0.057		Mexico.
59	Pint.....	....do.....	30.20	53.6	+0.15	+0.174	—0.024			
		March 17	29.70	53.7	+0.25	+0.1985	+0.0515	+0.0137		
59	Half pint.	March 10	30.17	48.5	—0.28	—0.3042	+0.0242			
		March 18	29.55	51.0	—0.1	—0.154	+0.0509	+0.0375		
60	Half gall.	March 11	30.19	50.7	—1.4	—1.4530	+0.053			
		March 13	30.13	52.5	—0.3	—0.2355	—0.0645	—0.006		
60	Quart...	March 3	30.08	49.6	—1.05	—0.997	—0.053			
		March 14	30.20	53.6	+0.45	+0.348	+0.102	+0.025		
60	Pint.....	March 13	30.18	52.6	—0.05	—0.039	—0.011			
		March 17	29.70	53.6	+0.20	+0.174	+0.026	+0.008		
60	Half pint.	March 10	30.17	48.4	—0.3	—0.307	+0.007			
		March 18	29.55	51.0	—0.17	—0.154	—0.016	—0.005		
61	Half gall.	March 27	30.30	54.7	+1.6	+1.754	—0.154	—0.154		
61	Quart...	March 22	30.10	51.2	—0.55	—0.562	+0.012			
		March 25	30.10	52.8	+0.03	+0.024	+0.006	+0.009		
61	Pint.....	March 21	29.99	50.4	—0.48	—0.405	—0.075			
		March 26	30.48	52.3	—0.1	—0.09731	—0.00269	—0.0388		
61	Half pint.	March 21	29.59	50.6	—0.21	—0.188	—0.022			
		April 11	30.40	55.4	+0.37	+0.3134	+0.0606	+0.0193		
62	Half gall.	March 27	30.30	54.7	+1.73	+1.754	—0.024	—0.024		
62	Quart...	March 22	30.10	51.2	—0.7	—0.562	—0.138			
		March 25	30.10	52.7	—0.07	—0.0275	—0.0425	—0.09		
62	Pint.....	March 22	30.10	51.4	—0.17	—0.250	+0.080			
		March 26	30.48	52.3	—0.05	—0.09731	+0.04731	+0.064		
62	Half pint.	March 24	29.85	50.2	—0.15	—0.222	+0.072			
		April 11	30.40	55.6	+0.4	+0.3441	+0.0559	+0.0639		
63	Half gall.	March 27	30.30	54.7	+1.63	+1.754	—0.124	—0.124		
63	Quart...	March 24	29.85	49.9	—1.05	—0.934475	—0.115525			
		March 26	30.48	52.3	—0.3	—0.19462	—0.10538	—0.11		
63	Pint.....	March 22	30.10	51.4	—0.15	—0.250	+0.10			
		March 26	30.48	52.2	—0.25	—0.116	—0.134	—0.017		

Ex. Doc. 27——13

Comparison of parts of gallon measures—Continued.

No. of standard.	Denomination.	Date.	Barometer.	Temp. of water.	Difference from standard.	Corrections for temp.	Result: —too large; +too small.			Destination.
							Single.	Mean.	Corrected mean.	
		1851.	Inches.	Fah.	Grains.	Grains.	Grains.	Grains.	Gr'ns.	
63	Half pint.	March 22	30.10	51.4	—0.14	—0.125	—0.015			
		April 11	30.40	55.5	+0.35	+0.3287	+0.0213	+0.003		
64	Half gall.	......do.....	30.40	55.4	+2.45	+2.5075	—0.0575			
		April 14	29.82	51.2	—0.95	—1.125	+0.175	+0.0587		
64	Quart...	March 25	30.10	52.8	—0.05	+0.024	—0.074			
		March 26	30.48	52.2	—0.4	—0.233	—0.167	—0.12		Alexandria, Va., Sept., 1853.
64	Pint.....	March 22	30.10	51.3	—0.35	—0.2657	—0.0843			
		March 26	30.48	52.2	—0.2	—0.116	—0.084	—0.084		
64	Half pint.	March 21	29.99	50.5	—0.17	—0.181875	+0.011875			
		April 11	30.40	55.5	+0.35	+0.3287	+0.0213	+0.0166		
65	Half gall.	April 12	30.55	48.8	—2.47	—2.333	—0.137			
		April 14	29.82	51.1	—0.83	—1.19285	+0.36285	+0.1129		
65	Quart...	April 18	29.76	54.8	+0.95	+0.970	—0.020	—0.020		
65	Pint.....	April 17	29.62	54.2	+0.35	+0.316	+0.034	+0.034		
65	Half pint.	April 15	29.77	53.2	+0.10	+0.060	+0.040	+0.040		
66	Half gall.	......do.....	29.78	52.8	+0.1	+0.048	+0.052	+0.052		
66	Quart...	April 17	29.62	54.3	+0.80	+0.676	+0.124	+0.124		
66	Pint.....	April 18	29.76	54.7	+0.50	+0.4385	+0.0615	+0.0615		
66	Half pint.	April 15	29.77	53.2	0.00	+0.060	—0.060	—0.060		
67	Half gall.	Nov. 18	30.31	54.1	+1.18	+0.070				
		Nov. 28	29.75	49.7	—1.7	—1.9521	+0.2521	+0.161		
67	Quart...	Dec. 5	30.38	50.3	—0.8	—0.8372	+0.0372			
		Dec. 16	30.10	49.0	—1.3	—1.1314	—0.1686	—0.0657		
67	Pint.....	Dec. 23	30 25	49.4	—0.62	—0.5206	—0.0994			
		1852.								
		Jan. 3	29.93	50.9	—0.45	—0.3491	—0.1179	—0.1086		
67	Half pint.	Jan. 7	29.90	49.6	—0.27	—0.2494	—0.0206			
		Jan. 15	29.65	51.8	—0.12	—0.0939	—0.0261	—0.023		
		1851.								
68	Half gall.	Nov. 18	30.31	54.1	+1.27	+1.18	+0.090			
		Nov. 28	29.75	49.7	—1.73	—1.9521	+0.2221	+0.156		
68	Quart...	Dec. 5	30.38	50.3	—0.83	—0.8372	+0.0072			
		Dec. 16	30.10	49.0	—1.03	—1.1314	+0.1014	+0.054		
68	Pint.....	Dec. 23	30.25	49.4	—0.55	—0.5206	—0.0293			
		1852.								
		Jan. 3	29.93	50.8	—0.43	—0.3491	—0.0809	—0.055		
68	Half pint.	Jan. 7	29.90	49.6	—0.25	—0.2494	—0.0006			
		Jan. 15	29.65	51.8	—0.07	—0.0939	+0.0239	+0.0166		
		1851.								
69	Half gall.	Nov. 20	30.16	53.6	+0.87	+0.696	+0.174			
		Nov. 29	30.07	51.9	—0.6	—0.6804	+0.0804	+0.127		
69	Quart...	Dec. 8	30.13	48.7	—1.12	—1.1842	+0.0642			
		Dec. 17	30.26	49.6	—1.2	—0.9978	—0.2092	—0.0725		
69	Pint.....	Dec. 27	30.66	49.0	—0.63	—0.5657	—0.0643			
		1852.								
		Jan. 3	29.93	50.8	—0.4	—0.3491	—0.0509	—0.0576		
69	Half pint.	Jan. 9	29.70	49.5	—0.3	—0.259875	—0.040125			
		Jan. 15	29.65	51.8	—0.1	—0.0939	—0.0061	—0.023		
		1851.								
70	Half gall.	Nov. 22	29.87	54.8	+1.87	+1.940	—0.070			
		Nov. 29	30.07	51.8	—0.63	—0.7518	+0.1218	+0.0259		
70	Quart...	Dec. 6	30.62	50.8	—0.62	—0.6982	+0.0782			
		Dec. 17	30.26	49.5	—0.9	—1.0193	+0.1193	+0.0987		
70	Pint.....	Dec. 26	30.33	50.0	—0.53	—0.4573	—0.0727			
		1852.								
		Jan. 3	29.93	50.8	—0.23	—0.3491	+0.1191	+0.023		
70	Half pint.	Jan. 10	29.92	50.9	—0.2	—0.1660	—0.034			
		Jan. 15	29.65	51.7	—0.1	—0.1018	+0.0018	—0.016		
		1851.								
71	Half gall.	Nov. 19	30.23	53.2	+0.37	+0.485	—0.115			
		Nov. 29	30.10	51.8	—0.6	—0.7518	+0.1518	+0.0184		
71	Quart...	Dec. 8	30.13	48.6	—1.25	—1.2018	—0.0492			
		Dec. 17	30.24	49.3	—1.17	—1.0638	—0.1062	—0.0777		
71	Pint.....	Dec. 30	30.17	50.6	—0.33	—0.3774	+0.0474			
		1852.								
		Jan. 5	29.67	50.3	—0.5	—0.4186	—0.0814	—0.017		
71	Half pint.	Jan. 13	30.13	49.6	—0.17	—0.1887	—0.0187			
		Jan. 16	29.81	50.5	—0.12	—0.1982	+0.0782	+0.0297		
		1851.								
72	Half gall.	Nov. 19	30.23	53.2	+0.46	+0.485	—0.035			
		Nov. 29	30.10	51.8	—0.67	—0.7518	+0.0818	+0.023		
72	Quart...	Dec. 8	30.13	48.6	—1.22	—1.2018	—0.0182			
		Dec. 17	30.24	49.1	—1.22	—1.1589	—0.0611	—0 0396		

WEIGHTS AND MEASURES.

Comparison of the parts of gallon measures—Continued.

No. of standard.	Denomination.	Date.	Barometer.	Temp. of water.	Difference from standard.	Corrections for Temp.	Result: — too large + too small. Single.	Mean.	Corrected mean.	Destination.
		1851.	Inches.	Fahr.	Grains.	Grains.	Grains.	Grains.	Gr'ns.	
72	Pint.....	Dec. 26	30.40	50.0	—0.53	—0.4573	—0.0727	......	......	......
		1852.								
		Jan. 5	29.67	50.3	—0.53	—0.4186	—0.1114	—0.092		
72	Half pint.	Jan. 10	29.92	51.2	—0.17	—0.1406	—0.0294	....		......
		Jan. 16	29.81	50.5	—0.2	—0.1982	—0.0018	—0.0156		......
		1851.								
73	Half gall.	Nov. 20	30.16	53.4	+0.75	+0.566	+0.184	....		......
		Dec. 1	30.32	49.5	—1.75	—2.0386	+0.2886			
		Dec. 2	30.10	49.5	—2.00	—2.0386	+0.0389	+0.170		.. ...
73	Quart ...	Dec. 9	30.33	52.9	+0.05	+0.0761	—0.0261	....		......
		Dec. 17	30.24	49.0	—1.05	—1.1314	—0.0814	—0.0537		......
73	Pint.....	Dec. 26	30.40	50.0	—0.55	—0.4573	—0.0927	....		......
		1852.								
		Jan. 5	29.67	50.3	—0.52	—0.4186	—0.1014	—0.097		
73	Half pint.	Jan. 12	30.18	50.4	—0.25	—0.2028	—0.0472	....		......
		Jan. 16	29.81	50.4	—0.22	—0.2028	—0.0172	—0.032		. ....
		1851.								
74	Half gall.	Nov. 18	30.31	53.7	+0.89	+0.794	+0.096	....		......
		Dec. 1	30.32	49.4	—1.9	—2.0826	+0.1826			
		Dec. 2	30.10	49.6	—1.82	—1.9956	+0.1756	+0.151		
74	Quart ...	Dec. 9	30.33	52.8	+0.07	+0.0242	—0.0458	....		......
		Dec. 18	30.18	49.3	—0.9	—1.0638	+0.1638	+0.059		......
74	Pint.....	Dec. 27	30.66	48.8	—0.65	—0.5823	—0.0667	....		......
		1852.-								
		Jan. 5	29.65	50.2	—0.5	—0.4315	—0.0685	—0.067		
74	Half pint.	Jan. 12	30.18	50.3	—0.27	—0.2093	—0.0607	....		......
		Jan. 16	29.81	50.4	—0.15	—0.2028	+0.0528	—0.004		......
		1851.								
75	Half gall.	Nov. 25	30.08	52.0	—0.7	—0.609	+0.091	....		......
		Dec. 1	30.32	49.4	—1.8	—2.0826	+0.2826	+0.0958		......
75	Quart ...	Dec. 6	30.65	50.6	—0.8	—0.7548	—0.0452	....		......
		Dec. 18	30.18	49.4	—1.1	—1.0413	—0.0587	—0.052		......
75	Pint.....	Dec. 30	30.17	50.6	—0.37	—0.3774	+0.0074	....		......
		1852.								
		Jan. 5	29.65	50.2	—0.53	—0.4315	—0.0985	—0.0456		
75	Half pint.	Jan. 13	30.13	49.6	—0.15	—0.1887	—0.0387	....		......
		Jan. 16	29.81	50.4	—0.17	—0.2028	+0.0328	—0.003		......
		1851.								
76	Half gall.	Nov. 24	30.07	50.6	—1.37	—1.509	+0.139	....		......
		Dec. 1	30.32	49.4	—1.95	—2.0826	+0.1326	+0.1358		......
76	Quart ...	Dec. 11	30.04	52.7	+0.05	—0.0275	+0.0775	....		......
		Dec. 18	30.18	49.4	—1.08	—1.0413	—0.6387	+0.019		......
76	Pint.....	Dec. 29	30.16	51.1	—0.32	—0.2984	—0.0216	....		......
		1852.								
		Jan. 6	29.14	49.5	—0.6	—0.50975	—0.09025	—0.0559		
76	Half pint.	Jan. 9	29.70	50.2	—0.22	—0.2157	—0.0043	....		......
		Jan. 10	29.92	51.4	—0.13	—0.1250	—0.005	....		
		Jan. 16	29.81	50.3	—0.2	—0.2093	+0.0093	0.000		
		1851.								
77	Half gall.	Nov. 24	30.07	50.6	—1.67	—1.509	—0.160	....		
		Dec. 1	30.32	49.3	—1.97	—2.1276	+0.1576	—0.001		
77	Quart ...	Dec. 17	30.25	49.6	—1.05	—0.9978	—0.0522	....		
		Dec. 18	30.18	49.3	—1.2	—1.0638	—0.1362	....		
		Dec. 19	30.00	49.0	—1.2	—1.1314	—0.0686	—0.086		{ Wisconsin, November 11, '54.
77	Pint.....	Dec. 31	29.93	52.6	—0.05	—0.03965	—0.01035	....		
		1852.								
		Jan. 6	29.14	49.6	—0.48	—0.4989	+0.0189	+0.004		
77	Half pint.	Jan. 10	29.92	51.3	—0.12	—0.1328	—0.0128	....		
		Jan. 17	30.10	50.3	—0.22	—0.2093	—0.0193	—0.016		
		1851.								
78	Half gall..	Nov. 28	29.80	49.6	—2.1	—1.9956	—0.144	....		
		Dec. 1	30.32	49.2	—2.15	—2.1727	+0.0237	—0.061		
78	Quart ...	Dec. 16	30.03	49.1	—1.12	—1.1589	+0.0389	....		
		Dec. 18	30.18	49.4	—1.07	—1.0413	—0.0287	+0.005		......
78	Pint.....	Jan. 2	30.10	50.2	—0.35	—0.4315	+0.0815	.. ..		
		Jan. 6	29.14	49.6	—0.45	—0.4989	—●.0489	+0.065		
78	Half pint	Jan. 15	29.65	50.7	—0.15	—0.1816	+0.0316	....		
		Jan. 17	30.10	50.3	—0.13	—0.2093	+0.0793	+●.055		
		1851.								
79	Half gall.	Nov. 25	30.05	51.8	—0.67	—0.751	+0.081	....		
		Dec. 1	30.32	49.2	—1.97	—2.1727	+0.2027	+0.142		
79	Quart ..	Dec. 11	30.04	52.4	—0.13	—0.1512	+0.0212	....		......
		Dec. 18	30.18	49.4	—0.93	—1.0413	+0.1113	....		

Comparison of the parts of gallon measures—Continued.

No. of standard.	Denomination.	Date.	Barometer.	Temp. of water.	Difference from standard.	Corrections for temperature.	Result: — too large, + too small. Single.	Mean.	Corrected mean.	Destination.
		1851.	Inches.	Fah.	Grains.	Grains.	Grains.	Grains.	Gr'ns.	
79	Quart..	Dec. 19	30.00	49.0	—1.03	—1.1314	+0.1014	+0.078	......	
		1852.								
79	Pint....	Jan. 2	30.10	50.2	—0.35	—0.4315	+0.0815			
		Jan. 6	29.14	49.5	—0.5	—0.50975	+0.00975	+0.0456	......	
79	Half pint	Jan. 14	29.88	50.1	—0.23	—0.2222	—0.0078			
		Jan. 17	30.10	50.3	—0.17	—0.2093	+0.0393	+0.0157	......	
		1851.								
80	Half gall.	Nov. 26	29.95	50.7	—1.64	—1.453	—0.187			
		Dec. 1	30.32	49.1	—2.3	—2.2178	—0.0822	—0.135	......	
80	Quart..	Dec. 15	29.96	49.6	—1.0	—0.9978	—0.0022			
		Dec. 18	30.18	49.4	—0.97	—1.0413	+0.0713	+0.0345	......	
		1852.								
80	Pint.....	Jan. 5	29.70	50.7	—0.3	—0.3632	+0.0632			
		Jan. 6	29.14	49.5	—0.55	—0.50975	—0.04025			
		Jan. 7	29.84	49.6	—0.52	—0.4989	—0.0213	+0.0005	......	
80	Half pint	Jan. 14	29.88	50.0	—0.25	—0.2286	—0.0214			
		Jan. 17	30.10	50.3	—0.17	—0.2093	+0.0393	+0.009	......	
		1851.								
81	Half gall.	Nov. 29	30.05	52.2	—0.6	—0.4661	—0.1339			
		Dec. 1	30.32	49.1	—2.18	—2.2178	+0.0378			
		Dec. 2	30.10	49.5	—2.1	—2.0386	—0.0614	—0.052	......	
81	Quart..	Dec. 15	29.96	50.7	—9.75	—0.7261	—0.0239			
		Dec. 18	30.18	49.4	—0.93	—1.0413	+0.1113	+0.0437	......	
81	Pint.....	Dec. 31	29.93	52.3	—0.2	—0.0973	—0.0027			
		1852.								
		Jan. 6	29.15	49.5	—0.47	—0.50975	+0.03975	+0.0185		
81	Half pint	Jan. 17	30.10	50.2	—9.2	—0.2157	+0.0157	+0.0157	......	
		1851.								
82	Half gall.	Nov. 26	29.99	50.6	—1.45	—1.5096	+0.0596			
		Dec. 2	30.10	50.0	—1.73	—1.8292	+0.0992	+0.079	......	
82	Quart..	Dec. 16	30.03	49.1	—1.2	—1.1589	—0.0411			
		Dec. 19	30.00	49.3	—1.15	—1.0638	—0.0862	—0.0636	......	
		1852.								
82	Pint.....	Jan. 2	30.10	50.1	—0.42	—0.4444	+0.0244			
		Jan. 6	29.15	49.5	—0.42	—0.50975	+0.08975	+0.057	......	
82	Half pint	Jan. 14	29.88	49.6	—0.27	—0.2494	—0.0206			
		Jan. 17	30.12	50.2	—0.22	—0.2157	—0.0043	—0.012	......	
		1851.								
83	Half gall.	Nov. 29	30.05	52.1	—0.53	—0.5375	+0.0075			
		Dec. 2	30.10	49.9	—1.95	—1.8689	—0.0811	—0.0368	......	
83	Quart..	Dec. 15	29.96	50.4	—0.73	—0.8114	+0.0814			
		Dec. 19	30.00	49.3	—0.93	—1.0638	+0.1338	+0.1076	......	China.
		1852.								
83	Pint.....	Jan. 5	29.70	50.7	—0.35	—0.3632	+0.0132			
		Jan. 7	29.84	49.6	—0.45	—0.4989	+0.0487	+0.0310	......	
83	Half pint	Jan. 15	29.65	51.6	—0.17	—1.1097	—0.0603			
		Jan. 17	30.12	50.2	—0.23	—0.2157	—0.0143	—0.0373	......	
		1851.								
84	Half gall.	Nov. 28	29.80	49.6	—2.0	—1.9956	—0.044			
		Dec. 2	30.10	49.8	—2.05	—1.9087	—0.1413	—0.0926	......	
84	Quart..	Dec. 17	30.25	49.4	—1.12	—1.0413	—0.0787			
		Dec. 19	30.00	49.3	—1.2	—1.0638	—0.1362	—0.107	......	
		1852.								
84	Pint.....	Jan. 3	29.93	50.9	—0.33	—0.3321	+0.0021			
		Jan. 7	29.84	49.6	—0.4	—0.4989	+0.0987	+0.050	......	
84	Half pint	Jan. 14	29.86	49.6	—0.22	—0.2494	—0.0294			
		Jan. 17	30.12	50.1	—0.25	—0.2222	—0.0278	—0.0286	......	
		1851.								
85	Half gall.	Nov. 29	30.05	52.0	—0.7	—0.6090	—0.0910			
		Dec. 2	30.10	49.7	—2.27	—1.9522	—0.1178	—0.104	......	
85	Quart..	Dec. 18	30.18	49.3	—0.95	—1.0638	+0.1138			
		Dec. 19	30.00	49.2	—1.05	—1.0863	+0.0363	+0.075	......	Iowa, Nov. 6, 1856.
		1852.								
85	Pint.....	Jan. 6	29.14	49.6	—0.55	—0.4989	—0.0511			
		Jan. 7	29.84	49.6	—0.55	—0.4989	—0.0513	—0.051	......	
85	Half pint	Jan. 17	30.12	50.0	—0.2	—0.2286	+0.0286	+0.0286	......	
		1851.								
86	Half gall.	Nov. 29	30.05	51.9	—0.75	—0.6804	—0.0696			
		Dec. 2	30.10	49.6	—2.05	—1.9956	—0.0544	—0.062	......	
86	Quart..	Dec. 17	30.26	49.2	—1.03	—1.0863	+0.0563			
		Dec. 19	30.00	49.0	—1.00	—1.1314	+0.1314	+0.094	......	
		1852.								
86	Pint.....	Jan. 7	29.84	49.6	—0.5	—0.4989	—0.0013			
		Jan. 8	30.10	50.0	—0.47	—0.4573	—0.0127	—0.007	......	
6	Half pint	Jan. 17	30.10	50.4	—0.2	—0.2028	+0.0028			
		Jan. 19	30.03	49.4	—0.25	—0.2603	+0.0103	+0.0065	......	

APPENDIX No. 26.

Experiments on the weight of various liquids at different temperatures.

With a view of ascertaining the practicability of gauging by weight, experiments were made on the weight of various liquid articles of commerce, such as oils, syrups, &c., at different temperatures. The substances were weighed in glass bottles, containing rather more than a quart, with narrow necks, the tops of which were ground so as to admit of being accurately closed by a small plate of glass. The weighings were made with one of the middle-sized balances furnished to the States.

The bottles, with the plates, were first accurately weighed, (see Table I, A; they were next filled with water near the temperature of 62° Fahr., or 17° Cent., and thus weighed, the operation being repeated several times, (Table I, B.) After being carefully dried, they were filled with samples of the following substances, furnished by Mr. Charles Ellis, druggist, of Philadelphia:

Series I. Castor oil, olive oil, linseed oil, lard oil.

Series II. Spirits of turpentine, Barbadoes tar, copaiba.

After each weighing a portion of the liquid was removed from the bottle for the purpose of inserting a thermometer. The temperature of the room being at all times very nearly the same as that of the substances in the bottles, the temperatures of the latter thus obtained were not supposed to differ materially from the actual temperatures during the weighings. A Fahrenheit thermometer by Green was used at first, for which a centigrade thermometer by Griener, reading to two-tenths of a degree, was afterwards substituted. The two instruments were carefully compared, and in the table of results the readings of the former were converted into the centigrade scale. Table 1. C and D, gives an abstract of the weighings, the weight being in ounces, troy.

The barometer was noted in every instance, but the correction for the change in buoyancy of the air is entirely masked by the uncertainty of temperature. The greatest buoyancy correction would amount to but 0.0005 of an ounce, while a variation of one-tenth of a degree of the centigrade thermometer corresponds to 0.0014 of an ounce on the average.

The experiments were made by *Mr. Woods Baker* up to April 16, 1852, when they were taken up by *Mr. E. Liomin.*

A discussion of these first experiments showed that a desirable degree of accuracy could be reached, and that the principal difficulty consisted in ascertaining the true temperature of the liquid.

In making additional experiments, therefore, bottles were procured having thermometers inserted into them in such a manner that the bulb occupied nearly the middle of the vessel, the stem coming out at the side, so as to have the scale entirely outside, the top of the neck remaining unobstructed. These thermometers were graduated to the centigrade scale, and carefully compared with the Greiner standard. The table of corrections thus obtained is given with the experiments. (See table II, A, B, C.)

With these vessels the experiments were repeated on some of the substances previously used, two of them (castor oil and copaiba) being those with which very regular results had been obtained, and two others (lard oil and spirits of turpentine) those that had given irregular results. In the case of the latter substance, this was doubtless owing to an increase of density by evaporation of volatile parts; while the experiments with lard oil showed some irregularity near the point of congelation, as might be expected. The following substances experimented on were obtained from Mr. Ben. R. Smith, of Philadelphia, viz: East India castor oil, copaiba, refined English castor oil, lard oil, spirits of turpentine.

In addition to these, a number of samples of molasses were procured by Prof. R. S. McCulloh, and analyzed by him in reference to the amount of crystallizable sugar contained in them. The brief notes of their importation and results of the analyses are given below.

Table II D and E gives the weighings made with these substances. All the experiments made are graphically represented on plate No. 3, each series having been multiplied by a constant factor, so as to obtain a convenient scale, and make the rates of expansion readily comparable by the eye.

The annexed table of results gives the *specific gravity* and *weight of one gallon* of the substances experimented on at 15° C., and the rate of expansion for 1° C. within the range of temperature observed, or within which uniform results were obtained. In making the reductions, the specific gravity of water is assumed as unity at 15° C., and the weight of one gallon of water at that temperature equal to 8.3316 pounds avoirdupois, it being equal to 8.3389 pounds at the maximum density of water, and *less* in the proportion of 1.000875 to 1 at 15° C., according to DESPRETZ, whose table was also used in reducing the observed weights of water to 15° C. For the expansion of the glass vessels, allowance has been made at the rate of 0.0000258 for 1° C.

Table of results of weighings.

Substance.	Specific gravity at 15° C.	Weight of one gallon at 15° C.	Rate of expansion for 1° C.	Between temperatures.
		Pds.		
Castor oil, (series 1)	0.9647	8.037	0.00069	0 to 27
(series 3)	0.9645	8.035	0.00069	— 1 to 28
East India	0.9666	8.053	0.00068	— 2 to 28
Linseed oil	0.9326	7.770	0.00078	1 to 27
Olive oil	0.9167	7.637	0.00073	1 to 27
Lard oil, (series 1)	0.9187	7.654	0.00071	6 to 27
(series 3)	0.9186	7.654	0.00071	14 to 28
Barbadoes tar	0.9530	7.940	0.00068	0 to 27
Copaiba, (series 2)	0.9755	8.128	0.00072	0 to 27
(series 3)	0.9873	8.226	0.00068	— 2 to 29
Spirits of turpentine, (series 3)	0.8695	7.244	0.00099	6 to 27
(series 4)	0.8730	7.274	0.00073	0 to 20
Molasses, No. 1	1.3626	11.353	0.00041	0 to 28
No. 2	1.3864	11.551	0.00047	0 to 22
No. 3	1.3595	11.327	0.00042	0 to 28
No. 4	1.3640	11.365	0.00041	0 to 28
No. 5	1.3644	11.368	0.00040	0 to 28
No. 6	1.3739	11.447	0.00049	0 to 22
No. 7	1.370	11.456	0.00038	0 to 28

Results of the analysis of samples of molasses; by Prof. R. S. McCulloh.

The cane or crystallizable sugar in each was determined by the method of circular polarization of light. The proportion of water was obtained by dessiccation. It is difficult, however, to know when this is done completely, or to perform it, even with the aid of the air-pump, without liability to chemical change or decomposition. The results, therefore, are somewhat uncertain, and only approximate.

The solid matter other than cane sugar, being residual, is given by subtraction. The specific gravity is in each instance referred to that of water as unity at its maximum density.

No. I. Gimbernat & Esconaza, importers; by Narraguages, St. John's, Porto Rico; Muscovado.
Flavor sweet; specific gravity, 1.3640 at 45° Fah.; per cent. of sugar, 49.86; other solid matter, 21.51; water, 28.63.

No. II. Yznaga & Etulam, importers; by Oleronzaza, Cuba; Muscovado.
A sediment in the bottom of the bottle; specific gravity of the supernatant molasses, 1.3663 at 45° Fah.; flavor sweet; per cent. of sugar, 48.78; other solid matter, 23.93; water, 27.29.

No. III. G. S. Stephenson, importer; by Edward, Cardenas, Cuba; clayed.
Flavor sweet; specific gravity, 1.3615 at 45° Fah.; per cent. of sugar, 51.35; other solid matter, 20.86; water, 27.79.

No. IV. Agmar & Co., importers; by Rose & Matilde, Ponce, Porto Rico; Muscovado.

Flavor sweet; slightly burnt; specific gravity, 1.3675 at 45° Fah.; per cent. of sugar, 57.06; other solid matter, 16.64; water, 26.30.

No. V. Wardwell & Knowlton, importers; by John Bird, Sagua a Grande, Cuba; Muscovado.

Flavor sweet; specific gravity, 1.3661 at 45° Fah.; per cent. of sugar, 49.93; other solid matter, 22.84; water, 27.23.

No. VI. Wooding, importer; by Xenephon, Cardenas, Cuba; Muscovada.

Flavor sweet, slightly acid; specific gravity, 1.3626 at 45° Fah.; per cent. of sugar, 48.35; other solid matter, 23.70; water, 27.95.

No. VII. M. Taylor & Co., importers; by Azores, Sagua la Grande, Cuba; clayed.

Flavor sweet, slightly acid; specific gravity, 1.3646 at 45° Fah.; per cent. of sugar, 50.90; other solid matter, 21.85; water, 27.25.

TABLE I. A.—*Weighings of bottles covered with plates.*

No. of bottle.	Temperature of room.	Weight of bottle and plate.	No. of bottle.	Temperature of room.	Weight of bottle and plate.
		Ounces.			*Ounces.*
No. 1	15.5	8.7824	No. 4	17.2	.4534
	16.6	.7823	No. 5	16.2	8.8031
No. 2	15.7	8.6409		15.5	.8032
	16.4	.6408	No. 5	16.1	9.3783
No. 3	16.1	8.0251		15.5	.3783
	16.6	.0250	No. 7	16.0	9.7911
No. 4	16.5	9.4534		15.5	.7912

TABLE I. B.—*Weighings of bottles filled with distilled water.*

No. of bottle.	Substance afterwards contained.	Barometer.	Temperature of room.	Weight.	Temperature of water.
		Inches.	°	*Ounces.*	°
No. 1	Castor oil	30.33	16.4	27.0630	15.0
		30.19	17.6	.0567	16.6
		30.10	17.0	.0569	16.9
No. 2	Olive oil	30.33	16.9	29.3980	15.0
		30.10	17.4	29.3929	16.6
		30.10	16.9	29.3925	17.2
No. 3	Linseed oil	30.33	16.9	27.4696	15.0
		30.10	17.2	.4647	17.2
		30.10	16.9	.4646	17.2
No. 4	Lard oil	30.33	16.9	29.6812	15.5
		30.10	17.0	.6771	17.2
		30.10	16.9	.6771	17.2
No. 5	Turpentine	29.83	14.3	27.4887	13.4
		29.73	17.3	48.48135	16.9
No. 6	Barbadoes tar	29.83	10.9	30.2382	13.5
		29.73	16.3	.2294	17.0
No. 7	Copaiba	29.83	14.5	27.9086	13.6
		29.73	17.2	.9009	17.0

WEIGHTS AND MEASURES.

TABLE I.

C.—Weighings of liquids at different temperatures: series I.

No.	Date.	Bar.	Temp. of room.	Castor oil. Weight.	Temp.	Olive oil. Weight.	Temp.	Linseed oil. Weight.	Temp.	Lard oil. Weight.	Temp.
	1852.	Inches.	°	Ounces.	°	Ounces.	°	Ounces.	°	Ounces.	°
1	Mar. 15	29.74	16.4	26.3958	16.5	27.6428	16.0	26.1425	16.6	28.0700	16.0
2	....do....	29.14	24.3	26.3162	24.4	27.5620	21.6	26.0533	22.9	27.9343	22.2
3	Mar. 16	30.00	16.1	26.4030	15.6	27.6494	15.5	26.1507	15.5	28.0253	15.5
4	....do....	30.00	16.4	26.4010	16.1	27.6474	15.8	26.1465	16.1	28.0209	16.2
5*	....do....	30.00	25.0	26.3300	22.2	27.5755	21.1	26.0647	22.2	27.9445	21.1
6	Mar. 18	29.87	13.5	26.4365	13.0	27.6870	12.7	26.1844	13.3	28.0585	12.9
7	....do....	29.87	13.7	26.4327	13.6	27.6808	13.3	26.1804	13.3	28.0524	13.3
8	....do....	29.87	16.5	26.3845	17.5	27.6228	17.2	26.1296	16.9	28.0043	16.3
9	Mar. 19	30.20	11.5	26.4584	11.1	27.7155	10.8	26.2102	10.8	28.0856	10.8
10	....do....	30.20	11.4	26.4543	11.5	27.7084	11.1	26.2049	11.1	28.0827	11.0
11	Mar. 26	30.20	18.0	26.4100	17.4	27.7134	19.1	26.1147	18.9	27.9892	19.0
12	June 3	29.78	22.8	26.3107	23.5	27.5445	23.6	26.0501	23.7	27.9237	23.6
13	June 16	30.09	24.0	26.3029	24.5	27.5343	24.6	26.0417	24.6	27.9120	24.7
14	June 22	29.76	25.0	26.2891	25.4	27.5203	25.3	26.0309	25.2	27.9021	25.3
15	July 7	30.16	25.5	26.2817	26.1	27.5125	26.0	26.0222	26.0	27.8923	25.9
16	July 12	30.10	26.7	26.2681	27.4	27.4960	27.4	26.0074	27.4	27.8761	27.3
17	Dec. 2	30.43	11.6	26.4538	11.8	27.7096	11.6	26.2094	11.7	28.0856	11.6
18	Dec. 3	30.23	11.7	26.4487	12.1	27.7058	12.0	26.2050	12.0	28.0810	12.0
19	Dec. 4	29.74	13.3	26.4343	13.4	27.6873	13.4	26.1900	13.4	28.0619	13.5
20	Dec. 6	30.07	12.6	26.4490	12.8	27.6959	12.8	26.1989	12.8	28.0708	12.8
21	Dec. 8	29.91	15.1	26.4116	15.3	27.6644	15.2	26.1688	15.2	28.0385	15.3
22	Dec. 10	29.97	14.4	26.4187	14.7	27.6733	14.6	26.1786	14.6	28.0480	14.6
23	Dec. 13	30.05	10.6	26.4661	10.6	27.7271	10.6	26.2276	10.7	28.0995	10.7
24	Dec. 14	30.44	10.1	26.4720	10.0	27.7355	10.0	26.2373	10.0	28.1075	10.1
25	Dec. 16	30.50	09.4	26.4815	9.2	27.7467	9.2	26.2474	9.3	28.1176	9.3
26	Dec. 21	29.99	18.1	26.3715	19.0	27.6275	18.4	26.1263	18.9	27.9895	19.0
27	Dec. 22	30.52	7.2	26.4858	8.5	27.7569	8.2	26.2605	8.0	28.1332	7.9
28	Dec. 23	30.52	8.5	26.4845	8.8	27.7534	8.8	26.2543	8.8	28.1276	8.6
	1853.										
29	Jan. 5	30.20	8.3	26.4966	8.0	27.7647	8.2	26.2642	8.2	28.1349	8.2
30	Jan. 6	30.14	6.7	26.5155	6.4	27.7858	6.4	26.2855	6.6	28.1577	6.4
31	Jan. 7	30.07	7.4	26.5034	7.6	27.7802	6.8	26.2816	7.0	28.1522	7.0
32	Jan. 14	30.16	6.2	26.5134	6.4	27.7848	6.4	26.2861	6.4	28.1571	6.4
33	Jan. 17	30.10	2.9	26.5671	2.0	†27.8446	2.2	26.3399	2.4	‡28.2105	2.6
34	....do....	30.11	2.8	26.5450	4.0	27.8202	4.0	26.3207	4.0	§28.1939	4.0
35	Jan. 18	29.97	3.0	26.5644	2.2	27.8444	2.4	26.3394	2.6	....	.....
36	....do....	30.00	3.9	26.5530	3.4	26.8320	3.5	26.3271	3.4	28.2226	3.3
37	....do....	29.90	4.6	26.5418	4.2	27.8231	4.2	26.3185	4.3	28.2170	4.2
38	Jan. 19	30.20	4.5	26.5432	4.0	27.8209	4.0	26.3174	4.3	28.2124	4.8
39	....do....	30.20	5.6	26.5308	5.0	27.8148	5.4	26.3068	5.3	28.2099	4.9
40	Jan. 27	30.68	1.4	26.5812	.9	27.8656	.9	26.3612	.9	28.2676	1.2
41	....do....	30.65	2.1	26.5705	1.6	27.8558	1.8	26.3483	2.0	28.2635	2.0
42	Jan. 28	30.78	.9	26.5809	.5	27.8694	.8	26.3643	.8	Solid....	.9

* Fire having been made in the room, this set of weighings was made three hours afterwards.
† Olive oil slightly congealed.
‡ Lard oil slightly congealed.
§ Some appearance of congelation still remaining in the lard oil; it had the appearance of melting snow.

TABLE I.

D.— Weighings of liquids at different temperatures: series II.

No.	Date.	Bar.	Temp. of room.	Turpentine. Weight.	Turpentine. Temp.	Barbadoes tar. Weight.	Barbadoes tar. Temp.	Copaiba. Weight.	Copaiba. Temp.
	1852.	Inches.	°	Ounces.	°	Ounces.	°	Ounces.	°
1	April 16	29.82	17.5	24.9449	18.8	29.1907	18.7	27.4064	18.6
2	April 17	29.86	15.5	24.9886	15.5	29.2391	15.6	27.4455	15.7
3	April 19	29.34	16.4	24.9739	16.8	29.2123	17.2	27.4222	17.3
4	April 20	29.43	13.0	25.0277	13.5	29.2645	13.6	27.4730	13.4
5	April 23	29.63	13.9	25.0227	14.1	29.2527	14.5	27.4658	14.3
6	May 7	30.22	19.2	24.9341	20.1	29.1790	20.0	27.3935	20.1
7	May 10	29.99	20.8	24.9215	21.3	29.1644	25.5	27.3836	21.4
8	May 17	29.75	22.0	24.9022	22.8	29.1463	22.8	27.3655	22.7
9	June 3	29.81	22.9	24.9026	23.5	29.1377	23.7	27.3580	23.6
10	June 16	30.09	24.0	24.8960	24.6	29.1255	24.6	27.3444	24.6
11	June 22	29.76	24.7	24.8898	25.2	29.1163	25.4	27.3393	25.2
12	July 7	30.14	25.1	24.8905	25.9	29.1075	25.8	27.3298	25.8
13	July 12	30.10	26.6	24.8737	27.3	29.0902	27.2	27.3150	27.2
14	Dec. 2	30.43	11.7	25.2112	11.7	29.2888	12.0	27.5006	11.8
15	Dec. 3	30.18	11.7	25.2061	11.9	29.2888	12.0	27.4982	12.0
16	Dec. 4	29.74	13.4	25.1841	13.4	29.2707	13.6	27.4820	13.6
17	Dec. 6	30.07	12.7	25.1901	12.8	29.2776	13.0	27.4897	13.0
18	Dec. 8	29.94	15.1	25.1539	15.2	29.2473	15.2	27.4617	15.4
19	Dec. 10	30.01	14.4	25.1639	14.6	29.2559	14.6	27.4690	14.7
20	Dec. 13	30.05	10.7	25.2194	10.6	29.3049	10.7	27.5160	10.8
21	Dec. 14	30.45	10.2	25.2265	10.0	29.3117	10.2	27.5231	10.3
22	Dec. 16	30.44	9.4	25.2362	9.3	29.3206	9.3	27 5322	9.4
23	Dec. 21	29.97	17.3	25.1018	18.4	29.2140	17.8	27.4290	18.3
24	Dec. 22	30.55	7.2	25.2551	7.7	29.3352	8.1	27.5502	8.1
25	Dec. 23	30.50	8.6	25.2473	8.8	29.3269	8.7	27.5386	8.7
	1853.								
26	Jan. 5	30.22	8.3	25.2560	8.2	29.3348	8.3	27.5473	8.4
27	Jan. 6	30.14	6.0	25.2793	6.4	29.3576	6.3	27.5723	6.3
28	Jan. 7	30.07	7.8	25.2711	7.2	29.3476	7.3	27.5631	7.4
29	Jan. 14	30.17	6.2	25.2840	6.4	29.3550	6.4	27.5724	6.4
30	Jan. 17	30.11	3.6	25.3492	2.8	29.4029	2.9	27.6153	3.0
31	....do....	30.11	4.5	25.3187	4.2	29.3875	4.2	27.6006	4.3
32	Jan. 18	29.97	3.5	25.3406	2.9	29.4027	3.0	27.6161	3.2
33	....do....	30.00	4.0	25.3256	3.8	29.3936	3.8	27.6078	3.8
34	....do....	29.90	4.9	25.3173	4.5	29.3857	4.6	27.5997	4.8
35	Jan. 19	30.22	4.5	25.3192	4.3	29.3865	4.4	27.5920	4.4
36	....do....	30.18	5.6	25.3015	5.5	29.3731	5.4	21.5907	5.3
37	Jan. 27	30.70	1.6	25.3711	1.2	29.4228	1.3	27.6373	1.4
38	....do....	30.65	2.3	25.3578	2.0	29.4150	2.1	27.6292	2.1
39	Jan. 28	30.78	.9	25.3816	.4	29.4290	.5	27.6441	.5

NOTE.—The spirits of turpentine evidently increased in density (probably by evaporation) the weighings on April 20 and December 4, and those on April 16 and December 21, made at nearly the same temperatures, showing an increase in weight of 0.1566 of an ounce.

TABLE II.

A.—*Table of corrections to thermometers inserted into bottles.*

Temp.	No. 1.	No. 2.	No. 3.	No. 4.	No. 5.
°	°	°	°	°	°
0	— .2	— .2	— .2	— .2	— .2
1	— .2	— .2	— .2	— .2	— .2
2	— .2	— .2	— .2	— .2	— .2
3	— .2	— .2	.0	— .2	— .2
4	— .1	— .1	— .1	.0	— .2
5	— .1	— .1	— .1	— .2	— .2
6	— .1	— .1	+ .2	— .2	— .2
7	.0	— .1	+ .1	— .2	+ .2
8	.0	.0	+ .1	— .1	+ .2
9	.0	.0	+ .2	— .1	+ .2
10	.0	.0	+ .1	.0	— .3
11	+ .1	+ .1	+ .2	.0	— .4
12	+ .1	+ .1	+ .2	.0	— .4
13	+ .1	+ .1	+ .2	.0	— .2
14	+ .1	+ .1	+ .2	— .1	— .2
15	+ .1	+ .1	+ .2	— .1	— .2
16	+ .2	+ .2	+ .2	— .1	— .2
17	+ .2	+ .2	+ .2	— .1	— .2
18	+ .2	+ .2	+ .2	.0	— .2
19	+ .2	+ .2	+ .2	— .1	— .2
20	+ .2	+ .2	+ .2	— .1	— .1
21	+ .3	+ .2	+ .2	.0	— .1
22	+ .3	+ .3	+ .2	+ .1	— .1
23	+ .3	+ .3	+ .2	+ .1	— .1
24	+ .3	+ .3	+ .2	+ .1	— .1
25	+ .2	+ .3	+ .2	+ .1	— .1
26	+ .2	+ .3	+ .2	+ .1	— .1
27	+ .2	+ .3	+ .2	+ .1	— .1
28	+ .2	+ .3	+ .2	+ .1	— .1
29	+ .2	+ .3	+ .2	.0	— .1
30	+ .1	+ .4	+ .3	+ .2	— .1
31	+ .1	+ .4	+ .3	+ .2	— .1
32	+ .1	+ .4	+ .3	+ .2	— .1

TABLE II.

B.—Weighings of bottles covered with plates.

No. of bottle.	Temp. of room.	Weight.	No. of bottle.	Temp. of room.	Weight.
No. 1	19.0°	15.5251	No. 5	19.2°	14.5445
	19.2	.5251	No. 6	5.8	12.3790
	19.2	.5251		6.3	.3790
	19.2	.5252		7.4	.37905
No. 2	19.1	14.7622	No. 7	5.9	14.4232
	19.2	.7622		6.4	.4231
	19.2	.7621		7.3	.4232
	19.2	.7621	No. 8	6.0	23.9523
No. 3	19.1	15.46835		6.5	.9524
	19.3	.4684		7.3	.9524
	19.2	.4684	No. 9	6.2	14.9022
	19.2	.4685		6.7	.90215
No. 4	19.2	14.4014		7.2	.90225
	19.2	.4015	No. 10	6.4	13.7980
	19.2	.40155		6.8	.7979
	19.2	.4014		7.3	.7980
No. 4, (new bottle)	5.7	15.0551	No. 11	6.6	14.08865
	6.3	.0551		7.0	.08865
	7.2	.0551		7.3	.0887
No. 5	19.2	14.5446	No. 12	6.8	16.0962
	19.0	.5446		7.0	.0960
	19.2	.5446		7.4	.0961

TABLE II—C. Weighings of bottles filled with distilled water.

No. of bottle.	Substance afterwards contained.	Barometer.	Temp. of room.	Weight.	Temp. of water.	Temp. corrected.
		Inches.	°		°	°
1	Castor oil	30.45	18.3	37.1513	17.8	18.0
		30.44	18.6	.1508	17.9	18.1
		30.16	18.4	.1503	18.1	18.3
		30.14	19.0	.1507	17.9	18.1
		30.13	19.2	.1501	18.2	18.4
		30.10	19.4	.1456	19.2	19.4
		29.82	16.5	.1554	16.7	16.9
		29.81	16.8	.1551	16.8	17.0
6	East India castor oil	30.10	15.6	31.7651	15.5	15.6
		30.05	17.2	.7615	16.9	17.1
		30.05	16.8	.7638	16.0	16.2
		30.00	17.1	.7612	17.1	17.3
2	Lard oil	30.45	18.4	34.1265	17.9	18.1
		30.44	18.6	.1269	18.0	18.2
		30.16	18.6	.1267	18.2	18.4
		30.14	19.0	.1265	17.9	18.1
		30.13	19.2	.1261	18.3	18.5
		30.10	19.4	.1236	19.1	19.3
		29.82	16.5	.1310	16.6	16.8
		29.81	16.8	.1307	16.8	17.0

WEIGHTS AND MEASURES. 205

Table II.—C—Continued.

No. of bottle.	Substance afterwards contained.	Barometer.	Temp. of room.	Weight.	Temp. of water.	Temp. corrected.
		Inches.	°		°	°
3	Copaiba	30.45	18.5	38.3738	17.8	18.0
		30.44	18.7	.3729	18.0	18.2
		30.16	18.6	.3726	18.2	18.4
		30.14	19.1	.3730	18.1	18.3
		30.13	19.2	.3728	18.3	18.5
		30.10	19.5	.3673	19.2	19.4
		29.82	16.6	.3779	16.6	16.8
		29.81	16.8	.3777	16.7	16.9
4	Turpentine	30.45	18.5	35.2679	17.9	17.9
		30.44	18.7	.2672	18.0	18.0
		30.16	18.7	.2669	18.0	18.0
		30.14	19.1	.2672	18.0	18.0
		30.13	19.2	.2666	18.2	18.2
		30.10	19.5	.2633	19.0	18.9
		29.82	16.7	.2712	16.6	16.5
		29.81	16.9	.2713	16.6	16.5
4	Turpentine (new bottle)	30.10	15.5	32.4786	15.1	15.0
		30.05	16.5	.4734	16.9	16.8
		30.05	16.2	.4769	16.3	16.2
		30.00	16.7	.4732	17.0	16.9
5	Molasses, I	30.45	18.6	36.9695	18.2	18.0
		30.44	18.8	.9692	18.3	18.1
		30.16	18.8	.9687	18.4	18.2
		30.14	19.1	.9689	18.2	18.0
		30.13	19.3	.9688	18.6	18.4
		30.10	19.6	.9655	19.5	19.4
		29.82	16.7	.9743	16.9	16.7
		29.81	16.9	.9741	16.9	16.7
7	Molasses, II	30.09	15.2	31.5568	15.0	14.8
		30.05	17.3	.5533	16.4	16.2
		30.05	16.6	.5552	15.8	15.6
		30.00	17.3	.5529	16.6	16.4
8	Molasses, III	30.10	15.3	31.7537	14.9	14.7
		30.05	17.1	.7506	16.3	16.1
		30.05	16.2	.7530	15.5	15.3
		30.00	17.1	.7503	16.4	16.2
9	Molasses, IV	30.09	15.3	33.4519	15.1	14.9
		30.05	16.8	.4481	16.6	16.4
		30.02	16.1	.4512	16.0	15.8
		29.98	16.9	.4477	17.0	16.8
10	Molasses, V	30.09	15.1	31.6162	15.4	15.2
		30.05	16.7	.6131	16.9	16.7
		30.02	16.3	.6136	16.1	15.9
		29.98	16.7	.6129	17.0	16.8
11	Molasses, VI	30.09	15.0	32.0613	15.3	15.1
		30.05	16.5	.0584	16.5	16.3
		30.02	16.4	.0610	15.8	15.6
		29.98	16.6	.0581	16.6	16.4
12	Molasses, VII	30.09	14.8	31.9365	16.4	16.2
		30.05	16.3	.9329	17.7	17.5
		30.02	16.6	.9364	16.6	16.4
		29.98	16.4	.9334	17.5	17.3

TABLE II.

D.—*Weighings of liquids at different temperatures: series III.*

Number.	Date.	Barometer.	Temp. of room.	Castor oil.		Lard oil.		Copaiba.		Molasses I.		Turpentine.	
				Weight.	Temp.	Weight.	Temp.	Weight.	Temp.	Weight.	Temp.	Weight.	Tem
	1854.		°		°		°		°		°		°
1	Oct. 23	30.37	14.6	36.3991	14.1	32.5662	14.3	38.0981	14.2	45.1330	14.3	32.5581	14.4
2	Oct. 23	30.34	15.0	36.3864	14.7	32.5558	14.9	38.0865	14.9	45.1280	14.8	32.5472	15.0
3	Oct. 24	30.38	16.5	36.3818	15.5	32.5323	16.6	38.0606	16.5	45.1088	16.0	32.5120	17.0
4	Oct. 24	30.35	17.0	36.3545	16.9	32.5199	17.6	38.0526	17.2	45.1016	16.9	32.5028	17.8
5	Oct. 24	30.32	21.1	36.3121	19.6	32.3813	20.3	38.0048	20.1	45.0537	20.4	32.4455	20.9
6	Oct. 24	30.30	20.5	36.3050	20.2	32.4781	20.8	38.0000	20.8	45.0521	20.9	32.4453	21.0
7	Oct. 25	30.40	15.4	36.3858	15.2	32.5564	15.1	38.0888	15.3	45.1210	15.7	32.5486	15.1
8	Oct. 25	30.40	16.1	36.3816	15.4	32.5493	15.7	38.0810	15.6	45.1185	15.8	32.5426	15.5
9	Oct. 26	30.49	16.8	36.3727	16.1	32.5400	16.2	38.0709	16.3	45.1099	16.7	32.5283	16.2
10	Oct. 26	30.49	17.5	36.3625	16.5	32.5323	16.8	38.0618	16.8	45.1036	17.0	32.5103	17.5
11	Oct. 26	30.46	18.1	36.3497	17.5	32.5227	17.6	38.0485	17.8	45.0925	17.9	32.5004	18.0
12	Oct. 26	30.44	18.7	36.3380	18.2	32.5092	18.5	38.0413	18.3	45.0845	18.7	32.4925	18.6
13	Oct. 27	30.41	16.7	36.3715	16.2	32.5408	16.2	38.0750	16.1	45.1125	16.5	32.5310	16.2
14	Oct. 28	30.29	25.0	36.2355	24.7	32.4147	25.0	37.9307	24.9	45.0272	23.7	32.3555	26.2
15	Oct. 28	30.26	25.3	36.2265	25.7	32.4057	25.9	37.9215	25.8	45.0189	24.4	32.3549	26.4
16	Oct. 28	30.21	24.2	36.2435	25.0	32.4272	24.8	37.9429	25.0	45.0114	24.8	32.3866	24.9
17	Oct. 28	30.17	23.2	36.2721	22.9	32.4513	22.8	37.9673	23.2	45.0288	23.3	32.4115	23.4
18	Nov. 4	30.37	16.9	36.3605	17.1	32.5294	16.9	38.0651	16.9	45.1080	17.2	32.5237	16.8
19	Nov. 6	30.26	11.4	36.4352	11.8	32.6215	12.1	38.1434	11.8	45.1675	12.3	32.6143	11.5
20	Nov. 6	30.18	12.7	36.4182	12.3	32.5977	12.4	38.1277	12.6	45.1544	12.8	32.5956	12.5
21	Nov. 6	30.14	13.6	36.4078	13.0	32.5945	13.1	38.1116	13.3	45.1505	13.2	32.5888	13.5
22	Nov. 6	30.05	14.1	36.4023	13.7	32.5801	13.8	38.1041	13.9	45.1436	13.9	32.5665	14.2
23	Nov. 7	29.58	13.0	36.4246	12.5	32.5976	12.6	38.1289	12.7	45.1583	13.0	32.5976	12.4
24	Dec. 9	30.58	6.4	36.5031	7.4	32.7113	7.2	38.2160	6.9	45.2263	7.4	32.7114	6.5
25	Dec. 9	30.58	8.0	36.4768	7.8	32.6933	7.8	38.1981	7.3	45.2160	7.8	32.6843	7.9
26	Dec. 9	30.55	8.0	36.4721	8.7	32.6906	8.4	38.1904	8.0	45.2122	8.1	32.6751	8.5
27	Dec. 11	30.14	9.7	36.4617	9.1	32.6946	9.1	38.1714	9.1	45.2003	9.1	(a)	....
28	Dec. 11	30.13	10.1	36.4560	9.7	32.6873	9.6	38.1633	9.7	45.1954	9.6	....	....
29	Dec. 11	30.11	10.3	36.4491	10.3	32.6781	10.1	38.1560	10.3	45.1883	10.2	....	....
30	Dec. 11	30.10	10.9	36.4402	11.0	32.6657	10.9	38.1457	11.1	45.1801	11.0	....	....
31	Dec. 21	30.00	16.0	33.5844	1.3	Solid.	1.5	38.3004	1.2	45.2951	1.6	....	....
32	Dec. 21	30.01	2.5	36.5713	2.2	...do....	2.2	38.2846	2.3	45.2856	2.4	....	....
33	Dec. 22	30.29	2.1	36.5761	2.0	...do....	......	38.2927	1.9	45.2890	2.1	....	....
34	Dec. 22	30.31	3.6	36.5606	3.0	...do....	3.0	38.2736	2.9	45.2755	3.0	....	....
35	Dec. 23	30.76	0.0	36.6168	−.7	...do....	......	38.3346	−.8	45.3181	−.5	....	....
36	Dec. 23	30.75	.9	36.6006	0.0	...do....	......	38.3162	−.1	45.3087	0.0	....	....
37	Dec. 23	30.69	1.5	36.5877	.9	...do....	......	38.3026	1.0	45.3005	.9	....	....
38	Dec. 26	30.10	5.2	36.5342	5.0	Melting.	5.0	38.2479	4.9	45.2560	5.0	....	....
39	Dec. 26	30.02	5.9	36.5256	5.5	Melted, but thick.	5.5	38.2358	5.6	45.2485	5.7	....	....
40	Dec. 27	29.95	6.8	36.5115	6.4	32.7610	6.9	38.2219	6.3	45.2370	6.7	....	....
41	Dec. 28	30.02	8.6	36.4881	8.1	32.7383	8.2	38.1969	8.2	45.2174	8.4	....	....
42	Dec. 30	30.12	4.0	36.5555	3.5	31.8151	3.6	38.2610	3.7	45.2712	3.7	....	....
	1855.												
43	Jan. 2	30.68	4.4	36.5443	4.2	32.8114	4.1	38.2581	4.1	45.2634	4.4	....	....
44	Feb. 8	29.82	−.9	36.6318	−1.3	Solid.	−1.7	38.3366	−1.5	45.3239	−1.1	....	....
45	Apr. 25	30.09	18.8	36.3353	18.7	32.5121	18.8	38.0373	18.9	45.0954	19.0	....	....
46	Apr. 25	30.08	18.9	36.3346	18.9	32.5094	18.9	38.0347	19.0	45.0945	19.1	....	....
47	June 25	29.93	25.1	36.2500	25.0	32.4250	24.9	37.9495	25.0	45.0239	25.1	....	....
48	June 26	30.13	24.5	36.2602	24.1	32.4312	24.2	37.9594	24.3	45.0310	24.5	....	....
49	June 27	30.24	25.8	36.2417	25.4	32.4145	25.4	37.9358	25.9	45.0145	25.8	....	....
50	June 28	30.18	27.0	36.2234	26.9	32.4000	26.8	37.9170	27.3	44.9977	27.1	....	....
51	June 29	30.14	27.7	36.2130	27.4	32.3933	27.3	37.9129	27.8	44.9936	27.6	....	....
52	June 29	30.10	28.2	36.2064	28.1	32.3852	28.0	37.9010	28.3	44.9846	28.3	....	....
53	June 30	30.05	28.6	36.2016	28.5	32.3791	28.3	37.8988	28.9	44.9814	28.7	....	....

(a) The bottle containing the turpentine was accidentally broken, December 11. Another one was substituted and weighed in the next series.

WEIGHTS AND MEASURES.

TABLE II.

E.—Weighings of liquids at different temperatures: series IV.

No.	Date.	Bar.	Temp. of room.	Turpentine. Weight.	Turpentine. Temp.	East India Castor Oil. Weight.	East India Castor Oil. Temp.	Molasses II. Weight.	Molasses II. Temp.	Molasses III. Weight.	Tem.
	1855.		°		°		°		°		°
1	Feb. 6	30.05	.9	30.4201	.6	31.2523	.5	38.3002	.6	38.2784	1.0
2	...do....	30.04	1.8	30.4036	2.0	31.2390	1.7	38.2924	1.5	38.2714	1.9
3	Feb. 7	30.14	—2.4	30.4690	—2.7	31.2929	—2.3	38.3255	—2.3	38.3075	—2.0
4	....do....	30.08	— .5	30.4416	— .8	31.2724	—1.1	38.3155	—1.2	38.2960	—1.0
5	Feb. 9	29.86	+ .2	30.4301	+ .1	31.2602	0.0	38.3078	— .2	38.2878	+ .1
6	Feb. 13	30.27	2.4	30.4078	1.7	31.2403	1.2	38.2943	1.2	38.2736	1.6
7	....do....	30.25	4.2	30.3792	4.0	31.2146	3.6	38.2766	3.3	38.2553	3.7
8	Feb. 14	29.82	5.1	30.3695	4.9	31.2019	4.7	38.2678	4.7	38.2470	4.9
9	....do....	29.81	6.4	30.3553	6.0	31.1807	6.3	38.2584	5.9	38.2360	6.0
10	Feb. 15	29.80	5.7	30.3639	5.5	31.1921	5.6	38.2620	5.5	38.2399	5.6
11	Feb. 16	29.90	4.6	30.3760	4.4	31.2070	4.3	38.2717	4.2	38.2512	4.4
12	Feb. 20	30.10	3.8	30.3933	3.5	31.2154	3.6	38.2763	3.5	38.2590	3.8
13	....do....	29.89	7.0	30.3499	6.6	31.1764	6.4	38.2542	6.2	38.2325	6.5
14	Mar. 5	29.90	8.2	30.3427	7.7	31.1710	7.4	38.2458	7.3	38.2245	7.4
15	Mar. 6	29.83	9.7	30.3232	9.1	31.1519	9.2	38.3319	9.0	38.2103	9.0
16	....do....	29.80	10.1	30.3152	9.9	31.1449	9.6	38.2273	9.4	38.2057	9.4
17	....do....	29.77	10.7	30.3042	10.7	31.1351	10.3	38.2195	10.2	38.1986	10.1
18	Mar. 9	29.65	11.6	30.2965	11.5	31.1253	11.0	38.2124	10.9	38.2026	10.7
19	April 10	30.05	12.7	30.2917	12.2	31.1157	12.1	38.1927	12.1	38.1820	12.0
20	....do....	29.90	13.1	30.2889	12.8	31.1110	12.9	38.1890	12.6	38.1773	12.4
21	April 17	30.27	13.6	30.2838	13.2	31.1037	13.4	38.1737	13.1	38.1690	13.0
22	....do....	30.20	14.3	30.2782	13.9	31.0934	14.2	38.1665	13.9	38.1614	13.8
23	April 18	....	15.2	30.2743	14.5	31.0908	14.5	38.1592	14.2	38.1559	14.1
24	....do....	29.95	16.0	30.2610	15.4	31.0770	15.4	38.1505	15.1	38.1473	15.0
25	April 19	29.89	17.0	30.2493	16.6	31.0653	16.4	c 38.1254	16.3	c 38.1359	16.1
26	....do....	29.85	17.4	30.2412	17.2	31.0555	17.1	38.1540	17.1	38.1345	17.0
27	....do....	29.80	18.5	30.2285	18.2	31.0422	18.1	38.1450	18.0	38.1260	17.8
28	April 20	29.73	19.3	30.2201	19.0	31.0294	19.0	38.1310	18.9	38.1154	18.8
29	....do....	29.65	20.2	30.2121	19.8	31.0217	19.8	38.1237	19.5	38.1088	19.2
30	April 24	30.10	18.8	30.2255	18.9	31.0340	18.6	38.1413	18.3	38.1230	18.1
31	April 25	30.03	19.5	30.2229	19.2	31.0254	19.2	38.1295	19.0	38.1138	18.9
32	May 16	30.01	21.5	30.2060	21.1	31.0032	21.0	38.1096	21.0	38.0916	20.9
33	....do....	29.95	22.3	30.1988	21.8	30.9950	21.8	38.1002	21.8	38.0849	21.5
34	....do....	29.90	23.0	30.1877	22.6	30.9837	22.5	38.0934	22.4	38.0766	22.1
35	May 18	30.15	20.8	30.2193	20.7	31.0080	20.5	d	....	38.1033	20.3
36	June 25	29.94	25.2	30.1760	26.3	30.9502	25.0	....	....	38.0591	24.9
37	June 26	30.13	24.8	30.2025	24.4	30.9585	24.3	....	....	38.0600	24.1
38	June 27	30.24	26 0	30.1989	25.8	30.9436	25.5	....	....	38.0501	25.2
39	June 28	30.17	27.2	30.1865	27.0	30.9288	26.8	....	....	38.0454	26.5
40c	June 29	30.14	27.8	30.1834	27.6	30.9213	27.3	....	....	38.0416	27.2
41	....do....	30.08	28.4	30.1769	28.2	30.9126	28.0	....	....	38.0355	27.9
42	June 30	30.05	28.8	30.1747	28.5	30.9091	28.3	....	....	38.0332	28.2

TABLE II—E, (bis.)

Number.	Date.	Barometer.	Temp. of room.	Molasses, IV. Weight.	Molasses, IV. Temp.	Molasses, V. Weight.	Molasses, V. Temp.	Molasses, VI. Weight.	Molasses, VI. Temp.	Molasses, VII. Weight.	Molasses, VII. Temp.
1	....	30.05	1.1	a40.3356	1.0	38.2328	1.2	38.9173	.8	37.9896	.8
2	....	30.04	1.9	40.3298	2.1	38.2237	2.1	38.9079	1.7	37.9815	2.0
3	....	30.14	—1.9	(b)	....	38.2619	—2.1	38.9498	—2.3	38.0161	—2.3
4	....	30.06	— .2	40.3552	— .9	38.2467	— .6	38.9335	— .9	38.0011	— .7
5	....	29.86	+ .4	40.3472	+ .2	38.2415	+ .3	38.9280	— .1	37.9959	+ .2
6	....	30.27	2.4	40.3305	1.8	38.2240	2.0	38.9097	1.6	37.9796	2.0
7	....	30.20	4.3	40.3115	3.9	38.2068	4.1	38.8913	3.7	37.9649	4.1
8	....	29.82	5.4	40.3025	5.2	38.1999	5.3	38.8820	4.8	37.9582	5.1
9	....	29.81	6.6	40.2916	6.3	38.1882	6.6	38.8705	6.0	37.9475	6.5
10	....	29.80	6.0	40.2960	5.8	38.1930	6.0	38.8767	5.4	37.9537	5.8
11	....	29.90	4.8	40.3077	4.8	38.2040	4.8	38.8887	4.1	37.9637	4.4
12	....	30.12	3.9	40.3155	3.9	38.2114	3.9	38.8967	3.3	37.9709	3.6
13	....	29.92	7.1	40.2874	6.8	38.1854	7.0	38.8684	6.4	37.9452	6.9
14	....	29.90	8.4	40.2780	7.8	38.1759	8.0	38.8579	7.5	37.9345	8.1
15	....	29.81	9.9	40.2629	9.5	38.1630	9.7	38.8430	9.1	37.9242	9.5
16	....	29.80	10.3	40.2581	9.9	38.1586	10.0	38.8387	9.5	37.9199	9.9
17	....	29.74	11.1	40.2500	10.7	38.1503	10.9	38.8294	10.4	37.9125	10.9
18	....	29.67	11.6	40.2456	11.2	38.1462	11.4	38.8232	11.0	37.9092	11.4
19	....	30.05	12.8	40.2356	12.4	38.1363	12.6	38.8041	12.0	37.9045	12.3
20	....	28.99	13.3	40.2313	13.0	38.1315	13.1	38.7987	12.7	37.8987	13.0
21	....	30.27	13.9	40.2242	13.7	38.1261	13.8	38.7820	13.1	37.8945	13.5
22	....	30.15	14.5	40.2170	14.2	38.1193	14.4	38.7731	13.9	37.8865	14.4
23	....	....	15.4	40.2126	14.7	38.1149	14.8	38.7635	14.4	37.8825	14.9
24	....	29.93	16.3	40.2032	15.4	38.1055	15.8	38.7526	15.2	37.8731	15.9
25	....	29.89	17.1	40.1919	16.8	38.0951	17.0	c38.7354	16.5	37.8650	17.0
26	....	29.83	17.7	40.1848	17.4	38.0898	17.7	38.7595	17.1	37.8613	17.8
27	....	29.78	18.8	40.1750	18.3	38.0785	18.7	38.7447	18.3	37.8492	18.9
28	....	29.70	19.5	40.1662	19.2	38.0714	19.5	38.7259	19.0	37.8453	19.5
29	....	29.60	20.4	40.1595	19.8	38.0640	20.0	38.7145	19.8	37.8373	20.3
30	....	30.05	18.9	40.1707	18.6	38.0751	18.9	38.7430	18.5	37.8501	18.9
31	....	30.02	19.7	40.1644	19.2	38.0697	19.6	38.7245	19.1	37.8445	19.7
32	....	30 00	21.6	40.1459	21.2	38.0533	21.5	38.7078	21.2	37.8323	21.4
33	....	29.93	22.5	40.1408	21.8	38.0473	22.0	38.6962	22.0	37.8237	22.2
34	....	29.86	23.3	40.1342	22.3	38.0403	22.7	38.6858	22.5	37.8179	22.9
35	....	30.15	21.0	40.1534	20.6	38.0595	20.8	(d)	....	37.8399	20.8
36	....	29.95	25.4	40.1088	25.1	38.0192	25.3	....	....	37.8059	25.0
37	....	30.14	24.8	40.1185	24.5	38 0264	24.6	....	....	37.8124	24.4
38	....	30.24	26.1	40.1049	25.5	38.0101	25.8	....	....	37.8011	25.5
39	....	30.17	27.4	40.0903	26.8	37.9950	27.0	....	....	37.7912	26.9
40	....	30.14	27.9	40.0845	27.3	e38.0000	27.5	....	....	37.7867	27.3
41	....	30.08	28.6	40.0783	28.0	37.9940	28.2	....	....	37.7798	28.2
42	....	30.05	28.8	40.0780	28.3	37.9911	28.6	....	....	37.7796	28.3

a This weighing is to be rejected, a bubble of air having appeared after it was made.
b Mercury below scale of thermometer.
c April 19. Bubbles of air were found in the bottles containing molasses Nos. II, III, and IV. They were carefully weighed before and after removing the air, and the differences were found to be, at the same temperature: for No. II, 0.0247 oz.; for No. III, 0.0144 oz.; for No. VI, 0.0326 oz.
It is uncertain how long these bubbles may have been in the bottles, which are badly formed, being too flat on top, and not allowing the air to escape.
d Molasses Nos. II and VI had fermented so much that it was impossible to remove the foam.

ABSTRACT OF CONTENTS OF REPORT.

Weights and measures for the States, pages 2—7. Weights and measures for the customhouses, pages 7—9. Weights and measures, miscellaneous, pages 9, 10. Division and comparison of standard yards, pages 11—16. Comparisons of foreign standards with those of the United States, pages 17—19. Balances for the States, pages 20—23. Weights, measures, and balances, for foreign governments, pages 23—29. Hydrometers for the custom-houses, pages 29—33. Gauging, pages 33, 34. Laws of the States of the Union relating to weights and measures, pages 34—85. Appendix, pages 88—208.

Ex. Doc. 27——14

ERRATA.

Page 22, line 19 from below: For four read seven.
Page 165, line 21 from below: For 01. l read 0. 1 l.
Page 175, last line: For February 22 read June 29.
Page 187. Gallon No. 111, mean: For — read +.
Page 191. Quart No. 29, mean: For + read —.
Page 194. Half pint No. 68, mean: For +0. 0166 read +0. 0116.

CONTENTS OF THE APPENDIX

TO THE

REPORT ON WEIGHTS AND MEASURES.

PART I.—RELATING TO OFFICE BUSINESS.

		Page.
No. 1.	Resolution of Congress providing for the distribution of weights and measures	88
No. 2.	Act of Congress of 1799 directing a semi-yearly comparison of weights and measures used in custom-houses	89
No. 3.	Act of Congress of 1825 authorizing the Secretary of the Treasury to adopt a new hydrometer for ascertaining the proof of liquors in the custom-houses	89
No. 4.	Circular to the governors of States in regard to balances	89–90
No. 5.	Form of the labels accompanying standards of weight and measure issued from the office of weights and measures	90
No. 6.	List of reports made in relation to analyses of sugars, molasses, &c., and hydrometers for the custom-houses	91
No. 7.	Report of Woods Baker, esq., upon the delivery of hydrometers, and the condition of the standard weights and measures furnished to the custom-houses	91–104
No. 8.	Table showing the States, foreign governments, &c., to which balances have been delivered, with those on hand ready for delivery, and the number yet to be completed	104–105
No. 9.	List of States and custom-houses to which standard weights, measures, and balances have been furnished, December 31, 1856	106–109
No. 10.	Miscellaneous distribution of standard weights and measures	110

PART II.—LAWS OF THE STATES IN REGARD TO WEIGHTS AND MEASURES.

No. 11.	Circular to governors of States requesting copies of laws on weights, measures, and gauging	111–112
No. 12.	Titles of laws passed by the several States of the Union in relation to weights and measures during the period intervening between the years 1819 and 1857, with statements showing their authenticity	112–127
No. 13.	Letter of E. R. Potter, esq., of Providence, R. I., giving a brief account of the legislation of that State prior to 1819	127–128
No. 14.	Table showing the weight of a bushel of different grains and other substances, as established by law in the different States and Territories, in pounds avoirdupois	129

CONTENTS.

PART III.—SCIENTIFIC PAPERS, REPORTS, CORRESPONDENCE, AND TABLES.

Page

No. 15. Circular to the ministers of the United States in England, France, the Netherlands, Prussia, and Belgium, asking for information in regard to the methods of gauging officially practiced in those countries, and correspondence in relation thereto 130
    (1.) Papers received from Hon. Abbott Lawrence, United States minister at London: 1. Letter of Thomas Memanter, esq., of the Board of Customs, London; 2. Memorandum of R. Troughton, esq., chief officer of the Gauging Department of the Customs 131–133
    (2.) Letter received from Hon. George Folsom, chargé d'affaires at the Hague, enclosing one to him from M. Van Borp, Minister of Finance of the Netherlands 133–135
    (3.) Papers received from the government of Prussia, comprising a translation of the official instructions for gauging casks, by M. Von Düesberg, Minister of Finance, with table 135–137
No. 16. Letter of M. Moreau, Sub-director of International Exchanges, transmitting a complete collection of standard weights and measures as a present from France to the United States 137–138
No. 17. Letter of M. Silbermann, Superintendent of the Conservatory of Arts and Trades of France, to M. Vattemare, agent of International Exchanges, in relation to the standards of the United States and France. 138–148
No. 18. Letter of General A. Morin, Administrator of the Conservatory of Arts and Trades, transmitting the report of M. Silbermann upon the French weights and measures presented to the United States 148–169
No. 19. Letter of W. H. Vesey, esq., United States consul at Havre, transmitting books and instruments illustrative of the French system of gauging 169–170
No. 20. Letter of D. K. McRae, esq., consul at Paris, transmitting books, papers, and instruments in relation to the French system of gauging 170
    (1.) Letter from M. Alex. Vattemare, Agent of International Exchanges, to D. K. McRae, esq., consul at Paris, in relation to the French system of gauging 171–172
    (2.) Letter from Mons. M. F. Hausemann, Prefect of the Seine, to Mons. Alex. Vattemare, in relation to the instruments used in gauging tuns at the gates of Paris 172–173
    (3.) Price current of the instruments employed in gauging casks in the French custom-houses 173–174
No. 21. Table showing the result of the comparisons of standard yard measures. 175
No. 22. Comparisons of foreign standards with those of the United States 176–181
No. 23. Comparison of the half bushel measures 181–185
No. 24. Comparison of the gallon measures 186–189
No. 25. Comparison of the parts of gallon measures 190–196
No. 26. Abstract of experiments on the weight of liquids at different temperatures 197–208

INDEX.

A.

Adams, Hon. John Quincy. Abstract of report on weights and measures, 1821, 34—36.
Alabama. Abstracts of laws on weights and measures, 36, 65, 66; Titles of laws, 122; Standards destroyed by fire and replaced, 5.
Alexandria, Virginia. Standards replaced, 9.
Apples, Dried. Weight of the bushel, by law, in different States, 129.
Arkansas. Abstracts of laws on weights and measures, 81; Titles of laws, 125.
Astoria, (custom-house,) supplied with standards, 8.

B.

Bache, Professor A. D. Examination of standards, 9.
Baker, Woods. Observations on gauging, 2; Delivery of hydrometers, 2; Examination of standards, 9, 102, 103; Death, 2.
Balances. Distribution, 8, 20—23, 104, 105; Number made and on hand, 105; Description of balance suitable for testing county standards, 7.
Barley. Weight of the bushel, by law, in different States, 129.
Beans. Weight of the bushel, by law, in different States, 129.
Blue grass seed. Weight of the bushel, by law, in different States, 129.
Bran. Weight of the bushel, by law, in different States, 129.
Buckwheat. Weight of the bushel, by law, in different States, 129.
Bushel. Capacity of United States standard, 5; Weight of grain, &c., by law, in different States and Territories, 129.

C.

California. Supplied with balances, 8; With yard measure for Land Office, 10; Abstracts of laws on weights and measures, 82, 83; Titles of laws, 126.
Castor beans. Weight of the bushel, by law, in different States, 129.
Circulars. Sent with hydrometers to custom-houses, 92, 93; To United States revenue officers, with Tralles' hydrometer, 93, 94; To governors of States, requesting copies of laws, 111, 112; Relative to balances, 89, 90; To United States ministers in Europe relative to gauging, 130.
Clover seed. Weight of the bushel, by law, in different States, 129.
Coal. Weight of the bushel, by law, in different States, 129.

Comparisons, (Office.) Of British yard with United States standard, 17, 176, 177 ; Of British pound with United States standard, 17, 177 ; Of Silbermann's with committee kilogramme, 178 ; Of Fortin's with committee kilogramme, 179 ; Of Mexican vara with United States standard yard, 180 ; Of United States yard measures, 175 ; Of United States half bushel measures, 181—185 ; Of United States gallon measures, 186—189 ; Of United States half gallon, quart, pint, and half pint measures, 190—196.

Connecticut. Abstracts of laws on weights and measures, 35, 48, 49 ; Titles of laws, 116.

Copaiba. Weight at different temperatures, 202.

Corn, (shelled and unshelled.) Weight of the bushel, by law, in different States, 129 ; Of corn meal, 129.

County standards. Description of sets suitable for, 6, 7.

Custom-houses. Description of standards provided for, 7, 8 ; To be compared semi-annually, 89 ; Distribution of standards, 8, 106—109 ; Condition of sets in use, 9, 102, 103 ; Sets to be supplied, 9, 106—109 ; Hydrometer adopted, 89 ; Provision for supply of instruments, 2 ; Number of hydrometers furnished, 29—32, 95, 96.

Cwt. (100 lbs.) Adopted, by law, in different States, 85.

D.

Delaware. Abstracts of laws on weights and measures, 35, 57—59 ; Titles of laws, 120.

District of Columbia. Abstracts of laws on weights and measures, 36.

Dividing engine. Description of, 11—15.

E.

Engineer Bureau. Supplied with standard yard, 10.

Expansion. Of brass, for 1° Fahrenheit, 5.

F.

Flaxseed. Weight of the bushel, by law, in different States, 129.

Florida. No laws on weights and measures, 65.

Foster, Captain J. G., U. S. Corps of Engineers, 2.

France. United States standards presented, 23—27 ; Standards received from, 28, 137, 138, 143—147 ; Verification of standards, 148—166 ; Remarks on adoption of the metre, 141, 142.

G.

Gallon. Capacity of United States standard, 5 ; Office comparison of United States gallon measures, 186—189.

Gauging. Defective methods in use, 103 ; Collection of data for rules, 33, 34, 130 ; System in London, 131—133 ; in Prussia, 135—137 ; in Netherlands, 133—135 ; in France, 169—174.

Georgia. Abstracts of laws on weights and measures, 35, 64, 65 ; Titles of laws, 122.

Georgetown, S. C. Standards destroyed, 9.

Great Britain. United States standards presented to, 23.

INDEX. 215

H.

Hair, (*plastering*.) Weight of the bushel, by law, in different States, 129.
Half bushels, (*United States.*) Office comparison of, 181—185.
Half gallons, (*United States.*) Office comparison of, 190—196
Half pints, (*United States.*) Office comparison of, 190—196.
Hemp seed. Weight of the bushel, by law, in different States, 129.
Hundred weight, (100 *lbs.*) Adopted, by law, in different States, 85.
Hydrometers. Law adopting Tralles', 89 ; Supply procured and distributed, 2, 29—32, 91—96 ; Additional purchase, 10, 96 ; Opinions of port surveyors, 103 ; Comparison of old instruments, 96—99.

I.

Illinois. Abstracts of laws on weights and measures, 36, 74—76 ; Titles of laws, 125.
Indiana. Abstracts of laws on weights and measures, 36, 73, 74 ; Titles of laws, 124.
Indian Corn. Weight of the bushel, by law, in different States, 129.
Instructions. For using hydrometer, 93 ; For use and preservation of standards, 100, 101.
Iowa. Abstracts of laws on weights and measures, 76, 77 ; Title of law, 126 ; Yard measure supplied for land office, 10.

K.

Kansas. Yard measure supplied for land office, 10.
Kilogramme. Verification of standards presented by France, 156—162 ; Office comparison of Silbermann's with committee kilogramme, 18, 19, 178 ; Of Fortin's with committee kilogramme, 19, 179.
Kentucky. Abstracts of laws on weights and measures, 35, 68, 69 ; Titles of laws, 124.

L.

Labels. Accompanying standards, Appendix No. 5.
Laborers. Number in Office of Weights and Measures, 2.
Laws. Notice of adoption of United States standards, 5 ; For distribution of standards to States, 88 ; For comparison of custom-house standards, 89 ; adopting Tralles' hydrometer, 89 ; Abstracts and titles of acts relative to weights and measures passed in Maine, 38—41, 112, 113 ; New Hampshire, 35, 41, 42, 113, 114 ; Vermont, 35, 42, 43, 114 ; Massachusetts, 35, 44—46, 114 ; Rhode Island, 35, 46, 47, 115, 116, 127, 128 ; Connecticut, 35, 48, 49, 116 ; New York, 35, 49—53, 116—118 ; New Jersey, 35, 53, 54, 118 ; Pennsylvania, 35, 54—57, 118—120 ; Delaware, 35, 57—59, 120 ; Maryland, 35, 59—61, 120 ; Virginia, 35, 61, 62, 120, 121 ; North Carolina, 35, 62, 63, 121 ; South Carolina, 35, 64, 121, 122 ; Georgia, 35, 64, 65, 122 ; Alabama, 36, 65, 66, 122 ; Mississippi, 36, 66, 67, 122, 123 ; Louisiana, 36, 67, 68, 123 ; Texas, 81, 123 ; Arkansas, 81, 125 ; Missouri, 36, 79—81, 125 ; Tennessee, 36, 68, 124 ; Kentucky, 35, 68, 69, 124 ; Ohio, 36, 69—72, 123, 124 ; Indiana, 36, 73, 74, 124 ; Illinois, 36, 74—76, 125 ; Michigan, 72, 73, 126 ; Iowa, 76, 77, 126 ; Wisconsin, 77—79, 126 ; California, 82, 83, 126 ; Minnesota Territory, 83, 127 ; Territory of New Mexico, 83, 84, 127 ; Washington Territory, 84, 85, 127.

216 INDEX.

Litre. Verification of standard presented by France, 163—166.
Louisiana. Abstracts of laws on weights and measures, 36, 67, 68 ; Titles of laws, 123.

M.

Maine. Abstracts of laws on weights and measures, 38—41 ; Titles of laws, 112, 113.
Mangel Wurzel. Weight of the bushel, by law, in Maine, 129.
Manual. To accompany hydrometers, notice, 10, 31.
Maryland. Abstracts of laws on weights and measures, 35, 59—61 ; Titles of laws, 120.
Massachusetts. Abstracts of laws on weights and measures, 35, 44—46 ; Titles of laws, 114, 115.
McCulloh, Prof. R. S., 2, 91.
Measures. Of length and capacity, description of sets, 4, 7, 8 ; Distribution to States and custom-houses, 106—109 ; Miscellaneous distribution, 110 ; Forms of labels accompanying standards, Appendix No. 5.
Mechanics. Number in Office of Weights and Measures, 2.
Metre. Adoption in France, 141 ; By other nations, 142 ; How related to French coins 167 ; Verification of standard presented by France, 150—156 ; Expansion of, 28 ; Nomenclature of metrical system, 168.
Mexican Boundary Commission. Supplied with standard of length, 10.
Michigan. Abstracts of laws on weights and measures, 72, 73 ; Titles of laws, 126.
Minnesota Territory. Abstracts of laws on weights and measures, 83 ; Titles of laws, 127.
Mississippi. Abstracts of laws on weights and measures, 36, 66, 67 ; Titles of laws, 122.
Missouri. Abstracts of laws on weights and measures, 36, 79—81 ; Titles of laws, 125.
Molasses. Weight at different temperatures, 197—208.
Monterey, Cal. Custom-house supplied with standards, 8.

N.

Naval Academy. Supplied with balance and ounce weights, 10.
Nebraska. Yard measure furnished for land office, 10.
New Hampshire. Abstracts of laws on weights and measures, 35, 41, 42 ; Titles of laws, 113, 114.
New Jersey. Abstracts of laws on weights and measures, 35, 53, 54 ; Titles of laws, 118.
New Mexico, (Territory.) Abstracts of laws on weights and measures, 83, 84 ; Titles of laws, 127 ; Yard measure supplied to land office, 10.
New York. Abstracts of laws on weights and measures, 35, 49—53 ; Titles of laws, 116—118.
North Carolina. Abstracts of laws on weights and measures, 35, 62, 63 ; Titles of laws, 121.

O.

Oats. Weight of the bushel, by law, in different States, 129.
Ohio. Abstracts of laws on weights and measures, 36, 69—72 ; Titles of laws, 123, 124.
Oils. Weight at different temperatures, 197—208.
Olympia, W. T. Custom-house supplied with standards, 8.
Onions. Weight of the bushel, by law, in different States, 129.
Ordnance and Hydrography, (Bureau of.) Supplied with standards, 9.
Oregon Territory. Balance furnished, 8 ; Yard measure for land office, 10.

P.

Peaches, (dried.) Weight of the bushel, by law, in different States, 129.
Pennsylvania. Abstracts of laws on weights and measures, 35, 54—57; Titles of laws, 118—120.
Pint measures, (U. S.) Office comparison of, 190—196.
Post Office Department. Furnished with small weights, 10.
Potatoes. Weight of the bushel, by law, in different States, 129.
Pound. Derivation of United States standard, 5; Office comparison of standard presented by Great Britain, 18, 177.
Pyrometer, (Saxton's.) Description of, 15, 16.

Q.

Quart measures, (U. S.) Office comparison of, 190—196.

R.

Rhode Island. Abstracts of laws on weights and measures, 35, 46, 47, 127, 128; Titles of laws, 115, 116.
Reports. On analyses of sugars, &c., and hydrometers, (titles,) 91.
Rye. Weight of the bushel, by law, in different States, 129.

S.

San Diego, Cal. Custom-house supplied with standards, 8.
Scottsville, W. T. Custom-house supplied with standards, 8, 9.
Saxton, Joseph, 2, 8, 11, 15, 16.
Sonoma, Cal. Custom house supplied with standards, 8.
South Carolina. Abstracts of laws on weights and measures, 35, 64; Titles of laws, 121, 122.
Standards, (U. S.) How derived—of length, 4; Of capacity, 5; Of weight, 5; Date of adoption, 5; Resolution providing for distribution, 88; States and custom-houses furnished, 8, 106—109; Form of label accompanying, Appendix No. 5; Presentations to foreign governments, 23, 105; Condition of custom-house sets, 102, 103; Law directing comparison, 89; Description of sets suitable for counties, 6, 7; M. Silbermann's remarks on set presented to France, 139—141; Office comparisons of foreign standards, 17—19, 176—180; Verification of sets presented by France, 148—166; Uniformity in standards recommended, 86, 87.
Sugar beet. Weight of the bushel, by law, in Maine, 129.

T.

Tar, (Barbadoes.) Weight at different temperatures, 202.
Tennessee. Abstracts of laws on weights and measures, 36, 68; Titles of laws, 124.
Texas. Abstracts of laws on weights and measures, 81; Titles of laws, 123.
Timothy seed. Weight of the bushel, by law, in different States, 129.
Titles. Of reports of analyses of sugars, distribution of hydrometers, &c., 91; Of laws in States and Territories relative to weights and measures, 112—127.
Ton, (2,000 pounds.) Adopted, by law, in different States, 85.
Topographical Engineers, (Bureau.) Furnished with standard yard, 10.

Treasury Department. Supplied with standards of length for public works, 10.
Turpentine, (spirits.) Weight at different temperatures, 197—208.

U.

Utah Territory. Yard measure furnished for land office, 10.

V.

Vara, (Mexican.) Compared with United States standard yard, 19, 180.
Vermont. Abstracts of laws on weights and measures, 35, 42, 43; Titles of laws, 114.
Virginia. Abstracts of laws on weights and measures, 35, 61, 62; Titles of laws, 120, 121.

W.

Washington Territory. Law on weights and measures, 84, 85, 127.
Weights, (U. S. standard.) Description of set and arrangement in boxes, 3, 4; Instructions for using and preserving, 100, 101; Distribution of, 106—109, 110; Condition of sets at custom-houses, 9, 102, 103.
Wheat. Weight of the bushel, by law, in different States, 129.
Wisconsin. Abstracts of laws on weights and measures, 77—79; Titles of laws, 126; Yard measure furnished for land office, 10.
Workshop. Number of mechanics and laborers, 2.

Y.

Yard, (U. S. standard.) How derived, 4; Office comparison of United States yard measures, 175; Of British yard with United States standard, 17, 18, 176, 177.

Printed in Dunstable, United Kingdom